Scotland and the Indian Empire

Scotland and the Indian Empire

Politics, Scholarship and the Military in Making British India

Alan Tritton

BLOOMSBURY ACADEMIC
LONDON • NEW YORK • OXFORD • NEW DELHI • SYDNEY

BLOOMSBURY ACADEMIC
Bloomsbury Publishing Plc
50 Bedford Square, London, WC1B 3DP, UK
1385 Broadway, New York, NY 10018, USA

BLOOMSBURY, BLOOMSBURY ACADEMIC and the Diana logo are trademarks of
Bloomsbury Publishing Plc

First published in Great Britain 2020

Cover design: Terry Woodley
Cover image: A portrait of Colonel John Baillie and Mary Martin in
Durbar at the Oudh Court at Lucknow. By an Indian artist.

A catalogue record for this book is available from the British Library.

ISBN: HB: 978-1-7883-1809-9
ePDF: 978-1-7867-3661-1
eBook: 978-1-7867-2655-1

Typeset by Newgen KnowledgeWorks Pvt. Ltd., Chennai, India
Printed and bound in Great Britain

To find out more about our authors and books visit www.bloomsbury.com
and sign up for our newsletters.

Contents

Illustrations

Unless otherwise stated, images are the author's own or in the public domain.

Maps

Plates

Acknowledgements

It is a most pleasant task to sit down and write my acknowledgements and also my appreciation for all the assistance that I have been given in writing and publishing this Scottish Indian historical biographical book and we will do so, but first of all, to my mind, I do think that it would be both right and proper to give due acknowledgement to the two men about whom this book is written – Baillie and Edmonstone – because, without them, there would have been no book. This goes for all the men, women and children – both Indian and Scottish – mentioned in the book. To me in researching and writing about them, these people who lived and died nearly two hundred years ago, in some extraordinary sense, seem to have become both alive and familiar. Indeed, I often think about the Scots and their Military, domestic and political lives in that then far distant land during that tumultuous period in the eighteenth and nineteenth centuries and, at the same time, I think about the Indian men and their wives and children, who were also and even more involved during that same tumultuous period and who bore the heat and burden of the day, as they confronted their external and internal enemies in their vast subcontinent.

But, for the present, let us start in Scotland, where there still exists in various libraries and archives and private collections a wealth of material on the matter in hand – a wealth of material which hardly ever emerges into the light of day, until someone comes along and starts digging it all out. My first port of call was once again, as with my previous book *When the Tiger Fought the Thistle: The Tragedy of Colonel William Baillie of the Madras Army*– the Highland Archive Office on the outskirts of Inverness, where the Staff could not have been more helpful.

Moving south from Inverness to Edinburgh, I need to acknowledge with gratitude the assistance of the Edinburgh University Library, to whom all of Colonel John Baillie's magnificent Collection of Persian Papers and Manuscripts were bequeathed – and one wonders again how well this magnificent Collection is known. Still in Edinburgh, I am very grateful for the help of the National Archives of Scotland, who had also assisted me with my earlier book, recalling that Colonel William Baillie of the Madras Army was the uncle of Colonel John Baillie of the Bengal Army.

Moving south again, I need to extend my warmest thanks to the Cambridge University Library, which holds the Elmore Papers, bequeathed to them by

Mrs Browne, a granddaughter of Edmonstone, who confirmed that the Anglo-Scottish and Scottish-Indian children of Neil Edmonstone had never met or even knew that their stepbrothers and stepsisters existed. Many of these papers, or rather letters, from Miss Margaret Baillie of Leys Castle, Inverness, the spinster sister of Colonel John Baillie, to the Edmonstone family and their replies show her dedication to the upbringing and education of not only the Scottish-Indian children of Edmonstone but also the Scottish-Indian children of Baillie and his Lucknow children by Mary Martin.

And then, of course, the India Office Library, which overflows with records, archives, information and paintings about the Honourable East India Company; my heartfelt and grateful thanks go out to the Staff there, with whom my Research Assistant Justine Taylor was in frequent contact; I certainly owe her an enormous depth of gratitude because, without her, this book would not have seen the light of day. It always remains a constant source of wonder and surprise even, that whenever I required some obscure piece of information from the entrails of the Library, Justine always seemed to find it without difficulty.

Moving on, I would like to thank my former History Editor, Dr Lester Crook, who, with his unfailing courtesy and kindness, provided me with much excellent advice as did his successor, Olivia Dellow; then there is Professor Francis Robinson, Professor of the History of South Asia at London University who also gave me sound advice; and then there is Dr Alison Ohta, the Director of the Royal Asiatic Society and her Staff, who could not have been more helpful – both Baillie and Edmonstone were Founder Members of the Society.

I would also like to thank Dr Richard Bingle, who serves on the BACSA – British Association for Cemeteries in South Asia – Committee and who is responsible for the Records and Archives of that Association, of which I was once President. He most kindly pointed me in the direction of the *Journal of the Uttar Pradesh Historical Society* and Dr Chatterjee's important article regarding the affair of the Oudh loans and the involvement therein of Lord Hastings – the then Governor General – and John Baillie then Resident at Lucknow – a most important and relatively unknown historical document.

I have also to thank Dr Rosie Llewellyn-Jones, former Hon. Secretary of BACSA and now Editor of Chowkidar, the BACSA House Journal, who researched the Oudh Archives for me and who is, without doubt, the leading Authority on the Oudh Royal Family and Lucknow and who provided me with details of the construction by Major John Baillie, as he then was, when the British Resident of Lucknow, of the Baillie Guard Gate of the Residency. This was constructed in 1815 during Baillie's last year as Resident, – the year of Waterloo – much to the irritation of the then Nawab Ghazi-ud-din Haidar, but which almost certainly saved the day for the besieged residents and garrison of the Residency in 1857.

Moving on again, I would like to extend my warmest thanks to Dr William Pinch, Professor of History at the Wesleyan University in Middletown, Connecticut, for his generous help and advice in introducing me to his book entitled *Warrior Ascetics and Indian Empires* and revealing to me the full part that Captain Baillie, as he then was, played in Bundelkhand, as the Political Agent there. This part was the transfer of the political and Military allegiance of the Gosain Anupgiri – also known as Himmat Bahadur – from the Mahrattas to the Company, which thereby enabled Captain John Baillie to bring the pivotal State of Bundelkhand under British control.

I think it would be right also to acknowledge the immensely valuable contribution provided by Wikipedia – as an example of this, when I was researching a vast but relatively unknown and obscure Fortress by the name of Kalinjar in Bundelkhand, which was well known to Captain Baillie, Wikipedia came to the rescue with a very fine painting of the Fortress in 1814, by a certain Colin Mackenzie from Stornoway, shortly after it was captured by the British in 1812. Interestingly enough, Mackenzie was appointed the first Surveyor General of India.

I would also like to thank the various members of the current Baillie family for all their help and assistance with this book.

Finally, this book would never have been written without the patient, loyal and persevering support of my wife Diana, and for that I would like to thank her from the bottom of my heart.

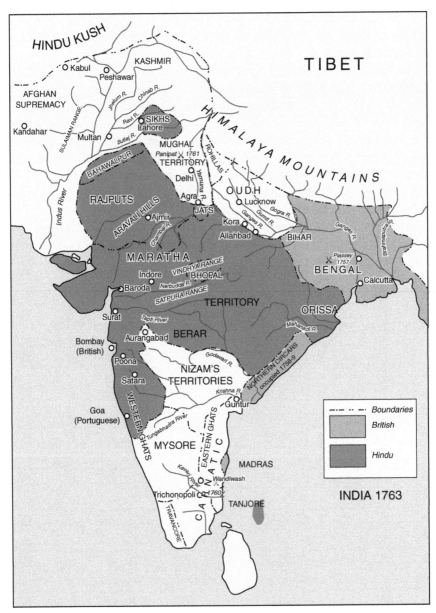

Map 1 India, 1763.

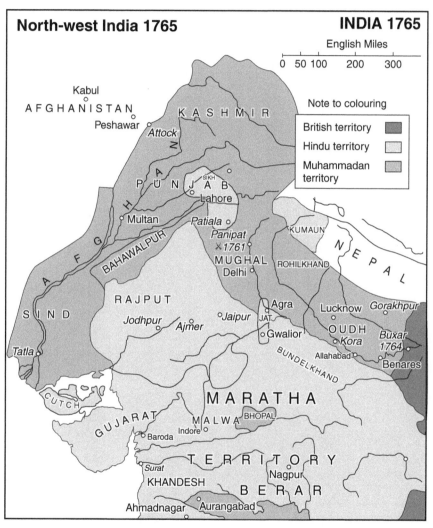

North-west India 1765

INDIA 1765

English Miles

0 50 100   200   300

Note to colouring

British territory

Hindu territory

Muhammadan territory

Kabul
AFGHANISTAN
Peshawar
Attock
KASHMIR

PUNJAB
SIKH
Lahore
Multan

AFGHAN

BAHAWALPUR

Patiala
Panipat
×1761
MUGHAL
Delhi

KUMAUN

NEPAL

ROHILKHAND

SIND

RAJPUT
Jodhpur   Ajmer   Jaipur
JAT
Gwalior

Agra

Lucknow   Gorakhpur

OUDH
Kora
Allahabad
Buxar
1764
Benares

BUNDELKHAND

Tatla

CUTCH

GUJARAT
Baroda
MALWA
Indore
BHOPAL

MARATHA

TERRITORY

Surat
KHANDESH
Ahmadnagar   Aurangabad

Nagpur

BERAR

Map 2 North West India, 1765.

Introduction

John Baillie, from Inverness in Scotland, went out to India as a Cadet of the East India Company in May 1791. In Calcutta, he was appointed an Ensign of the 4th Native Infantry Regiment of the Bengal Army, rising through the ranks to be promoted Colonel of his Regiment in 1816. He held a number of important Military, academic and political positions in the Service of the Company, and in 1823 following his return from India he was appointed a Director of the Company and served a number of years as a Member of Parliament, while also being elected a Fellow of the Royal Society. He was a Founder Member of the Royal Asiatic Society.

Neil Edmonstone, also from Scotland, went out to India in 1783, as a Writer of the East India Company. In Calcutta, he was at various times Persian Translator to the Government, Chief Secretary to the Government, Secretary of the important Secret Foreign and Political Department, Vice President of the Supreme Council of India and acting Governor General on two occasions. He was the Company's Chief Intelligence Officer for more than twenty years. On his return from India in 1818, he was appointed a Director of the Company in 1820 and remained so until his death in 1841. Like Baillie he was a Founder Member of the Royal Asiatic Society.

These were two Scots from well-known Highland families and we need to place their careers in India in three contexts: the first being in the context of the Honourable East India Company and its early history; the second being in the context of the Scots and their affinity for India; and the third being in the context of what was going on in India while they were there, during those crucial years between 1780 and 1820. All this should become clear as we go along, but let us paint here with a broader brush.

First, the Company was founded in the year 1600 at the end of Queen Elizabeth the First's reign and by the late eighteenth century had taken the lead over its European rivals in the Indian trade – bearing in mind that it had been ousted by the Dutch from the more profitable trade with the Spice Islands further east. Its trade with India consisted mainly of the import of Indian cotton, and to a lesser extent Indian silk, and all this was financed by the City of London in the form initially of remittances of substantial capital to India – although this changed after Robert Clive was given the Diwani of Bengal in 1765 – at that time there was very little demand for English goods in India.

The French came along later in 1668, and like the English, who had established their main trading posts at Bombay, Madras and Calcutta – to use the old spellings of these cities – the French had established theirs at Pondicherry, Mahe and Chandernagore, upstream from Calcutta. Up until the year 1744, the rivalry between the two countries in India had been relatively muted, but then, in that year, war broke out between the two countries in Europe. At first, this did not spread to India and neutrality was seen as the best bet – after all, they were trading companies and nobody wanted to lose money and ships, and they needed to make the money to make profits and remit dividends to Europe. At that time, Joseph François Dupleix was the Governor of Pondicherry and Director General of the French East Indies, and in those particular circumstances, he proposed that there should be a formal agreement of neutrality with the English at Madras – a little distance north of Pondicherry. However, the English were cautious and replied that they did not have the authority to enter into such an agreement – in other words, they would await instructions from London.

In London, the Directors of the Company then heard that the Government was sending out to India a Royal Squadron and bearing this in mind, the Directors came to the conclusion that this might be helpful, inasmuch as their trade could be hopefully protected and the French trade hopefully despoliated, as there were no French naval ships operating at that time in East Indian waters. They, therefore, rejected Dupleix's approach and instructed the Madras Government accordingly. The Royal Navy squadron duly arrived and began wrecking the French trade. Unfortunately, one could say, the squadron attacked a number of what were termed 'country ships' in which Dupleix had heavily invested personally and these were either captured or sunk. At a stroke, Dupleix lost most of his money and became almost incandescent with rage at the English, and thus war between the English and the French in India commenced.

A very complicated series of events was now set in motion, but to cut a long and involved story short, Dupleix came to grief and his ambitions of becoming the Lord of the Carnatic failed to materialize, as did his imperial pretensions of *La Gloire Francaise en Inde*. He was recalled to Paris where he died a pauper. All this is related in the author's earlier book entitled *When the Tiger Fought the Thistle*. However, although the French had been defeated in the Carnatic, this was not the case further north in the Deccan and elsewhere in India, and it became clear that eventually either the English or the French in India would need to be defeated. Thus it was that, although the English never, unlike the French, thought in terms of an Indian Empire, up at least till then, the competition between the two countries set this in train and, as we all know, the English were successful in the end. Nevertheless the French continued their machinations in India for many years to come, as will become evident, and you will find constant references to them in this book with Sir Richard Wellesley, Lord Mornington, the Governor General at the turn of the nineteenth century, becoming paranoid about them and one can understand why – after all the French were supporting his enemies, not only the Mysoreans in the south of India, but also the Hyderabadis and the Mahrattas.

Second, why did the Scots, and perhaps in particular the Highland Scots, have such an affinity for India? The short and immediate answer to this was the impoverishment of the Scots both before, but particularly after, the Battle of Culloden in 1746, so much so that many were desperate to leave – particularly the younger sons of the Lairds, who were themselves in difficulty, as were the author's own Highland Baillie family. Thus, the lure of the East became compelling, and the prospect of success and consequent financial independence took them there in astonishing numbers.

When James Boswell was on his way to London in 1762, he was amazed to find that his young Scottish travelling companion was not interested in going to London, but he was only going there to receive instructions from the Honourable East India Company to go out to Bengal. This affinity of the Scots for India was often noticed by English contemporaries, and in India an Englishman was heard to remark – one has to say in some disgust – that no man of any other nation can serve and survive in an Indian province, where the Chief is a Scot and where there is a Scot to be found. In Scotland itself, the result of the connection with India was seen 'as a little stream of East India gold spreading cultivation and fertility and plenty along its narrow glens'.

Charles Grant, whom we will meet later, was a Highland Scot. He had had what you would call a successful career in India for a number of years with the Board of Trade there and on his return, he was appointed a Director of the Company and later Chairman. He used his patronage for many years to send out many young Scots to India and John Baillie, the joint subject of this book, was one of them. So did his Scottish friend Henry Dundas, Lord Melville, who for many years was the Member of Parliament for Inverness-shire but, more importantly, the President of the Board of Control for India between 1793 and 1801. For those who know their Edinburgh, you will see his 150 feet high Column in St Andrew's Square, modelled after the Trajan Column in Rome and only a few feet shorter than that of Nelson's Column in Trafalgar Square. At the end of the day, one could perhaps say that it was fortunate for the Scots that the growth of British territorial power in India, and for that matter elsewhere in the world, provided many of them, not only with an escape from Scotland, but also with many other opportunities – both Civil and Military – after the Culloden defeat. The relative impoverishment of many Highland families, which included that of the Baillie family, made India 'a life prospect'. It perhaps needs to be said that the Irish were in a not dissimilar position and it will be noted, as we go along, that at the end of the eighteenth century, the Governor General of India – namely, Sir Richard Wellesley, Lord Mornington, and his Generals were nearly all Irish, including, of course, his younger brother Arthur Wellesley, later the Duke of Wellington, who commanded the Army in the Deccan, while the Irish Lord Lake commanded the Army in Hindustan.

The third and final context is what was going on in India when Baillie and Edmonstone arrived there at the end of the eighteenth century – Edmonstone as a Writer and Baillie as a Cadet – Writer being the Civil role and Cadet being the Military role. This book gives a description of all this, but it can be argued that it was in 1780 or thereabouts that the British Empire in India began to take shape. It was the loss of the American colonies that precipitated this and, in India itself, the expansionary activities of the then Governor General Warren Hastings – who was taking an increasing interest in the States beyond Bengal, Orissa and Bihar – were becoming better known in Britain. Baillie's and Edmonstone's Scottish Indian generation served the Company, as it changed from a defensive commercial Company to an aggressive commercial Company spanning the subcontinent. It was 1818 – the year of Edmonstone's departure from Calcutta and India after his thirty-four years there – that witnessed the final victory of the Company over the Mahrattas, the last great independent native power remaining in India.

Thus it was that Edmonstone, Baillie and their colleagues set in train the first organized expansionist Government in the Company's history with Edmonstone playing a leading role in all this, given his close proximity to successive Governor Generals. What they accomplished was not haphazard, but a carefully considered strategy to forge a British Empire in India. It certainly was not created 'in a fit of absent mindedness', as someone once put it. However, there was one particular episode in 1799, which could have and might well have, propelled Edmonstone into taking a more decisive and aggressive imperial line, and that was the murder at Benares of his best friend George Cherry by Wazir Ali Khan, the deposed Nawab of Oudh – a decisive imperial line, which resonated with Sir Richard Wellesley, Lord Mornington, the then Governor General, and the most imperial of all the Governor Generals of India, but not so much with the Company's Directors in London.

Chapter 1
Setting the scene

Neil Edmonstone was born on 6 December 1765, the year of the significant battle of Buxar, about which more later, and it will also be recalled that it was during that year that Robert Clive attained the Diwani of Bengal, which conferred the right of the Company to collect the revenues of that State and to administer, therefore, one of the most fertile and, therefore, richest regions of India, technically for the Mughal Emperors but in reality for the Company. Importantly, this revenue replaced the requirement to finance the Company's Indian trade from London.

The following year, the British Government in London conceived of the bright idea of abolishing the Company and taking control of its Indian possessions, which included the £2 million a year in estimated tax revenues from the Diwani of Bengal – this with the laudable intention of paying off the National Debt. This attempt was partly successful, because in 1767, the Company, in order to avoid being taken over, reluctantly agreed to pay the huge annual amount of £400,000 to retain its independence. However, there was, needless to say, a significant desire for the reform of the Company on the part of the Government, and young Edmonstone might just have been familiar with all this, given his father's, Sir Archibald's, part in the process. The 1773 Regulating Act had given the Government, for the first time, considerable powers of control over the Company and this mainly arose as a result of the Company requiring a significant loan, which was needed to pay its debts to the Crown. For this, the quid pro quo was the Government's power to nominate the Governor General and Members of the Supreme Council, which would take precedence over the Governments in Calcutta, Bombay and Madras.

It was hoped that this would result in a more effective supervision over the Company and put an end to its now well-known abuses. However, it then became clear that more measures were required and these were again supported by Sir Archibald. This resulted in the East India Bill of 1783, which was initially resisted by King George 111, who thought that the Council should be appointed by himself and not by the Parliament. The King managed to persuade the House of

Lords to throw the Bill out, but William Pitt's compromise Bill, supported by Sir Archibald, became law as the East India Act of 1784.

Under this Act, the Company retained the right to appoint the civil and Military officers sent out to India and to set out its major policies – however, a Board of Control composed of Members of Parliament was given powers of overall supervision. Despite, however, the provision in this Act calling for a cession of Company interference, there was a strong feeling of imperialist sentiment, resulting from the loss of America, which, so to speak, fed into the system. Henry Dundas, who was the President of the Board of Control from 1788 to 1801, and who was Pitt's great imperialist ally, strongly favoured the extension of the Company's sphere of control by whatever means were necessary.

Chapter 2

Edmonstone's family: His voyage to and arrival at Calcutta

Neil Edmonstone was the fifth and youngest son of Sir Archibald. The Edmonstones' family life centred round a large greystone house in the central Highlands called Duntreath Castle. Sir Archibald was fascinated to the point of obsession with his ancestry, and his one major ambition was to restore the family's fortunes to their apparent past glory. He noted, 'I own that I felt from the beginning that my family fortune was inferior to its Rank,' and went on to say that 'the Purse has often become the Pedigree especially about London'. His wife was half-French – her name, Susanna Mary Harene. The Harenes were an ancient French noble family from Normandy, who had moved to England in 1720. The family had prospered in England and, when his daughter married Sir Archibald, her father was able to provide her with a dowry of £10,000 – a significant sum in the value of money at that time. When she died in 1776, Sir Archibald remarried a certain Hester, the daughter of Sir John Heathcote and young Neil Edmonstone became unusually very fond of his stepmother. When he left for India, she gave him a gold watch and this remained one of his most treasured possessions all his life. In 1783, Sir Archibald was 66 years old and a portrait of him shows a grim old man wearing a wig and a tri-cornered hat. He had a long somewhat sagging face that appears devoid of humour, and on his finger is a heavy signet ring with the family motto inscribed thereon: *Virtus Auget Honorum*. He was always short of capital; his standard of living was too high for his income, and this was because he felt that he was obliged to support his 'Rank and Station in every respect'. Perhaps, one could say that he particularly wanted his sons to succeed financially, so that he could continue to live in the style to which he thought he and his family should be accustomed. Thus, the East India Company beckoned.

The eldest son, like his father, was called Archibald and it was reported that he was the apple of his father's eye. Indeed, he described him as the 'Pride, the Glory and the Comfort of my Heart'. In his case, he joined the Guards and was sent out to fight in America. He served there as ADC to General Riediesel, who was commanding the German division of the Army under General Burgoyne. Very sadly, he went down with consumption there and died two years later, aged 25.

Following the death of Archibald, his father turned to his next son William in the hope that he would be able to contribute something towards the financial support of the Edmonstone family. He went out to India in 1776 with instructions from his father to make a 'competent fortune'. However, whereas Archibald was, somewhat surprisingly, described by his father as 'modest and docile', he described William as 'secretive and reserved'. William had no wish to go out to India and once he was there, he hardly ever wrote home. He never felt well in India – he did not make much progress up the Company ladder and never went home, dying in India. Of the two remaining brothers, Charles was called to the Bar and appointed one of the six Clerks in Chancery, while George took Holy Orders and then became the curate in the Wiltshire parish of Pollerne. There were three daughters – the youngest Sarah was still at home at that time, while the other two daughters were married with families.

Neil Edmonstone went out to India on the East Indiaman, the *Stormont*, of 723 tons, sailing from Portsmouth in March 1783, reaching Madras in July and by September, the Hooghly River and then Calcutta's Diamond Harbour, in those days one of the world's most famous and busiest ports. On board the *Stormont* were 42 'Writers', all aged between 16 and 17. There the ship stopped, meaning that the last 41 miles had to be undertaken by a vessel called a *budgerow*, which was little more than a barge with a flat-roofed cabin. These last 41 miles were not particularly pleasant as the monsoon rains had not yet stopped and the passengers were assailed by hordes of mosquitoes. They also passed that island, where the son of Sir Hector Munro, who had commanded the Company's army at the famous battle of Buxar already mentioned, went ashore to have a picnic lunch only to have his head bitten off by a tiger, just as he was sitting down to eat his lunch. The remains of his body were never discovered.

As the budgerow neared Calcutta itself, the jungle gave way to garden houses, as they were called, with beautiful manicured lawns studded with roses, scarlet geraniums and mango trees and now, with Calcutta itself in full view, perhaps Neil could never have thought that this was to be his home for the next thirty-four years.

Edmonstone arrived in Calcutta close to a hundred years after it had been founded by Job Charnock and let us read the latter's opening words, which appeared in the first volume of the Fort William Factory Records: 'This day at Sankraul ordered Captain Brooke come up with his vessel to Chutanutte, where we arrived at noon, but found ye place in a deplorable condition, nothing being left for our present accommodation and ye rains falling day and night. We were forced to take ourselves to boats, which, considering the season of the year is very unhealthy.'

Chutanutte was situated on the east bank of the river, while somewhat further to the east was situated the well-known and extensive Salt Lake. This lake, unfortunately, overflowed during the months of September and October and this brought to it, as our old friend Captain Alexander Hamilton reported, 'prodigious numbers of fishes, but in November and December, when the floods receded, these fishes were left stranded high and dry with the result that their putrefaction affected the air with stinking vapours, which the north east winds bring to Fort William, so that they cause a yearly mortality'. The Captain reckoned that, when he was there one August, there were 460 burials registered in the Clerk's Book of Mortality, out of a total population of about 1,200 Englishmen then residing in Calcutta. The Captain was well known for a certain amount of exaggeration and embellishment, but he could not really have made up this figure, given his access to this Book of Mortality.

The Captain then went on to say,

Mr Charnock in choosing the ground for the colony, where it now is, reigned more absolutely than a Rajah, only he wanted much for their humanity, for when any poor ignorant native transgressed his laws, they were sure to undergo a severe whipping for a penalty and this penalty was carried out near to his dining room, so that the groans and cries of these poor delinquents served him for music at dinner. The custom of wives being burnt alive with their deceased husbands is also practised. Before the Moghul's war, Mr Charnock went out one day with his ordinary bodyguard to see a young widow act out that tragic catastrophe, but he was so smitten with her beauty, that he sent his guards to take her by force from the funeral fire and conduct her to his lodgings. They lived together for many years and had several children. He made no effort to try and convert her to Christianity and after she died, on the anniversary of her death, he always sacrificed a cock on her tomb after the pagan manner.'

Chapter 3

Baillie's family: His voyage to and arrival in Calcutta

The Baillie family originally came from Flanders and then branched out into four main lines, all of which were in Scotland. These were the Lamington Baillies, the Leys Baillies, the Dunain Baillies and, finally, the Dochfour Baillies, from whom my mother Iris Mary Baillie was descended.

John Baillie, the joint subject of this book, was born in Inverness, Scotland, in 1772 in a house by the River Ness. His father was a practising doctor there and it is interesting to note how many Baillies took up medical as well as Military careers, both in this country and also in India.

John Baillie's father George was born in 1727 and died in 1795. He married another Baillie, by the name of Annie, and she was the daughter of Alexander Baillie of Dunain – the small Baillie estate situated more or less between the Dochfour and Leys Baillie estates. Annie Baillie was a sister of Colonel William Baillie of Dunain, who joined the 89th Highland Regiment of Foot, then, when that Regiment returned to Scotland, transferred to the Coromandel Coast Army, which metamorphosed into the Madras Army. Why did he transfer to the Coast Army? The answer is that he had not made any money and, as it happens, never did. As, perhaps, some readers may know, this Colonel William Baillie was the subject of an earlier book of mine entitled *When the Tiger Fought the Thistle – the Tragedy of Colonel William Baillie of the Madras Army* – the Tiger being Tipu Sultan and the Thistle the Scots in the shape of William Baillie. He and his Brigade were defeated by the combined forces of Haidar Ali and his son Tipu Sultan at the battle of Pollilur near Conjeveram, now Kanchipuram, on 10 September 1780 – Conjeveram being situated approximately 50 miles or so west of Madras and well worth a visit to see its temples and its textile industry. He was captured, forced to watch his brother officers being decapitated by Tipu and then marched to his Fortress Palace of Seringapatam, where he was thrown into a dungeon, manacled to a wall and, denied medical help, died there two years later. At Seringapatam, his nephew Colonel John Baillie, the joint subject of this book, erected a magnificent Memorial to him in 1816 – his final year as the British Resident of Lucknow. This Memorial has recently been restored.

John Baillie's parents had seven children – the eldest of whom was Margaret Baillie, who was born in 1761 and died seventy years later in 1831. She never married but, as the Chatelaine of Leys Castle, which John Baillie had bought from his brother Alexander Baillie, she brought up not only John's four Scottish Indian children, all of whom had been born in Calcutta, as well as his three children born in Lucknow, but also two of Neil Edmonstone's Scottish Indian boys, born in Calcutta. The youngest of the Edmonstone sons was sent to a boarding school in London, as Margaret was by then probably too old to manage yet another boy – she had nine to bring up already, while John's daughter Eliza stayed behind in Calcutta. The surname of Edmonstone's Scottish Indian children was changed to Elmore, but whether or not his father Archibald influenced this decision is not known.

Going back to the children of Dr George and Annie Baillie: a son John was born in 1765 but died shortly afterwards; another son Alexander went out to India, where he rose through the ranks to command his Regiment as Colonel. Alexander had several Scottish Indian children, and it seems that these children were sent back to Scotland from India, but not to Leys. A daughter Anna was born in 1768; a son William, who was born in 1770 and tried his luck in the West Indies plantations, but died there; then John the joint subject of this book and then two more girls.

In 1786, Annie died and the widower married a certain Margaret Cummings, by whom he had one son George, who was born in 1787. He, like his father, qualified as a doctor, then, as an Assistant Surgeon, he seems to have joined the Bengal Army and took part in the capture of Java from the French in 1811, when Lord Minto was Governor General. In 1827, he was appointed the Personal Physician to the then Nawab of Oudh, but then resigned four years later, when his salary, which was paid by the Company, was reduced from 2,500 rupees a month to 1,000 rupees.

It is interesting to note that as Personal Physician to the Nawab, he had succeeded Dr John Gibson, who had died mysteriously. His wife, who also seems to have mysteriously died, was Ann. She was no less a person than Ann Baillie, the only surviving child of Colonel William Baillie by his Indian lady in Madras. She had been sent back to England by her father, to be brought up there, and we find just one single letter written by her to her father, which ends as follows: 'I remain with duty to Mama and Love to Brother, Dear Papa, Your Most Affectionate and ever Dutiful daughter, Ann Baillie'. It is sad to say that there were no children of that Gibson marriage – it is also sad to say that not many children, if any, would nowadays end their letters, if indeed they wrote them at all, to their parents as Ann did.

Colonel William Baillie had a younger brother John, who also went out to India to join the Madras Army in 1768. When his brother William was captured in 1780 and then died in that Seringapatam dungeon two years later, it was reported that before he died, he told a fellow officer prisoner, who was later murdered by Tipu Sultan: 'I hope my brother John will live and go home. Tell him to go home immediately and not be looking as high as I have been in this country'. John thereupon, resigned his commission and returned to Scotland, as he put it, 'an ill- used and disappointed man'. It is, perhaps, worth mentioning that after his return to Scotland, he was prevailed upon to 'raise' at very considerable personal expense to himself, a Scottish Territorial Regiment entitled the Inverness-shire Fencibles, which, later on, had its name changed rather grandly to the Duke of York's Royal Inverness-shire Highlanders. These territorial Fencible or rather Militia Regiments had been introduced by Pitt the Elder, when the country was in danger of being invaded by the French. Indeed, not long after they were raised, they were rushed to Ireland, where the Irish supported as usual by the French, were rebelling. However, it is sad to say that on a forced route march to Kilkenny to attack the Irish and French forces, he, the Colonel, dropped down dead from a heart attack and, if you go to the Church there, you will see a fine brass Memorial commemorating his death. He had two children – a boy William, who went out to India where he became deranged, and a daughter Catherine, who married a certain Hugh Rose of Kilravock, my grandmother's family.

As it happens, we know very little about John Baillie's early life – we assume that, like the Dunain Baillies, he went to school in Aberdeen and then on to Edinburgh University. He stayed on in Edinburgh to serve as an apprentice prior to becoming a Writer to the Signet, as had his grandfather, but this was not a success and it appears he rather took to the bottle and resigned. He then decided to apply to the East India Company, but first he required the necessary application money and the necessary sponsorship. The former seems to have been obtained from his uncle Colonel John Baillie of Dunain and the latter from a certain Richard Thornton, and therein lies an interesting story. Richard Thornton had become known to the Baillies via Charles Grant and his wife Jane, a Balnain Fraser, whose family also came from near Inverness. The Grants had left for India almost immediately after their marriage in 1773, and there he had been appointed Secretary to the Board of Trade in Calcutta – a lucrative appointment. With this money, he spent most of his time in Calcutta at the gaming tables. But then tragedy struck. They lost both of their two young children from smallpox, and this catastrophe changed their lives for ever. He abandoned the gaming tables, returned to England and became an evangelical Christian – in other words he and his wife saw the 'light'. He was appointed a Director of the East India Company and then Chairman, as we have mentioned and through his wife's Fraser connection, also sponsored John Baillie to be appointed a Cadet in the Bengal Army of the Company.

John Baillie was required to be interviewed by a Committee of the Directors in Leadenhall Street. We do not know how it went, except that he was successful, but it is interesting that Hickey, who was also interviewed, did describe in his famous diary how his went:

I attended before a Committee to undergo the usual examination as a Cadet. I was called in to one of the Committee rooms and there saw three old Dons, sitting close to the fire, with beside them a large table with pens and ink, papers and a number of books thereon. Having surveyed me, one of them said;

Well, young gentleman, what is your age and I answered nineteen. Have you ever served, I mean have you been in the Army, although I presume from your age and appearance, you have not? I replied that I had not.

Can you go through the manual exercise? I replied, No Sir.

Then you must take care and read it. I bowed.

Do you know the terms upon which you enter our service? I replied, Yes Sir.

Are you fully satisfied therewith?

Yes Sir.

A clerk then told me that I could now withdraw, so I went to Mr Coggan's office, who then presented me with my appointment as a Cadet of the Honourable East India Company.

Baillie then sailed out to Calcutta on the East Indiaman the *Bridgewater*, which had been constructed by Barnard and had been launched in 1775. She does not appear to have been a large vessel – 799 tons – only 143 feet long (the figure of 143 feet does look curiously short) and 36 feet wide with three decks. The description goes on – keel 116 feet, hold 14 feet, wing transom 23 feet, port cell 26 feet, waist I foot, between decks 6 feet, roundhouse, 6 feet, ports 13 middle and upper. Her Captain, a Scot, was a certain Gregory Moffat Lewin. She left Portsmouth on 25 May 1791, with no less than 426 people on board and one wonders how they all fitted in and also how they got on in such cramped quarters for the long six-month voyage to Madras and Calcutta. It was to be her last voyage to Calcutta. The crew consisted of no less than 112 sailors; there were 263 artillery gunners on board, 31 passengers and 20 Company recruits including Baillie. You can see a picture of her defending herself from an attacking American privateer, the *Hampden*, on 8 March 1778. The latter got the worst of it and retired after its Captain Pickering was killed.

It is, as always, of absorbing interest to read the passenger lists of these East Indiamen; in this case we see Mr and Mrs Sharp going out with their daughter; we see Mrs Cockburn the wife of Captain Cockburn of the Artillery with their three children; we see Mrs Ross, the wife of Captain Ross of the Artillery, who was going out to join her husband and then there were all the young Cadets and

Writers, some destined for Madras, where promotion was said to be quicker than at Calcutta, and one wonders what happened to all these people and the children.

Following a short stop at Madras, the ship continued and Baillie finally reached Calcutta on 5 December 1791, after having been at sea for six months. Unlike Edmonstone, who had his brother William waiting by the ghat to meet him off the boat, Baillie seems to have had nobody. However, shortly after his arrival, he did find lodgings with Colin Robertson, son of the Provost of Dingwall – a town to the north of Inverness and as it happens, the former Regimental Depot of the 11th Battalion (Territorial) Seaforth Highlanders. Interestingly enough, Colin Robertson had a sister who had married a certain Sir James Gladstone and she thus became the mother of the future Prime Minister, William Gladstone. Colin had an auctioneer's business close by at Tank Square and we must assume that it was a profitable business, given the number of deaths listed in the Calcutta Register of Mortality and the associated auction of the assets of the deceased. Who has not read that fascinating book by Theon Wilkinson entitled *Two Monsoons*, that being the average number of monsoons, which a new arrival to Calcutta could expect to live? And it was Theon Wilkinson who founded that most interesting association entitled the British Association for Cemeteries in South Asia (BACSA).

Baillie was assigned to the 4th Bengal Native Infantry Regiment, which seems to have been stationed in the barracks of Fort William, and he seems to have almost immediately taken up with an Indian lady. One wonders how he managed this and where she came from, and one also wonders whether she was allowed to live in the barracks and what sort of accommodation they had. One could also speculate on whether he received his Commanding Officer's permission, to which the answer must be presumably yes. If he had been a Writer, it would have been most likely that he would have been assigned to the Writers Building, where dormitory style accommodation was made available to new arrivals. Edmonstone was fortunate in that he was able to lodge with his brother William in Fort William itself, which had only been completed in 1778, just before his arrival. This new Fort William was huge – a 2-mile square irregular octagon with seven gates flanked by barracks with accommodation for some twenty thousand soldiers, although the usual complement was fifteen thousand. It is interesting to note that the number of gun emplacements as stipulated by the Architect/Engineer was 1,000, but when the Fort was completed, he walked round his Fort no less than three times and could count only 999 emplacements, whereupon he went home and shot himself. Outside the Fort was a huge open glacis, which could be swept by artillery fire in the event of an attack. It is now called the Maidan and is the main green lung of Calcutta.

On 30 January 1792, shortly after he arrived, Baillie wrote a letter to his uncle Colonel John Baillie of Dunain, which reads as follows:

My dear Uncle,

If to receive intelligence of me or my concerns can afford you any pleasure or satisfaction, or if this will serve to convey to you, the smallest idea of those principles of gratitude with which your affectionate attention to me as well as the general interests of my family can and have never ceased to inspire me, I shall conceive this part of my duty, the most fortunate as well as the most pleasant except that of addressing my immediate parent in which I have been engaged.

So little has transpired since the date of my last letter to you, that I should hardly have troubled you at this time, except as a duty and just tribute to that tender and parental attention, which you have always paid with pleasure to the most trifling interests of our family, I am convinced that you will be happy to see that, notwithstanding the many disadvantages which my own imprudence and your diffidence of my future conduct subjected me to, I have met with several friends and acquaintances whose kindness has enabled me to live most agreeably and comfortably without a farthing of expense.

The gentleman I now live with and most pleasantly is the son of the Provost of Dingwall. None of my pay has yet become due, as the Army are two months in arrears, but I do hope that shortly I will be able to draw an Ensign's allowances. When my promotion appears in General Orders, which is something I expect daily, and if I have the luck to join a corps in the field and even go up country, my allowances will be double. These are, as you know, far superior to those at Madras and I wisely chose this establishment of which I am now very glad, although the Madras cadets are sooner promoted.

The purport of both my letters was, I think, as nearly as possible as the subject of our conversation in London. I explained briefly the state of my father's family and mentioned his extreme anxiety and pressed him earnestly to write. I concluded with mentioning my own position and that if it was fully in his power, I should wish to be his debtor a short time for the small sum sufficient to furnish me the articles immediately requisite for my military appearance and which my own imprudence at home had prevented my friends from allowing me.

This was my sole motive, which you may perhaps condemn, but which I am sure my position justified. Were you to see a list of the articles and expenses attending the purchase, you would, I dare say, think as I do. You will be surprised when I tell you that my only Regimental coat and which I cannot appear without, will cost 80 Rupees and everything else in proportion. You do know very well the expense of European articles in India and I need not mention it. They are even more enormous than those at Madras and you may be assured that the sum I have mentioned and been obliged to draw would not go far. I will not say that I will be accepted, tho' if my affairs in Edinburgh have not turned out very pressing, you and my father may be restored in one obligation to my sisters, which, if sent out, I will most gratefully sign and, with my first ability, discharge. They are the chief if not the only sufferers of my extravagance and the greatest cause why I have no doubt of your forgiveness if I have failed.

You are, I hope, fully persuaded of my most sincere and most grateful good wishes which is all I can offer for the health and prosperity of you and your family. That the Supreme Being may for many years preserve you and bless you, my dearest parent and benefactor and every branch of your family, in which, as a mark of your goodness, I believe, many of my own are included, is, believe me, the most ardent and sincere wish of your ever grateful and affectionate nephew.

John Baillie
Calcutta 30th January 1792

A most remarkable letter for a young man of only 19 years to write – however, you will note that there is a certain whiff of pomposity about it – a trait, which seems to have demonstrated itself throughout his career and which perhaps could be said to have been his undoing, when he was the British Resident at Lucknow – a post which he assumed when he was aged only 35 years.

When Baillie arrived in Calcutta, he found other Baillies there, of which the most notable was Major William Baillie – whether they were related in any way, we do not know for certain, but they probably were. This William Baillie had been born in 1752 and had gone out to Calcutta in 1772 as a Cadet in the Bengal Native Infantry. He then transferred to the Bengal Engineers and took part in the all-important task of surveying the Hooghly River. After that, he went on leave without pay and on his return started up his own weekly newspaper entitled the *Calcutta Chronicle*. He then resigned from the Army in 1788 with a view to becoming a professional artist.

He was successful and you can see his wonderful set of hand-painted aquatints entitled *Twelve Views of Calcutta*, which he drew in 1794. These views were followed later by those of James Baillie Fraser, whose family home was situated just north of Inverness and not that far from the Baillie's Leys Castle Estate, which was situated just south of Inverness.

He did not make much money from his painting so, in order to make ends meet, he became Secretary of the Calcutta Free School and then it's Superintendent. In 1795, he told his old artist friend Ozias Humphrey that 'he had wasted a lot of time painting landscapes, but that it was a pleasing pursuit but not a pot-boiling one'. Of all the British miniature portrait painters, this somewhat enigmatic Ozias Humphrey was the most highly accomplished and highly skilled. He and William Baillie numbered among his artist friends William and Thomas Daniell, Claude Martin, Gavin Hamilton and others – all familiar names. Very sadly, this William Baillie died in 1799 at the early age of 46 and was buried in the South Park Street

Burial Ground. If you go there, you will see the Inscription on his Memorial: 'Sacred to the Memory of Major W Baillie of the Engineers who departed this life on the 6th June 1799, aged 46 years also Mrs A. M. Baillie, relict of the above, who died on the 27th August 1840 aged 67 years. This Tablet is erected by their three Children.' And one wonders what happened to those three children.

Chapter 4

Descriptions of late-eighteenth-century Calcutta

Now that we have reached the point where both Edmonstone and Baillie have arrived in Calcutta, we need some description of the City, before it became known as the City of Palaces, and here we are indebted to a certain wealthy Mrs Kindersley, who wrote in 1777, a few years before their arrival there:

I think I have never given you an account of the town of Calcutta; indeed after Madras, it does not appear worth describing, for although it is large, with a great many houses in it and has the advantage of standing upon the banks of a river, it is as awkward a place as can be conceived and so irregular that it looks like all the houses had been thrown up in the air and fallen down again by accident as they now stand; people keep constantly building; and everyone who can procure a piece of ground to build a house thereon, consults his own taste and convenience, without any regard to the beauty and regularity of the town; besides the appearance of the best houses is spoiled by the little straw huts, and such sort of encumbrances, which are built by the servants for themselves to sleep in, so that all the English part of the town, which is the largest, is a confusion of very wealthy and very shabby houses, dead walls, straw huts, warehouses and I know what not.

About the middle of the town, on the river's edge, stands the old Fort, memorable for the catastrophe of the Black Hole, much talked about in England; it was in one of the Fort's apartments that the wretched sufferers were confined. The Fort is now made a very different use of; the only apology for a church is in some of the rooms in it, where divine service is sometimes performed. In a different part of the town reside the Armenians and the people called Portuguese; each of them have their own churches; the Portuguese keep up the processions and pageantry of the Roman church, as far as they are permitted, but they are obliged to perform it all within their own walls. The chief connexion we have with these people is employing some of the women as servants or their men as writers or cooks. Here is not as at Madras a black town nearby for the servants of the English to reside in; therefore Calcutta is partly environed by their habitations which makes the roads rather unpleasant; for the huts they live in, which are built of mud and straw are so low that they can scarcely stand upright in them and having no chimneys, the smoke of the fires with which they dress their victuals comes out from all the doors and perhaps is more disagreeable to the passengers than to themselves.

The new Fort, an immense place, is on the river about a mile below the town. If all the buildings which are intended within the walls are finished, it will be a town within itself for besides houses for the engineers and officers, there are apartments for the Company's writers, barracks for the soldiers, magazines for the stores etc. The town of Calcutta is increasing in size daily, notwithstanding which the English multiply so fast that houses are extremely scarce. As I have given you a description of the houses at Madras, I need only say that these are very much in the same style, only that they do not have the beautiful chunam (plaster made from shell-lime and sand), for although they have the same shells brought from the coast of Coromandel and have mixed them with the same materials and in the same manner, it has not the least of that fine gloss, which is always so greatly admired in Madras; this owing to all the water of Bengal partaking so much of the salt-petre, with which all the earth here is impregnated. Paper or wainscot are improper, both on account of the heat, the vermin and also the difficulty of getting it done; therefore all the rooms have white walls but are plastered in panels, which has a pretty effect. The floors are likewise plastered, covered all over in fine matt, which is nailed down, for although carpets are manufactured in some parts of the country, they are such an addition to the heat, that they are seldom used; the rooms are few, but mostly large and lofty, many of the newly built houses have glass windows, which are pleasant to the eye, but are not so well calculated for the climate as the old windows, which are made of cane.

Mrs Kindersley then goes on at great length about her numerous servants, but then in another letter, she records her daily life:

As the morning and evening is cooler than during the day, it is usual to rise up early and sit up rather late; for after the morning, the heat is so intense that it is difficult to attend to any business and hardly possible to take any amusement. Ladies mostly retire to their own apartments where the slightest covering is almost intolerable. The most active disposition must be indolent in this climate. After dinner, everyone retires to sleep; every servant has gone to his habitation and all is silence and this custom is so universal that it would be as unreasonable to call on any person at three or four o'clock in the afternoon as at the same time in the morning. This custom of sleeping away the hottest hours of the day is necessary even for the strongest constitutions. After this repose, people dress for the evening and enjoy the sunset in their carriages. The rest of the evening is for society.

Living is very expensive on account of the great rent of houses, the number of servants, the excessive price of all European commodities, such as wine and clothes. The perspiration requires perpetual changes of clothes and linen, not to mention the expense of palanqueens, carriages and horses. Most of these things which appear as luxuries are in this climate real necessaries of life. It is remarkable that those Europeans who have good health enjoy a greater flow of spirits than in cooler climates. Except when parties become violent, which is sometimes the case, the society and the hospitality is general and there is no other part of the world, where people part with their money to assist each other as the English do in India.

Chapter 5
Marriages and mistresses

There was a severe dearth of European women, particularly young ladies, in Calcutta and there were hardly any at all in the 'mofussil' outside Calcutta. It was reported that, in the year 1800, there were in Calcutta only 250 British and European women as compared with some 4,000 British and European men. The unmarried single British women were often unattractive – otherwise they might not have braved the six-month voyage out to Bengal, presumably to find a husband. The first record of women being paid for by the Government – in this case, that of Bombay – to go out to India was in 1671 when twenty women sailed out east, and were paid the princely sum of £300 per annum, provided the Company approved their husbands – an allowance, which continued if and when they became widowed. These women later on had a collective – the 'Fishing Fleet' – and depending on their attractiveness or otherwise, they were generally looking for older men, particularly widowers, partly because the older men were more inclined to accept their lack of beauty, but also because when these older men died, they were entitled as widows to the all-important Widows Pension, as mentioned. The natural downside was that quite often these marriages were unhappy, although certainly not all, given the usual age difference. Young attractive girls were picked up almost immediately, and young widows were picked up just as quickly – sometimes even on the same day as their husband's death – such was the demand.

Clearly, these usually slightly older women were not interested in generally penniless young Writers and Cadets arriving from England, at least in terms of marriage, nor were the young Writers and Cadets very much interested in them. Most of them after their Regimental or Writers' duties were finished for the day, wandered round the streets and alleyways, drinking and gambling in the many taverns and visiting the many brothels lining the back streets, which, in turn, led to financial difficulties and disease. It is unlikely that either Edmonstone or Baillie went down this route, particularly as the latter had almost certainly learnt his lesson in Edinburgh. Instead, as we know, both of them took up with Indian ladies – Edmonstone much later than Baillie – and in both cases, proceeded to have Scottish Indian children with them – four each. Very sadly, we do not know the names of either of the two mothers, although we do know that Edmonstone's lady was described as being both charming and well educated, and was able to write to her children in English – possibly taught by Edmonstone. It is also the case that the entry for an Indian mother in the Baptismal Certificates was always left blank. However, we do know that it was not long after Baillie arrived in Calcutta that he took up with his Indian lady. We wonder where he found her, or for that matter, where she found him and how could he afford her and their four children on originally an Ensign's and then a Lieutenant's pay, and one still wonders where they lived – presumably somewhere in the capacious Fort William.

Going back to the later so-called 'Fishing Fleet', those women who did not marry and returned home were given the singularly infelicitous appellation of 'Returned Empties'. If they could not afford the fare home, they tended to end up as nannies, governesses or companions, and this is almost certainly what happened to two Baillie spinsters Henrietta and Anne Mary who died in 1845 and 1846, respectively, and were buried in the New Burial Ground, Circular Road, Calcutta.

General Charles Hindoo Stuart in his Calcutta book entitled *A Ladies Monitor* described going along to a dinner party in Calcutta, which was attended by a number of 'Returning Empties'. He reported that they were all complaining that Englishmen in India all preferred Indian women, and that very few were interested in marrying a white girl, everyone being apparently quite content and happy with their 'bibis' as they were called. For a portrait of a lovely bibi, you only have to go to the National Gallery in Dublin, and there you will see the famous portrait of William Hickey's beautiful bibi, Jemdanee, by Thomas Hickey. Hickey adored her and, sad it is to relate, she died in agony in childbirth along with her baby. Hickey was so heartbroken at losing them – it would have been his only child – that, unsurprisingly, he had to take six months off from his legal work to recover from depression.

General Stuart continued by saying that one of the 'Returning Empties' had remarked to him at the same dinner party

> that it would have been far better if they had stayed at home; that marriages were little in demand nowadays and that the bad taste of the Englishmen rendered unnecessary the introduction of any more foreign beauties, at least until that desire for novelty which scarcity always produces, should induce gentlemen to their own country women as an agreeable change, enhanced by the pleasure of variety.

English men in Calcutta, however, agreed with a Company official Samuel Brown, who wrote that they far preferred the more biddable Indian women to 'encountering the whims of an English woman and yielding to her furies'.

This General Stuart adopted Hindu customs including bathing in the river every day. He greatly encouraged European women to adopt the sari – a mistake because European women generally never looked right in a sari – and he published letters extolling the virtues of elegant, simple and sensual saris, comparing these with the prodigious structural engineering European women adopted at that time in the intense Bengali heat and humidity, namely, strapping themselves into busks in order to hold their bellies in, project their breasts out and allow their dresses to balloon grandly up and down towards the floor. One of his books was entitled *The Ladies Monitor Being a Series of Letters First Published in Bengal on the Subject of Female Apparel Tending to Favour a Regulated Adoption of Indian Costume and a Rejection of Superfluous Vesture by the Ladies of This Country – with Incidental Remarks on Hindoo Beauty, Whalebone Stays, Iron Busks, Indian Corsets, Man Milliners, Idle Bachelors, Hair Powder, Waiting Maids and Footmen*, which might be considered a somewhat long title.

It should be mentioned, however, that this is the somewhat eccentric Irish General who declared, 'Whenever I look around me regarding Hindu mythology, I discover Piety, Morality and as far as I can rely on my judgement, it appears the most complete and ample system of Moral Allegory, the world has ever produced.' He also left his remarkable collection of antiquities to the British Museum, where they form and continue to form the basis of the Museum's ancient Hindu and Buddhist sculpture collection from the subcontinent. Here we must, somewhat reluctantly, leave Hindoo Stuart and think of him travelling round India with his Indian bibi beside him in his buggy cart, followed, as it was put at the time, by a veritable cavalcade of children's carriages and 'palkee' loads of little babies.

Chapter 6

Baillie's and Edmonstone's bibis and their eight Scottish Indian children

We have mentioned that Baillie must have taken up with his Indian lady quite shortly after he arrived in Calcutta. Their first son, George, was born on 1 April 1795, meaning that he was conceived in the summer of 1794, when Baillie was aged 22, so clearly no time was wasted in getting together. As we have mentioned earlier, one wonders as an Ensign whether he had to request permission from his Commanding Officer, first, because of his age and second, because she was Indian.

The second son, Neil Benjamin Edmonstone Baillie, was born a few years later in November 1799. This son was baptized in Calcutta on 10 April 1801, but as his mother was Indian, her name on the Baptismal Certificate was left blank, although everyone knew who she was. He inherited his father's linguistic skills and after he returned to India from Scotland, where he had been brought up by Baillie's sister Margaret at Leys Castle, he was appointed Assistant Secretary to the Indian Law Commission and then the Government Pleader in the Court of Dewani Adawlut. He produced a number of publications on the Law and Land Tax of India and completed his father's treatise on Mohammedan Law. We can find no record as to whether he married and had children, or alternatively took up with an Indian lady – however, we do know that he did return to England and died aged 88, being buried at Kensal Green Cemetery, where he shares a stone with his widowed sister Margaret Catherine, who had also returned from India and who died aged 87 on 11 November 1890.

The third child, daughter Charlotte, was born in July 1801 and his last Calcutta child, Margaret Catherine was born in 1803, shortly before her father was appointed the Political Agent in Bundelkhand. Charlotte was married on 1 October 1819 to a certain Major Thomas Richard McQueen of the 45th Native

Infantry Regiment at Lucknow. He first came to be noticed, when as a Lieutenant of the 23rd Native Infantry, he attacked and dispersed some enemy on leaving Port Soony on 21 January 1818 – an engagement which was reported in *The London Gazette*. He was then promoted to be Adjutant of Baddely's Horse and then Captain of the 45th Native Infantry Regiment and then Major. In 1840 he, sadly, drowned in a river near Bhagalpur on 10 January 1840 – Charlotte was a widow for fifty-two years. However, they did have four children – three sons and one daughter – Thomas born at Dinapore in 1824; Charlotte born at Neemuch 1831; John Baillie born at Muttra in 1834; and finally, Arthur James born at Agra in 1836. One wonders again what happened to them.

Margaret Catherine married a certain Captain Henry Francis Caley of the 64th Native Infantry at Neemuch in Central India on 19 April 1823. He eventually was promoted to Major General in the Bengal Army. However, his ascent to that rank was not without certain alarums and excursions on the way, including being censured for passing into the Service recruits who were not fit for duty; being censured again this time by the Commander-in-Chief for having granted discharges to certain soldiers of the 4th Native Infantry, when the Regiment was under orders to proceed to Scinde on 30 March 1844. The following year, a certain Brevet Captain Becher accused him 'of an unusual intimacy with a band boy', whereupon he was court-martialled, but cleared of all charges, with the Brevet Captain being cashiered and dismissed the Service. Major-General Caley died at Rawalpindi in 1866 and you can see his Memorial there. Margaret herself died at Rawalpindi in 1890 – a widow for twenty-four years. Unfortunately, there were no children from the marriage.

George, Baillie's eldest son, was born in 1795 but never returned to India like his brother and sisters. He became a practising doctor in east London and later a Surgeon at the London Hospital; he was also appointed Surgeon to the Metropolitan Police Division in East London. He and his wife produced twelve children – six sons and six daughters. One son went out to India to join the Bengal Army, rising to be a Major General, but died in 1889 unmarried, while another son, who was born in 1828, went out to India as a Captain in the Engineers. He was stationed at Mhow, where he was engaged in building the railway line but died, when he fell off his horse. And there, I think, we must call a halt to Baillie's children by his Indian lady in Calcutta, but in all this we wonder what the feelings of the mother were when her children were taken away from her and sent off to Scotland, but we can well imagine them. It is almost certain that they were similar to those of Khair-un-Nisa, the Muslim wife of James Kirkpatrick, the Resident at Hyderabad, whose two children were sent back to England, much to her huge distress. You can see these two children, who had both Christian and Muslim names, in that superb portrait of them by George Chinnery, just before they left for England, and you can see that Catherine's eyes were bloodshot with tears at being taken away from her mother, who was never to see them again. At least, however, the Indian mother of Baillie's children might have seen three of her children again, assuming she was still alive, when they returned to India after leaving Leys Castle near Inverness.

It seems that it was not until 1795 that Edmonstone started his relationship with an Indian lady, so he appears to have been much slower off the mark than Baillie, who had wasted no time at all. He never revealed her name, despite having four children with her. It was reported that she was charming, intelligent and well-educated, which would mean that she came from an upper-class family, which had perhaps fallen on hard times or perhaps not. She was also literate in the sense that she could write letters in English and thus could communicate with her two boys, who were sent to Scotland to Margaret Baillie, and with her youngest son, who was sent to school in east London. It may have been the case that Edmonstone himself taught her English. We think it is almost certain that she was alive when he married his English girl in 1803, and it was even reported that when he left Calcutta in 1818, she and his daughter Eliza were at the dockside or rather ghatside to wave him and his English wife and children goodbye. How that must have hurt!

In 1796, Edmonstone's first Scottish Indian child was born and three others soon followed. The three sons were baptized in Calcutta and his name appeared on the Baptismal Certificate as the father. The eldest son was called John, and thereafter came Alexander and Frederick, and then a girl called Eliza. Another very hurtful matter was that Edmonstone refused to allow his four children to bear his name, so that their surname was changed to Elmore – something which Baillie, in his letters to Edmonstone, deprecated. It must have also been difficult for the two boys to write to their father, when they had a different name to his. The two eldest boys were, as we have noted, sent to Leys Castle near Inverness, to be brought up by Baillie's sister Margaret. The youngest son Frederick was sent to England in 1811 and placed in a school in Leyton run by a certain William Shepherd, as by then Margaret was almost certainly too old to cope with any more children – she already had nine to look after, bring up and arrange for their education. Interestingly enough, Mr Shepherd seems to have 'specialized' in half Indian children, including the son of Graeme Mercer, who accompanied Frederick from Calcutta to London. Graeme Mercer will appear again in this narrative, when he was involved with Baillie in Bundelkhand

We see two letters written by Frederick to his father in Calcutta – the first being dated 15 June 1811:

Dear Father

    With great pleasure, I inform you that we had a very quick and pleasant passage from India. I arrived in England at the beginning of last month. I have been quite well since I left Calcutta. On the 18th May, Mr Mercer put me to a school about six miles from London, where his son also is, together with several other East Indian boys and where I find myself comfortable. I should be happy to hear from you.

   With affectionate duty to you and Mother and love to my sister, I am, dear Father, your most dutiful Son

   Frederick Wm Ellmore

   Mr Shepherd's Academy, Leyton, Essex

Later we see another letter written to his father dated 19 February 1812 and you will note that he addresses his father this time as Sir and not Father – it is possible or even probable that he never received any letters from his father, although he did from his mother, and it is equally possible or even probable that his two older brothers in Scotland did not either – they were always complaining that they did not hear from him – see the letters in the Appendix.

Dear Sir,

   I had the pleasure of writing to you soon after I arrived in England. It is now some months since I had the pleasure of seeing Mr Mercer. He went to Scotland, I think, in last June, and has not been seen since. I have been very well until a month ago, when I was taken ill in my neck under my right ear. I am in the hands of a Surgeon and am being taken great care of, the complaint yields to the medicines which I take and I hope I shall be well soon; it does not prevent me from attending school or play.

   I am always, Dear Sir, Your very obedient humble Servant,

   Fred. Wm. Ellmore

   Leyton

   Essex

Unfortunately, Frederick did not recover and died from tuberculosis in 1815. We see a letter written by Mr Shepherd to Edmonstone in Calcutta dated 13 May 1813 – it reads as follows:

As the last East Indian fleet of this season is on the point of sailing and as Mr and Mrs Graeme Mercer left London for Scotland about 14 days ago, I think it my duty to take this opportunity of sending you the latest information respecting Master Elmore.

   He was sent to my school and committed to my care by Mr Mercer in May 1811 soon after his arrival and he is a boy of the most amiable disposition, good tempered, orderly, obliging and grateful. He was making good progress in his education.

   At the beginning of last year, a knot or gathering appeared to be forming under one of his ears. With the approbation of Mr Mercer, I immediately applied for the advice of an eminent surgeon in London, who attended him regularly and by whose direction, I sent him in July last year to Brighton for the benefit of sea bathing. At Brighton, he had the measles and returned to my house at Christmas in worse health and more emaciated than when he left.

Besides a running in the neck, there was a large gathering on the lower part of his back near the spine which broke some time ago and it has discharged most profusely. There are at this time three swellings of the same kind on the neck, which have also broken. In this distressing situation you may very well judge that his health has been much impaired and he has been reduced to a state of great disability.

About three weeks ago, he appeared to be a little better – he is now brought down every day and is drawn about in a little chaise in the garden for the benefit of fresh air and he can even stand and walk a little with some help. By the particular desire of his medical attendants, he has always been provided with the best and most nourishing articles that can be found for eating and drinking. I have engaged a nurse, who is with him night and day and whose sole employment is to attend him.

You may be assured that the most unabated care shall be taken of my poor afflicted pupil and, as the winter has now gone, I would willingly flatter myself that nature will make an effort to preserve his life. He is certainly a most engaging child and everybody in my family is seriously interested in him and I devoutly wish that my next letter to you may convey the pleasing intelligence of his being in an undoubted state of convalescence.

I have the Honour to be, Sir, Your most obedient and humble servant.
William Shepherd
Leyton
Essex

Alas, there was no more convalescence and he died shortly afterwards, all alone, no family near him, in effect an outcast for his mixed blood and without even his father's name. How this engaging, amiable, grateful and obliging boy must have suffered, as he lay dying, far from his beloved mother in Calcutta.

This leaves Eliza, who stayed with her mother in Calcutta. She was given a good dowry by the Edmonstone family and married a certain John Barker Plumb, an English merchant with the import firm Tulloh and Company. We do know that she had five children with Mr Plumb and that the first child, a son, was christened Neil Edmonstone Plumb. What we also know is that because of her birth and thus mixed blood and, despite her being married to an English merchant and being a wealthy woman, she could not or was not allowed to participate fully in Calcutta society and that the East India Company entertainments were generally out of bounds, although private entertainments were open. Later on, we will see what happened to the two boys John and Alexander, when we review the extensive correspondence, which Margaret Baillie had with the Edmonstones about them. Edmonstone seems to have been quite diffident about his Scottish Indian children – he denied them his name; he hardly ever, if ever, wrote to them; he never told them their birth dates; he kept their existence from his legitimate children and, as his granddaughter Mrs Browne attested, neither of the two families ever met or were, indeed, at all aware of the existence of their half-brothers and half-sisters – it was almost as if he was ashamed of them, and when Baillie wrote to him about this state of affairs, he never seems to have replied.

There were reasons for both Baillie and Edmonstone and many other families for sending their Scottish Indian children back to England or Scotland as the case may be, quite apart from the educational aspect. The reason was, as Edmonstone himself noted, and perhaps he was writing his own book here, that

the great number of that class of the community of India denominated half-caste are generally rejected and despised by the Europeans and, as it happens, held in very inferior estimation by the natives. They do not belong to one or the other. They are debarred from the rights and privileges of British subjects, being deemed in law natives of India, while at the same time, they are shut out from most of the advantages of their imputed nativity by their religion, habits, manners and education. Precluded from holding any offices under Government but those of the most subordinate description; without capital and consequently without the means of engaging in the commerce of the country, or establishing themselves as landholders, allied paternally with the European community and maternally with the native community and disavowed by both, they form an insulated, degraded and consequently discontented body.

This was not entirely true, of course, and three of Baillie's Scottish Indian children went back to India, his daughters marrying well and his son Neil Benjamin working in a senior position for the Government of India.

Chapter 7

Edmonstone's early days in Calcutta

When Edmonstone arrived in Calcutta, he was 'favourably introduced to the Governor-General Warren Hastings and experienced much personal kindness and attention from him during the remaining period of his administration'. He was immediately attached to the Secretary's Office as an Examiner and then appointed Assistant to the Judicial Office at the Presidency, called the Preparer of Reports.

Edmonstone wrote in his diary,

> From the time of my arrival in Bengal, I applied myself diligently to the study of Oriental languages, the knowledge of which, although at the time of the most essential importance to almost every branch of the Administration, especially the Political, was extremely rare among the Company's servants and of far more difficult of attainment than it has since become, by the institution of the College of Fort William. I was subsequently appointed to be the Assistant Persian and Bengali Translator to the Board of Revenue and the Second Assistant to the Registrar of the Sudder Dawaney Adawlut.

This was the Civil Court that tried cases exceeding 500 rupees. Later, he was appointed Persian and Bengali Translator to the Board of Revenue in January 1786.

Warren Hastings had resigned the previous year, but there was a long delay, while Lord Cornwallis made up his somewhat slow mind whether to succeed him or not. In a way, one could say that the choice of Cornwallis was surprising, bearing in mind that he was the General who had surrendered to General George Washington at Yorktown in 1781. Of course, there is a long story about that, but this is a book about India and not America. Curiously, his reputation did not greatly suffer as a result of his capitulation, although that of his superior officer

General Clinton did. It seems that he was forced to resign, and it was even reported that there was some scandal in that, during the campaign, he was thought to have been spending a lot of time with Mary Baddeley, his mistress in New York.

Cornwallis was regarded as being somewhat conventional and an unimaginative sort of fellow and a contemporary of his suggested that 'his mental constitution was the highest order of commonplace'. Be that as it may, he was respected for his honesty and common sense and he was generally regarded as a safe pair of hands. Warren Hastings agreed that he should succeed him and he is reported as saying, 'Here there is no broken fortune to be mended; here there are no beggarly mushroom kindred to be provided for; here there is no avarice to be gratified; here there is no crew of hungry followers to be gorged'. Cornwallis had originally declined the appointment, but when he was approached again a year later, he accepted it, provided that he was also appointed the Commander-in-Chief and that he was given powers to override the Council. He was, of course, very mindful of all the trials and tribulations, which Warren Hastings had experienced with the members of his Council, notably Sir Philip Francis, who so exasperated him, that he challenged him to a duel and shot him, although, perhaps somewhat unfortunately, not dead. The reason for this is that he was a key figure in the impeachment of Warren Hastings, which lasted no less than seven years.

While Lord Cornwallis was still making up his mind, there was naturally an interregnum in Calcutta and this was filled by the then senior member of the Council, namely a John Macpherson, who was, accordingly, appointed acting Governor General. Let us tell you a little about this relatively unknown man.

He was born at the Manse of Kilmour in the Isle of Skye, where his father, who was highly educated and cultured, was the Church of Scotland Minister. Interestingly enough for the Scottish reader, his mother was the daughter of Donald Macleod of Bernera and granddaughter of the Earl of Seaforth and Chief of the Clan Mackenzie. He was educated at King's College, Aberdeen, and then Edinburgh University, as were the Baillies at that time. He trained to follow his father's footsteps in the ministry of the Church of Scotland – however, his father suddenly died and equally suddenly there was no more money, and no prospect of entering the Ministry, for which apparently in those days money was required.

He found an alternative living as the Purser on the East Indiaman, the *Lord Mansfield*, which was captained by his uncle Alexander Macleod. He, therefore, went out to India in 1769 and landing at Madras, he was there introduced to the Nawab of the Carnatic, Mohammed Ali Khan, whom he described as a 'polite man of very agreeable address but at the same time the worst man in the world to do business with'. He was said to have amused him by introducing him to the magic lantern. As we know, the Nawab was heavily in debt to the Company and its servants and given this particular scenario, Macpherson saw the opportunity not only to assist the financially embarrassed Nawab, but also at the same time to feather his own nest, both of which he did successfully.

He then returned to England, partly to plead the Nawab's cause, and then returned to Madras, where his new-found friend Warren Hastings was about to embark for Calcutta, having been appointed the Governor General there. In 1775, he wrote to Hastings stating that 'it is my sincere opinion that if your Board does not speedily supersede the power of the Government of Madras, then one or two events must surely follow; either the ruin of the Nawab or a Convulsion in the ruined Government, from which the Company may never recover'. It nearly turned out to be both, and one can link this observation to the tragedy of Colonel William Baillie in 1780, five years later, at the battle of Pollilur, 50 miles west of Madras.

He again returned to England where he became the unopposed Member of Parliament for the rotten borough of Cricklade in Wiltshire in 1799, although his election was declared null and void – however, by that time he was back in India – this time in Calcutta, where, with the help of Laurence Sullivan and the then Lord North Government, he was appointed to the Supreme Council of India in the place of Richard Barwell. It was described as a disgraceful appointment, which was later condemned by a Select Committee in language of the greatest severity. Despite, therefore, having been brought up as a member of the Cloth, he was regarded as an unprincipled man. However, with Hastings leaving for England and with Lord Cornwallis still making up his mind, Macpherson as the, by now, Senior Member of the Council became the acting Governor General of India in 1785. This was a far cry from being the Purser on the *Lord Mansfield*, and there he ruled as the Governor General for nearly two years, at the end of which he was rewarded with a Baronetcy.

He remained on the Supreme Council under Cornwallis, but the latter became increasingly disillusioned with him. He told Dundas that 'he was certainly the most contemptible man that ever pretended to govern; that his Government was a system of the dirtiest jobbing and that he should consider himself lucky not to be impeached'. But then, Cornwallis had a personal grievance against Macpherson, as the latter had put it about in England that Cornwallis had remarried and that his bride was a young girl of 16 years of age – so some of his comments perhaps need to be discounted. What we do know is that, on his return to England, he received the unanimous approbation of the Court of Directors as well as the Baronetcy, received a very generous Pension, entered Parliament but was then unseated for bribery, but obtained another seat and became an intimate friend of the Prince Regent – by the use of all that money he had made in India. However, it needs to be said in his favour that, during his tenure as the acting Governor General, he dealt successfully with the Government's acute financial difficulties in all three Presidencies and by the time he left, he had managed to clear off all the arrears of Military pay before Cornwallis arrived.

Unlike Macpherson, Cornwallis knew nothing very much about India, nor did he seem to be particularly interested. He never developed any particular friendships with Indians, so perhaps it was the case that his mental constitution was the highest order of commonplace. He relied heavily on the opinions of those around him and his principal advisors. One of these was John Shore, later to succeed him as Governor General, who was a Member of his Council and a revenue expert, who, it was said, 'had many strong prejudices and a universal one against the natives of India'. He had also stated that 'the knowledge, such as it is, which I have acquired of the people of India, their customs and their manners, does not make me like them any better'. This mistrust could well have communicated itself to Cornwallis, who became convinced that 'unless they, the Indians, were confined to lowly posts, the administration was bound to be corrupt'.

Chapter 8

The Kennaway Embassy to Hyderabad

Cornwallis arrived in India in 1786. In South India, Tipu Sultan at Mysore was at war with both the Mahratta Peshwa and the Nizam of Hyderabad. Tipu had sent an Embassy to France, requesting Military support against the English, while Madras was reporting that he had designs on Travancore, which he was thinking of invading. In the Treaty of Bangalore, which had been made with Tipu, Travancore had been specifically named as an ally of the Company, so that if Tipu really did invade Travancore, then the Company would be honour-bound to come to the aid of the Rajah. Cornwallis then thought in terms of forming an alliance with the Mahrattas and requesting them to attack Tipu's territories from the north, but he then realized that, as he had withdrawn Macpherson's offer of aid to the Mahrattas, they were unlikely to respond positively, and they did not.

This, therefore, left Cornwallis no alternative but to seek the support of the Nizam of Hyderabad against Tipu. This resulted in a two-year Embassy there, led by Sir John Kennaway in order to confer, so to speak, with the Nizam and Edmonstone accompanied this Embassy as his Assistant and just as importantly as his Persian Translator. It was an honour which Edmonstone would later learn that he owed to a strong recommendation procured for him by the Duke of Argyll, and one wonders how the Duke of Argyll knew about this proposed Embassy to Hyderabad from as far away as Scotland. However, assuming this was somehow true, it does demonstrate the long reach of Scotland to India.

There were two main objectives – the first of which was to get the Nizam on side, so to speak, while the other was to request or rather to demand the surrender of the Guntoor Circar, the southernmost Circar adjacent to the Madras Presidency and to which the Company had a legitimate reversion negotiated by Clive.

This Guntoor Circar has a long and tortuous history and we need, perhaps, to put all this into some sort of context. The word 'Circar' was the Indian word applied to a Subah or Province, which was ruled by a Deputy Governor, responsible in this case to the Subahdar of the Deccan, who was the Nizam of Hyderabad, who, in his turn, was nominally responsible to the Emperor in Delhi. There were five of these Circars situated to the south of Orissa and to the north of the Carnatic on the east coast of India and the Guntoor was the southernmost. Of particular interest to the Baillie family was that Colonel William Baillie of the Madras Army with his Brigade column of three Sepoy battalions and, initially another two Circar Sepoy battalions, spent the last ten months of his active service life in 1780 marching, counter-marching and campaigning in the Guntoor Circar, before being ordered to march south to effect a junction with the Madras Army, commanded by Sir Hector Munro at Conjeveram, where he met his doom. When the order came through to march south, these two Circar battalions understandably deserted, as such a march would take them out of their home territory. This desertion, as it happens, saved their lives.

We need here to delve a little further, but perhaps not too deeply, into the history of the Guntoor Circar, which, for a long time, had been and was an explosive issue in Indian politics. The reason for this is that it has been fully explored in my previous book *When the Tiger Fought the Thistle*. However, as it was this dispute, which would almost certainly determine the allegiances of the great States of India for the forthcoming decisive period of British expansion in the subcontinent, it seems that some amplification is required. Perhaps it should to be pointed out that it was the presence of French troops there in the Deccan, as we have pointed out earlier in the 1750s, which had provided the Company with a motive for coveting the area and when the Seven Years War broke out between France and Britain in 1756, Madras took the opportunity of sending a force up into the Circars. At that point, Salabat Jang, one of the sons of the Nizam, who had succeeded to the throne, courtesy of the French, marched to defend his territory but, rightly concerned about the Nizam's intrigues in Hyderabad, while he was away, agreed to cede the Fortress of Masulipatam to the Company in return for peace. In the First Mysore War, Nizam Ali, now the ruler of Hyderabad, took the opportunity to invade the Carnatic but was pushed back by a British force, while another Company force took the opportunity to occupy the Circars. These hostilities, as well as the Farman, which Clive had personally obtained from the Moghul Emperor in 1765, gave the Company the opportunity to claim the area. In the end, the Nizam, reluctantly in 1768, came into line with the Emperor's 1765 Farman and agreed the cession of the Circars to the Company in return for an annual tribute payment called the 'Peishcush'. However, there was an exception and this was the southern Guntoor Circar, which had already been given to Basalat Jung, his brother. It was, therefore, decided that Basalat Jung would retain this Circar but that, on his death, it would revert to the Company.

But then it all went wrong and the reason for this was that the Madras Government persuaded Basalat Jung to rent them the Guntoor Circar in 1779, in return for a guarantee of protection against Haidar Ali and his son Tipu Sultan. The Nizam, when he heard about it, became particularly angry for a number of reasons: first of all, because he was thinking about taking it over himself, having decapitated his brother; second, because all this had been done without his permission; and third, because the Company had sublet the Guntoor to his arch enemy, the Nawab of the Carnatic, Mohammed Ali Khan. Haidar Ali was also upset, because he himself was on course to push up into the Guntoor and had been doing so for some time, with a view of taking it over himself for Mysore. He started to threaten Adoni, the capital of Basalat Jung, with a large force, which meant that the latter requested the Company for Military assistance and this was provided by a Brigade Column, as mentioned earlier, initially commanded by a certain Colonel Harper. He was then replaced by Colonel William Baillie, the uncle of Colonel John Baillie, who had to march through some of the territory in Cuddapah, which was occupied by Haidar Ali – a fact that helped prompt the Second Anglo-Mysore War, which, in its turn, led to the death of Colonel William Baillie after the battle of Pollilur on 10 September 1780.

Not, however, wishing to upset the Nizam, while the Company was still enmeshed in the Second Anglo-Mysore War, the Company did not initially insist on its reversion right. However, the Directors in London were keen to acquire the Guntoor, and, indeed, Cornwallis had instructions from the Directors of the Company to acquire it. In 1788, Cornwallis believed that the Company had never had a better opportunity for pressing its claim, as he informed Kennaway in a private conversation.

Accordingly, the Embassy paraded on the Maidan in front of Fort William on 30 April 1788, after a farewell dinner at the Old Court House given by Lord Cornwallis the previous evening; a salute was fired from the guns at the Fort and off they set for the three month journey down the east coast of India mounted on their horses, camels and elephants including a baby elephant, which had cost Edmonstone most of his annual salary. This elephant also required him to employ a mahout to drive the elephant and a grasscutter to enable the elephant to be fed daily on the journey and all this added to his expenses. Three months later, they arrived in Hyderabad. There, they discovered that the Nizam was, in a sense, hedging his bets, by planning an alliance with the French, by which, disregarding the reversion of the Guntoor to the Company, he would undertake to cede it to the French, in return for protection from the Company and also from Tipu. At more or less the same time, he was also making overtures to Tipu himself, proposing an alliance between the two States. Tipu's response to this was that, in return for such an alliance, he required the Nizam not only to make the Guntoor over to him – he had always coveted it, but also one of the Nizam's women as a bride. Tipu was, of course, of low birth, although he did not think so, and the result was that the Nizam turned him down flat.

Nevertheless, the Nizam was frightened of Tipu – more than that, he was perhaps mortally afraid of him – and perhaps rightly so after his defeat of Colonel William Baillie's Brigade Column near Conjeveram in 1780, so he therefore reverted back to Sir John Kennaway, who, perforce, had to give a somewhat noncommittal response, because if anything was taken further at that stage, it would place the Governor General in a difficult position. The reason for this was that, whereas the Nizam had now turned to the Company, requesting Military aid to defend his territories, the Government of India in Calcutta by various treaties, which had ended the previous Anglo-Mysore war, was bound to desist from aiding and abetting the enemies of that State. Thus, Cornwallis was forced to compromise by informing the Nizam via Kennaway that, whereas he was unable to sign a Treaty per se, nevertheless, the Company would in the event of an invasion of Hyderabad, contribute Military aid. And there the matter would have rested, except that Tipu did go ahead and invade Travancore, a neighbouring state, as it happens not particularly successfully, but Travancore was, indeed, an ally of the Company. This contravention of the Treaty forced Cornwallis to change his mind, and the result was that he later sailed down to Madras to conduct the war personally, taking along with him his Deputy Persian Translator George Cherry, which thus enabled Edmonstone, who had returned to Calcutta with the signed Treaty in his pocket, to take Cherry's place temporarily as Official Deputy Persian Translator to the Government of India – an astonishing responsibility for a young man aged 24.

How did all this end? On 9 September, Kennaway and Edmonstone visited the Nizam and presented him with a letter from Lord Cornwallis, which informed the Nizam that the Company troops would start marching into the Guntoor 14 days from the date of the delivery of His Lordship's letter. Naturally, there was an uproar, but in the end, the Guntoor Circar was transferred to the Company by the end of that month.

Edmonstone wrote,

The situation of Assistant to the Embassy, opened up a wide field of political instruction and experience and a favourable opportunity of practical acquaintance with the language, habits and Institutions of the Natives of India in every grade of Society. During the two years that I continued to be attached to this Embassy, I had, of course, the most favourable opportunity of improving myself in the knowledge of the Persian and Hindustani languages and at the end of that time, the Governor-General was pleased to select me to fill the Office of Deputy Persian Translator to the Government of India vacated by the promotion of Mr Cherry to be the Persian Translator in succession to Mr Edward Colebrooke.

He also wrote,

At that period of our comparatively very limited dominion in India, when numerous States and Principalities of all ranks and degrees of power and importance, with which all epistolary correspondence was conducted through the Persian Translator, that Office was of a peculiarly confidential and responsible nature. These political functionaries were in the habit of assembling daily at the Office of the Persian Translator for the purpose of communicating with him on the concerns of their respective Governments and Chiefs. The Persian Translator daily attended the Governor-General to impart information to him and receive instructions, whilst weekly levies were held and audiences given to the Natives of Rank and members of the Diplomatic Corps, who desired conferences with the Governor-General and at all of these, the Persian Translator was required to officiate.

Sir John Kennaway remained in Hyderabad as the first British Resident until ill-health forced his retirement in 1793. He wrote this end of term report on Edmonstone as follows:

I parted with him with great respect. His disposition is tractable, mild and good and he is very anxious to do right, but his want and knowledge and experience of the world, ceded to great modesty, renders him the most diffident man I know. Having always had some person or other on whose counsel he has depended, he is, on all occasions, unwilling to act from himself, although his understanding is a very good one and he possesses qualifications and talents which falls only to the lot of few.

Chapter 9

Sir John Shore, Governor General

The appointment of John Shore as the successor to Lord Cornwallis in 1793, not very long after Baillie had arrived in Calcutta, occasioned a certain amount of surprise. William Hickey, who was a snob but an amusing snob, regarded Shore as a man of low origins – without any particular connection or weight or influence – nor had he originally been thought much of by the Company's establishment in Leadenhall Street. Hickey also thought he was hideous – he was thin, slightly built, a former civil servant and a lawyer. Sir Richard Wellesley, Lord Mornington, his successor, complained bitterly about him having been appointed Governor General, saying, 'His low birth, vulgar manners, his eastern habits as well as his education in the Company's service, his shyness and awkwardness, added to timidity, indolence and bad health contributed to relax every spring of this Government of India and established a systematic degradation of the person, dignity and authority of the Governor-General,' all of which could be described as classic Wellesley.

We do need to ascertain whether Hickey's and Sir Richard Wellesley's criticisms was fair or not – it was not – on the contrary he was very able but, at the same time, diffident and somewhat self-effacing. We also need to remember that William Pitt, who had taken a great deal of interest in this Indian succession, as well as Shore's famous Indian Revenue Settlement, had been greatly struck by Shore's industry, his candour and his talent, so much so, that he recommended his name to the King who, in his usual ineffable manner, responded by saying, 'No one could be so properly thought of as Mr Shore, unless, of course, a more distinguished man can be found to be Governor-General of Bengal.'

Leadenhall Street soon had ample reason to be pleased with the choice of John Shore, because he actually did what he was asked to do by the Directors. He increased the profits of the Company, he kept the peace and, other than Oudh, he avoided any entanglements with the various Indian States and, in doing so, showed considerable strength of character. In particular, he refused to assist the Nizam of Hyderabad in a war against the Mahrattas, as it would have been a violation of Pitt's East India Act and we will deal with this in some detail later. He had admired Cornwallis, whom he described as 'manly, affable and of good judgement', and he also admired the young imperialists, whom Cornwallis had brought on and, in particular, Edmonstone and George Cherry, who became Edmonstone's best friend – and both of whom, importantly, were proficient in the Persian language as was Shore, although less so.

Edmonstone wrote that Shore was honest and had complete integrity, but that he lacked self-confidence and a forceful personality, all the while complaining about ill health – particularly insomnia, saying that in India, he rarely got more than two hours of sleep a night. Shore was well aware of his faults and wrote that 'the fact of the matter is that the duties of my situation are really too much for my abilities and I sometimes doubt my own judgement. How often have I wished that Lord Cornwallis was still at the head of the Administration here and that I was his co-adjutor as formerly and then all would have been well'. In his letters to London, he was often quite deferential and sometimes almost cringing in tone – constantly deploring his lack of ability and also writing that 'the Governor-General and the Commander-in-Chief ought to have more talents than either of us possess'. He consoled himself with the hope that his defects would be to some extent made up by his zeal and good intent, and he wrote, 'I shall do my duty and I will leave the rest to Providence.'

Indeed, his references to Providence were quite frequent, so much so, that he became, like Charles Grant and his wife, an evangelical Christian and a member of the Clapham Sect. Furthermore, he became the first President of the British and Foreign Bible Society. In Calcutta, he read and reread the New Testament and also many parts of the Bible, Warburton's *Divine Legation*, Jortin's *Ecclesiastical History*, his *Sermons* over and over again, Paley's Evidences and so on. Like both Edmonstone and Baillie, he had an Indian lady, with whom he had three children – John, Frances and Martha. When he returned to England, he married a certain Charlotte Cornish, with whom he proceeded to have another nine children, of whom, two, very sadly, died in infancy.

Shore faced his first real test with the politics of the Deccan and the Treaty of Alliance, which Cornwallis had concluded with both the Nizam and the Mahrattas. Here, this Treaty of Alliance stipulated that 'if after the conclusion of the peace with Tipu, he should attack or molest either of the two contracting parties, the others will join together to punish him'. Here, Cornwallis had been concerned that the grounds, on which the allied parties could request or perhaps demand mutual support, should be strictly defined. Accordingly, he sent a draft Guarantee to both Poona and Hyderabad, proposing that if any differences should arise between the parties and Tipu, the nature and the circumstances should be communicated to the other parties and that they should not take up arms, until he was convinced that every effort for conciliation had been exhausted. This proposal was quite acceptable to the Nizam, but not to the Mahrattas, who took the view that not only was the Company getting too powerful, but that this was also an arrogant assumption on its part – in any case, they were planning to invade the Nizam's territories themselves.

There were, of course, endless discussions about all this, which went on for a year or so and, in the end, the Governor General gave up any hope of obtaining the agreement of the Mahrattas and had to be content with some sort of vague assurance on their part, that they would abide by their engagements, which, in any case, they did not want to do, and nor did they.

In 1794, Mahdajee Scindia, the chief opponent of the Guarantee Treaty, died, and his great nephew Dowlat Rao aged 13 succeeded him as Peshwa. This did or might have represented some sort of opportunity for the Company to intervene to try and engender some sort of peace – however, Shore considered that any intervention to assist the Nizam in a conflict with the Mahrattas, when there was no particular Treaty obligation so to do, would have been a violation of the policy laid down by Pitt in his East India Act and, in any case, almost impossible to justify on any sort of grounds of expediency. He also, quite rightly, took the view that the combined armies of the Peshwa and Scindia were far stronger than those of the Nizam, whose Government he considered was 'a tottering fabric which would fall of its own weakness'.

To risk a war on the side of the Nizam against the Mahrattas, when they could also be joined by Tipu, he considered would be the height of folly. He reminded the Nizam that, in accordance with the conditions stipulated by Cornwallis, that the two battalions of the Company's Regiments, which were stationed at Hyderabad for his own protection, could not be used against the Mahrattas. This was too much for the Nizam, so he dismissed the Company's officers and replaced them with French officers, who were commanded by General Raymond – a French revolutionary, who flew the French Tricolour. Thus, the Governor General stood aside to let matters proceed between the Nizam and the Mahrattas.

So the Nizam's huge Army and all its many followers, including his harem and his dancing girls, lumbered slowly off in the direction of Poona, along the banks of the River Majirah, while the equally huge Mahratta Army lumbered slowly towards them. It is interesting to note that the Nizam's Army included his famous Regiment of women, two thousand strong, all dressed in their equally famous red-coats, their instructions being to see that the harem women came to no harm. These harem ladies were mounted in a long caravan of covered elephant howdahs and their presence ultimately decided the fate of the forthcoming battle, as we shall see. There were, of course, sundry negotiations along the way, but these came to nothing nor did the offers of vast bribes make any difference.

On 14 March 1795, the Nizam's Army arrived at the top of a ridge known as the Moori ghat and from there, they looked down on the Mahratta Army encamped below them. The following morning the Nizam gave the order to advance and descend the ghat, at the bottom of which the Mahrattas were waiting for them, and here one remembers one's Military training, when we were told never to lose height. After a leisurely lunch, some firing commenced but this was mainly between the two French battalions, who were fighting each other – the reason being that one battalion was fighting for the Nizam and the other one was fighting for the Mahrattas – one battalion being Bourbon French, the other Republican French. At this point the Women's red-coated Regiment were ordered to descend the ghat, which they did and when they came up against the right flank of the Mahrattas, they stopped. By the evening, the Nizam decided that his Army had got to more or less where he thought he wanted it, and thus the two armies settled down for the night.

But something terrible happened during that night in the Nizam's encampment. Later on, it transpired that the Nizam's senior wife Bakshi Begum had a nervous breakdown, when she heard some intermittent firing. She, therefore, insisted to the Nizam that she and the entire Zenana should be taken to the apparent safety of a small and, as it happens, indefensible and half-ruined fort by the name of Khardia and that, if he did not, she would take her clothes off and expose her naked body to the Mahrattas. This was too much for the Nizam, who, therefore, took them into this wretched fort.

During the night, and after the threat by the Begum to take her clothes off, a skirmish did take place and this precipitated such a panic among the Nizam's Army that most of them then fled, abandoning their guns, camels, baggage, stores and food behind them, much to the surprise of the Mahrattas the following morning. The wretched fort was then besieged until no food or water remained, and then the Nizam and his entourage surrendered. He was required to cede a large part of his extensive territories to the Mahrattas, but then the young Peshwa threw himself off a balcony or was it a defenestration. This led to so much in-fighting that this enabled the Nizam to evade most of the payments, which he had promised and also to evade the cession of most of those lands which he had also promised.

At the end of the day, Shore had been correct in adopting a neutral position, but, in any case, the Bengal Army was in no position to fight a battle, let alone a war. This was partly due to the Company being very short of money and partly because the Company Bengal Army was itself on the point of mutiny. Shore himself had no confidence or faith in his Commander-in-Chief, whose Military abilities were, as he put it, 'totally inadequate to being the Army's Commander', a view that had been echoed by Hickey when he heard of the appointment.

Chapter 10

Two missions to Lucknow

There have been countless books written about Oudh and its Nawabs and it is not my intention to write its history here – we will leave that until later when Captain John Baillie, as he then was, was appointed the Resident at Lucknow in 1807. Here we will deal with the two missions of the Governor General Sir John Shore to that State – the first of which was in 1796, when he was accompanied by Edmonstone his Persian Translator.

Let us see what he wrote:

In the early part of the year 1796, I attended the Governor-General Sir John Shore, as his Persian Translator, on his visit to Lucknow, whither we proceeded; first, for the purpose of entering into a negotiation with Assof-ud-Dowlah relative to the reform of the various systems of administration and the appointment of an efficient Minister; secondly to obtain the augmentation of the Subsidy. I then accompanied the Governor-General a second time to Lucknow, when his presence was required in consequence of the death of Assof-ud-Dowlah and the suspected invalidity of the title of his successor Vizier Ali, who was believed to be of spurious birth and whose succession was, in that case, a supercession of the right of Saadut Alli Khan, the brother of the late Vizier, then residing at Benares. Vizier Ali was a particularly unpleasant character and his abandoned habits and his profligate conduct threatened at that time, the most serious injury to the two States.

The history of the arduous, perilous and important proceedings, which terminated in the dethronement of the Vizier Ali and the elevation to the throne of Saadut Ali Khan, whose proceedings were conducted by the Governor-General with ability, fortitude and success and which received the highest approbation of the authorities at home, has long since been published and among persons conversant with events and transactions in India, is generally known. It is not going too far to say that this Revolution constituted one of the many perilous conjunctures in the history of British India, on the success of which the fate of our Eastern Empire was involved and it was mainly on the grounds of the great ability, judgement and fortitude manifested by the Governor-General on that critical occasion, that he was elevated to the Peerage as Lord Teignmouth.

The duties of my official situation were on that occasion of a nature peculiarly important, delicate and responsible. I had to examine individuals capable of giving evidence respecting the circumstances of the Vizier's birth, without betraying. if possible, the eventual purpose of such an investigation, as from the character of the Vizier and his dissolute and desperate companions, whom he had collected around him, a knowledge or even apprehension of the Governor-General's design would have been followed immediately by the destruction of every European in Lucknow.

At the close of these secret investigations, by which the spuriousness of the Vizier's birth was conclusively demonstrated, it became necessary to exchange written communications with Saadat Ali Khan at Benares on the subject of his succession, as well as to concert by correspondence with Mr Cherry, then filling the Office of Agent to the Governor-General at Benares, the means of conveying Saadat Ali Khan to Lucknow, so that he should arrive there simultaneously with the deposal of Vizier Ali.

Here, we need to shed a little light on Edmonstone's investigations into the birth of Vizier Ali. It was well known in Lucknow that he, Assof-ud-Dowlah, had taken to drink and drugs and that the women of his Court were mainly ladies of the town. There were also many people in Oudh who were ready to testify that Assof-ud-Dowlah was not Ali's father. His two natural children had died, and it was generally thought that through his excessive intake of opium, he had become impotent. Edmonstone, in his long search for what he hoped to be the truth, interviewed many people extremely discreetly, but without success. Eventually, he managed to have a private meeting with Tehseen Ali Khan, who was the Chief Eunuch in charge of the harem. He told Edmonstone that Assof had been totally distraught after the deaths of his two unquestionably legitimate children, and that he had then arranged for pregnant women to come and live in the Zenana, where their children were born. In this manner, Assof had acquired no less than sixteen so-called sons and daughters. Tehseen then went on to confirm that the mother of Wazir Ali was, in fact, a servant of the women in the Zenana, whom Assof-ud-Dowlah had never actually seen. Although this woman was married to another servant, she had given birth to Wazir Ali in his own house, whereupon Assof-ud-Dowlah, on hearing about the birth, had bought the child for 500 rupees on condition that the woman left the Zenana and never saw the child again. This was sufficient evidence for Edmonstone that Wazir Ali was indeed of spurious birth. There was the further concern that he wished to rule directly, rather than reign indirectly courtesy of the East India

Company, and that it was therefore necessary for him to be deposed – easier said than done.

At the end of the day, Edmonstone did admit to William Kirkpatrick that the real reason for preferring Saadat Ali Khan to Wazir Ali had nothing very much to do with questions of his legitimacy: 'it remained to determine whether our Government should continue to acknowledge him (Ali) as the legal heir to the Musnud or change the succession. The former might have been justified, but the situation of affairs certainly rendered the latter expedient.'

There were, of course, problems with the idea or rather proposal of appointing Saadat Ali Khan the Nawab in place of Wazir Ali. As it happens, he was not particularly popular in Oudh, mainly because of his perceived avariciousness and was especially so to the Begum, whose son he had wanted to depose and who realized that her hopes of influencing policy would end with his accession. Saadat Ali Khan also had no followers and no Army and was hardly known in Lucknow. According to Edmonstone, 'the question arose, by what right can we, who profess to consider the Kingdom of Oudh as an independent State, force upon the people a Prince obnoxious to them all. To this, it can be answered that Oudh is in fact not an independent State – its defence and protection by specific engagements depends on us.'

The decision to depose him was taken on 8 January 1798, although the Governor General then had second thoughts, so much so that he did not finally agree until a week later. Accordingly, Regiments were ordered up from the Cawnpore cantonments and a message was sent to Cherry at Benares to open up the sealed letter, which the Governor General had sent him. The contents amazed him. Saadat Ali Khan would only become the Wazir provided he agreed that the Company's army there would be increased to ten thousand men, for which an annual subsidy from the Nawab would be required in the sum of 76 lakhs; that the Oudh Army would be correspondingly reduced; that henceforth the security of the Oudh state was the responsibility of the Company; and that Saadat Ali Khan would need to swear that he would have no dealings with other powers without the consent of the Company. Surprisingly, Saadat Ali Khan agreed to all this and the only problem which remained was how to get him from Benares to Lucknow, without being spotted. Cherry then worked out a cunning plan to achieve this and, although the Governor General was extremely nervous about it, it nevertheless worked. When it became known that he had safely arrived in Lucknow, the Governor General summoned a Conference at which he duly announced that Saadat Ali Khan was now the rightful heir and that he had now arrived from Benares. A message was then sent to Wazir Ali, in which the Governor General promised that he would not be harmed, provided, of course, he accepted the instructions to him to abdicate in favour of Saadat Ali Khan. It was then that the Bahu Begum took control of Lucknow, and it was then at Bibiapur a refugee turned up that evening – it was Wazir Ali, who was so terrified by his 'grandmother' that he asked for asylum, which was duly granted. Thus, it was that night when the deposed and depressed Wazir Ali sat down to dinner with the Governor General, who, on that very same day, had forced him to abdicate.

We have mentioned that the Bahu Begum had temporarily taken over control of the city of Lucknow, and we now need to introduce her. She was the favourite foster child of the Moghul Emperor and, although she was illiterate, she was the most renowned and gifted of all the Oudh Begums. Her real name was Umrat-ul-Zohra and she had been brought up in the Moghul Court as the Emperor's daughter. He called upon his Chief Minister Safdar Jung to arrange a marriage between her and Shuja-ud-Daulah, the then Nawab of Oudh, and instructed a certain Amir Khan to make the marriage ceremony 'as pompous and magnificent as possible', and so it was. However, it was more of a political marriage than anything else, and physically she does not seem to have appealed to her promiscuous husband. Nevertheless, he was very fond of her and even went so far as to have dinner with her most evenings, before leaving her to visit the ladies of the town. If he did not return until the following day, she fined him the sum of 5,000 rupees. When Shuja was defeated by Major Hector Munro at the battle of Buxar in 1765 and lost every penny he had, she gave him nearly all her money, including her most precious nose ring with its bunch of pearls, which normally no married woman would ever part with. She loved him despite everything, and went so far as to tell her advisors, 'Whatever I have is no use to me as long as Shuja is safe. If he ceases to live, all these things would be of no use to me.'

The Begum was very fond of her only son Assof-ud-Dowlah and she spoilt him. His father did not think that he was a particularly promising son, because he engaged 'in disappointing acts', as they were described, and apparently he disgusted his tutors. Consequently, his father began to think in terms of nominating Mirza Mangli – the future Saadat Ali Khan as his successor but Bahu Begum disregarded her husband's wishes.

To begin with, she, therefore, supported the succession of Wazir Ali, although she knew perfectly well that he was not the son of Assof-ud-Dowlah. She did, in fact, continue to support him, although he greatly upset her by his indecent haste in occupying the Musnud – the throne. At Bibiapur, she took the almost unprecedented step of going out to meet the Governor General in an endeavour to negotiate with him with a view to her becoming the de facto ruler of Oudh. However, this did not work out, and the reason for this was that Wazir Ali was also present and the necessary etiquette and delicacy prevented her from putting her views across. However, once the Governor General knew that Saadat Ali Khan was safely in Lucknow, he called a meeting during which he said that he and the Company were very much the guarantors of the rights and dignity of the Begum. This surprised the gathering but so it was that the Begum felt mollified, and thus began to change her mind about the succession and therefore felt able to affix her Seal to the Accession Document of Saadat Ali Khan.

There were two particular results of Edmonstone's visit to Lucknow – one happy but perhaps not completely so, and the other tragic. The first was that at Lucknow, the then Resident was a certain James Lumsden, who was not only a friend of Edmonstone, but also some sort of distant relative. During all these investigations and exchanges, Edmonstone visited the Residency frequently. These visits started off as being quite formal, but became less and less formal as Edmonstone began to fall in love with the Resident's sister-in-law, namely Charlotte Friel and it was reciprocated. She was very attractive and the romance flourished. They eventually married and she bore him no less than ten children. The less happy aspect of all this was that Edmonstone already had an Indian lady in Calcutta and she had borne him four children – thus there was a new English bride and a now presumably deserted Indian bride and all the sensitivities and tensions that arose from such a 'bigamous' relationship. What we do know is that Edmonstone changed the name of his Scottish Indian children from Edmonstone to Elmore, although that, perhaps, may have been at the instigation of his father; that the three boys were despatched to Scotland and England and that Eliza remained behind in Calcutta and was paid off with a dowry to enable her to marry there, which she did; and that finally the Scottish Indian and the English children never met or even knew about each other's existence, according to Edmonstone's granddaughter.

The tragedy was that after the forced abdication, Edmonstone spent a lot of time with the sullen and angry Wazir Ali, before sending him off to Benares, where Cherry had been instructed to keep a close eye on him. On 13 January 1799, the Indian Superintendent of Police called on Mr Davis, the Judge and Magistrate there, to inform him that Wazir Ali was calling in a large number of armed men and that he feared that there was going to be an uprising. Davis was not entirely sure he believed him – however, he did feel relatively secure in the sense that a reserve of the Army under the command of a General Erskine was encamped not too far away.

That evening, a hircarrah presented himself at Cherry's house and advised him that Wazir Ali would like to take breakfast with him the following morning. Cherry cheerfully agreed, thinking that the discussion would be about his forthcoming move to Calcutta, which the new Governor General had ordered. The following morning Wazir Ali turned up and Cherry went out and invited him and his men to breakfast. Thereupon, Wazir Ali jumped up to tell Cherry that he had ruined his 'father's house', and that under no circumstances would he leave Benares for Calcutta. At that point, Cherry told him that it was not a matter for him and that he required the authority of the Governor General.

It was then that Wazir Ali seized him by the shoulders and Cherry suddenly realized that he was in mortal danger. He shouted out, 'For God's sake, do not strike me, what fault have I committed – I will write anything you want to the Governor General.' He then ran out of the house, where he was confronted by a band of mounted men, whereupon he ran back into the house and there was stabbed to death by Wazir Ali. A massacre ensued but, at last, an advance party of cavalry from the nearby encampment appeared, and Wazir Ali fled. After numerous escapes, he was handed in by the friendly Rajah of Jaynagar and taken to Calcutta, where he was locked up in an iron cage. He died in 1817 in Calcutta.

For those people who are visiting Benares, now Varanasi, you should go and see the old cemetery at Chaukaghat on Maqbol Alam Road, which is under the control of St Mary's Catholic Church at Benares. The cemetery lies just beyond the old fish market on the bridge and opposite the jail. There you will see a 50 feet tall obelisk, described as a 'colossal monument in the form of a square set on an immense platform of stone, ornamented at the four corners by large funeral urns'. The inscription reads, 'This Obelisk was erected in memory of George Frederick Cherry Esq; Captain Conway; Robert Graham Esq; Richard Evans Esq who were murdered by Wazir Ali January 14th 1799.' Perhaps it could be noted that this Cemetery now requires both restoration and conservation and donations for this and other similar work should be sent to the British Association for Cemeteries in South Asia (BACSA).

It happened that Cherry had been Edmonstone's best friend in India and he was devastated by his murder. It is possible, indeed probable, that from then on Edmonstone, who was, by instinct, more of a dove than a hawk, now became a hawk with regard to the British presence in India and this hawkish attitude resonated with the new Governor General Sir Richard Wellesley, Lord Mornington, so much so, that it was Edmonstone and his circle, who encouraged, aided and greatly influenced the new Governor General's plan of conquest of the subcontinent of India. By the time Wellesley left India in 1805 and Edmonstone in 1818, the British dominion in India was largely complete – so much for the supposition that India was won in a fit of absent-mindedness.

Chapter 11

Baillie's academic prowess: Sir Richard Wellesley, Governor General

The last few chapters have been preoccupied with the activities of Edmonstone rather than with Baillie, who was younger than Edmonstone and who had only arrived in India in 1792. He was finally commissioned as an Ensign in the 4th Native Infantry and then in 1795, he was promoted to Lieutenant. In Calcutta, like Edmonstone, he devoted his spare time to the study of Oriental languages and these he pursued with such perseverance and success that when the new Fort William College was established by Wellesley in 1800, he was appointed not only the Professor of the Arabic and Persian languages there but also Professor of Mohammedan Law, when he was aged 29. It was, while he was Professor there that he wrote 'Sixty Tables elucidatory of a Course of Lectures on Arabic Grammar', which he delivered to the College in its first year. He also wrote *The Five Books on Arabic Grammar That Is to Say the Meeut Ameel, Shuru Meeut Amel; Mesbah; Hedayut-oon-Nuhve and the Kafeea*. These books were issued in two volumes in 1802–3.

In 1798, in the minutes that Governor General Sir John Shore wrote shortly before he left India:

> Some time prior to the death of Sir William Jones, a compilation was begun under his direction of the Law and Doctrines of that Sect of Musulmen called Sheeas, but which was not completed until after his death. A translation of this useful work I conceive to be very desirable from a public point of view. I had an opportunity of conversing with Lieutenant John Baillie, an Officer in the Company's Service whom, from the great proficiency he has made in the study of the Arabic Language, I believe to be extremely well qualified for the task.

It was, therefore, agreed that Lieutenant Baillie be informed that he had been nominated, at the recommendation of the Governor General, to translate the Compilation of the Doctrines of the Sheeas under the Superintendence of the late Sir William Jones, and that he be acquainted that some recompense will be made to him relative to the extent of the undertaking. The recompense was 10,000 rupees.

Although he never was able to complete his translation of Mohammedan Law himself, nevertheless, it was completed by his son Neil Benjamin Baillie, who had a distinguished career in India, after his return there from Leys Castle, Inverness. Later on, Baillie amassed a large collection of paintings and illustrated manuscripts, including the exquisitely written and illuminated *History of the World* by Rashid al-Din, the Jami al-Tawarikh and the Poems of Hafiz of Sharaz and all these wonderful paintings and illuminated manuscripts numbering in all 165, were bequeathed in 1876 to the Edinburgh University Library by Baillie's grandson, where they were catalogued by Edward Robertson in 1912, and there they still remain – a very proud possession of the Library. We will come back later to Fort William College.

In 1797, Sir John Shore had written to the Directors that 'he was almost worn out and shall most gladly resign my station, either to Lord Hobart or to any other person, whom you may think proper to appoint'. At the time, Edmonstone wrote to his father, 'Shore's departure is a source of real regret that I have lost a friend and a benefactor'. It was, therefore, quite a shock when he heard that Cornwallis had been redirected by Parliament to deal with a rebellion in Ireland – this was the rebellion with which Colonel John Baillie of Dunain was involved, and where he died from a heart attack on his route march to Kilkenny. Richard Wellesley was the last-minute replacement as the Governor General for India – he had never been out East before and he was only five years older than Edmonstone.

Richard Wellesley was born in Ireland in 1760, the eldest of six sons and a daughter. Among his brothers were Arthur, the future Duke of Wellington and Henry Wellesley, the future Lord Cowley. Their father was a certain Garret Wellesley, an amateur musician and poet, whose artistic abilities did little to enhance the family's crumbling fortunes. Wellesley used to refer to his parents as 'frivolous and careless people like most of the Irish nobility'. He was sent to Harrow School, which was not a success as he was expelled for causing a riot, and then to Eton, which was a resounding success. His father died in 1781, when he was 21 years old and that was when he assumed the Mornington title and his father's debts. He entered politics and joined the Irish House of Lords, and here he became friendly with William Grenville, who was then the Chief Secretary of Ireland and perhaps, more importantly, William Pitt's first cousin.

In 1784, he became the Member of Parliament for Bere Alston in Devon and then Old Sarum, that famous rotten borough. It is, perhaps, interesting to note that he had sent his younger brother Arthur, who had failed at Eton, to the Royal

Academy of Equitation at Angers in France and when he had finished there, he bought him a Colonelcy in the Army.

Wellesley's interest in India had been noted and in 1793, he was appointed to the Board of Control for India. That was where he became a confidant of Lord Cornwallis, and when the latter was sent off to Ireland to take over as the new Governor General, the former was sent off to India as the new Governor General there. Wellesley's qualifications for the appointment were few, if any. He had never served in the Army; he had, therefore, never fought in battle. He had not served in the ranks of the Company, so that his sole experience of India were the reports he had heard at Board meetings in London. Therefore to be sent, at his comparatively youthful age – 39 years old – to oversee the Company's entire Indian operations might have seemed to be the height of folly, but it wasn't. And one can legitimately say that his appointment, supported by Edmonstone and Baillie and others, was the deciding factor and catalyst for the eventual imposition of British power and supremacy over India and South Asia.

He went out to Calcutta without his French wife – Hyacinthe-Gabrielle Roland, whom he had met when she was an actress at the Palais Royal in Paris, in those days when the Palais Royal had a reputation. They had lived together for a number of years without marrying, and she had borne him three sons and two daughters. They did, eventually, marry in 1794 and he moved her to London, where she was miserable. Virtually unable to speak or understand English, she was scorned by London's high society, and it was not only her inability to speak English that caused this. Lady Caroline Lamb, for instance, was warned by her mother-in-law Elizabeth Milbanke, who always noted who was socially acceptable or not, that no woman could ever afford to be seen in Hyacinthe's society.

She had turned down her husband's request for her to accompany him to India – the Channel sea crossing had been quite enough for her, let alone a six-month sea voyage out to Calcutta, and anyway, there was a feeling that she was not quite suitable as the wife of the Governor General of India. Shortly after he arrived in Calcutta, he wrote to her pleading that, if she would not come out, could he, please, have her permission to take on an Indian mistress, as the hot climate had so aroused his sexual appetite, that he could not live without 'it'. Hyacinthe initially demurred but later on replied in French, 'Prelaque [their codeword for "it"] if you are absolutely forced to, then with all the honour, prudence and kindness you have shown me.' Not all wives are so accommodating.

For those who are admirers of the portraits of Madame Vigee-Lebrun, you can see the lovely portrait of Hyacinthe painted by her in 1791. You can readily see why Richard Wellesley was so much in love with her and you can then imagine him as a grass widower, wandering around his huge new palace of Government House in Calcutta, which he had built at such huge expense, perhaps disconsolate and all alone. That is if anybody can be ever alone in that

Government House with its hundreds and hundreds of servants and guards, which state of affairs continues to this day.

As a footnote, Anne Wellesley, one of the daughters of Sir Richard and Lady Hyacinthe – now the Marquess and Marchioness. She was first married to Sir William Abdy, who was extremely rich and also extremely dull. She left him and eloped with Lord Charles William Cavendish Bentinck, a younger and somewhat impecunious son of the 3rd Duke of Portland, who completely captivated her. One of their sons was called Charley, who first married a gypsy girl Sinetta, who died very young – all her children having died soon after they were born – their deaths were attributed to the mixture she had taken to lighten the colour of her dark gypsy skin. Charley then married again a distant member of the author's family – a Burnaby – my mother's grandmother was a Burnaby, the sister of the True Blue – the famous Colonel Fred Burnaby – and they had four children. One of them a daughter, Nina Cecilia married Lord Strathmore, thus becoming the mother of the Queen Mother and you can see a photograph of her, Lady Strathmore, at the Christening of her granddaughter, the future Queen Elizabeth the Second. Thus Hyacinthe Gabrielle became the great great-grandmother of Queen Elizabeth, the Queen Mother, and thus the three times great grandmother of Queen Elizabeth II. Thus, the lovely Hyacinthe Gabrielle, the demi-mondaine of the Palais Royal, obtained her posthumous revenge on London Society.

The time when Wellesley was appointed Governor General in 1798 was a period of great difficulty for the British nation – not only was it at war with the French – nothing surprising in that, as it seemed to happen all the time – but it was also at war with the Dutch and the Spanish, while its ally Austria had been defeated by the French under the Emperor Napoleon. America, which had been supported by the French, had been lost and there was a risk that India might go the same way, aided and abetted by the French. Ireland was on the verge of rebellion supported by the French, as has already been mentioned; the Navy had mutinied and there was a general feeling in the country of constantly being in a nervous crisis.

In India, Tipu had recovered from his quasi defeat by Cornwallis and was once more on the warpath, assisted by the French; in western India, the Mahrattas assisted once again by the French were becoming more powerful; the Afghans were thinking of having another attempt at invading India; and then finally, there were the three Moghul successor states of Oudh, Arcot and Hyderabad, who were in touch with Tipu who, in his turn, was in touch with the French. It is, therefore, no surprise that all this put Wellesley in a difficult position – not only that, he became, understandably, quite paranoid about the French.

It was, however, becoming clear that London was beginning to consider that, in all this, India might be a useful tributary in its endless wars with the French, so much so, that it did indeed require a more aggressive policy against the Indian powers – the corollary being that, if the British did nothing very much, then the French most certainly would and were in a position so to do. Here, it is very possible that, if it had not been for the French presence in India, the English would never originally have really thought in terms of an Indian empire, being much more interested in trade than war. And here, one remembers again Dupleix's yearning and ambition for *La Gloire Francaise en Inde* and his dressing up as a Haft Hazari of the Deccan – a uniform which his successor Monsieur Godeheu described as *cet appareil comique*.

When Wellesley arrived at the Cape of Good Hope on his way out to Calcutta, he bumped into three people who gave him troubling reports on India. One was Lord Hobart, who was still smarting from the decision of the Directors not to appoint him as Governor General. He painted a grim picture of South India and warned him about the French mercenaries, who were being employed by both the Nizam and Tipu to train their armies. The second was General David Baird, who had fought with Colonel William Baillie in the Carnatic and had spent four years imprisoned by Tipu in that dungeon at Seringapatam, which he had shared for two years with Colonel William Baillie until his death. He described Tipu's new Army and the latter's expectations of receiving reinforcements from France. The third and perhaps more importantly, he met William Kirkpatrick, who was recuperating from an illness at the Cape, and who was a friend of both Edmonstone and Cherry. He had been the Resident at Hyderabad, where he was succeeded by his brother James, who was featured in William Dalrymple's book entitled the *White Moghuls*. Interestingly enough, when the Nizam was defeated by the Mahrattas, at what is now known as the battle of Khardia, previously known as the battle of the Moori ghat, William Kirkpatrick was among those taken prisoner at that dilapidated fort, in which the Nizam and his Begum, who had threatened to expose her naked body to the Mahrattas, took refuge but to no avail. Wellesley was so impressed with Kirkpatrick that he took him back with him to India, where subsequently he became his Military Secretary. Coming from the politically charged atmosphere of the British conflict with France in Europe, Wellesley became concerned almost to the point of paranoia, as we have already mentioned, over the possibility of French civil and Military aggression in India.

In his efforts as the Governor General, Wellesley was supported by his two brothers, Henry and Arthur, but also, as we have mentioned, by an extremely dedicated and able group of young men as his Military and Civil Assistants and these were led by Edmonstone, who had still not got over the murder of his great friend Cherry and never really did. Edmonstone wrote, 'That the temper of men's minds in this country in view of recent occurrences, which have betrayed that temper, proves that the necessity for boldness and exertion is greater than ever.' He also wrote,

They, the Muslims, entertain the utmost hatred towards us, having been annihilated by us and that they consider us to be polluted beings, as wretches devoted to damnation – by the tenets of their religion, the persecution and murder of infidels is a merit entitling them to the highest rewards in a future state – I have not withheld this view from the Government – indeed in conversation I have been much more explicit.

So Wellesley announced his intention of establishing complete British rule over South Asia, and it has to be said that to all intents and purposes, he did.

First, he reached an accommodation with the Mahrattas; second, he galvanized the Madras Presidency into some sort of action; third, he engineered a coup against the anti-British party in Hyderabad and persuaded the Nizam to disband his French-officered Corps of some fourteen thousand soldiers and replace them with British officers – and all of this was accomplished without any blood being spilt. Wellesley had now manoeuvred himself into a position where he could prod Tipu into war and, even more importantly, begin the expulsion of the French out of India. The French had told Tipu and the Mysoreans that the English tremble at the very name of Napoleon; that they will not be able to withstand his power and will be defeated in every quarter. Indeed, Napoleon had written a letter to Tipu, giving as his address the French Headquarters, Cairo, which read as follows:

Bonaparte, Member of the National Convention, General in Chief, to the most magnificent Sultan, our greatest friend TIPPOO SAIB;

You have already been informed of my arrival on the borders of the Red Sea, with an innumerable and invincible army, full of desire of relieving you from the iron yoke of England.

I eagerly embrace this opportunity of testifying to you the desire I have of being informed by you, by the way of Muskat and Mocha, as to your political situation.

I would even wish that you could send some intelligent person to Suez or Cairo, possessing your confidence, with whom I could confer.

May the Almighty increase your power and destroy your enemies.

Bonaparte

This letter ended up with the Sharif 'the Respected One' of Mecca, who promptly handed it over to a certain Captain Wilson, who translated it and then sent it on to the Governor-in-Council at Bombay, where it would then be used as evidence of Tipu's liaison with the French and therefore as ammunition against him.

Mercifully, all this changed when Nelson sank the French fleet off the coast of Egypt, and it was then that Tipu realized he was on his own and that no French aid would be forthcoming. At that point, Tipu should have remembered that he had found in his father's turban when he died, a small scrap of paper on which he, Haidar Ali, had written the words:

I have gained nothing by my wars with the English, but am now, alas, no longer alive. If you, through disturbances in your own kingdom, repair thither without having previously concluded peace with the English, they will certainly follow you and carry the war into your own country. On this account, therefore, it is better first to make peace on whatever terms you can procure and then go to your own country.

However, Tipu disregarded his father's advice, as his father knew he would, and this led to the fourth and final Anglo-Mysore War.

It was then that a series of letters were exchanged between the Governor General and Tipu. As was his wont, Tipu procrastinated, but eventually Edmonstone acting not only on the instructions of the Governor General, but also now the Mahratta Peshwa and the Nizam of Hyderabad, sent Tipu a six-page ultimatum, detailing all the reasons why the Company was finding it necessary to go to war with him. Tipu once again prevaricated, but then responded by stating that he was unwilling to submit to the English infidels; that, rather than grovel to the English, it would be better for him to die like a soldier than spend a miserable life dependent on the infidels. Thus it was that this fourth and final Anglo-Mysore War commenced and to cut a long story short, the Company's and the Nizam's armies were successful. Seringapatam was besieged and stormed with General David Baird, Tipu's former prisoner, leading the way into the breach and ended with finding Tipu's body still warm in the ruins – they also found the dungeon in which Colonel William Baillie had been confined, manacled to the wall and denied medical help, had died and his dungeon which is now a tourist attraction.

As a slight digression, it could be noted that immediately prior to the storming attack on Seringapatam, Colonel Arthur Wellesley – the future Duke – was instructed to capture and clear a small tope (derived from the Tamil word 'Toppu' meaning grove of trees), which was sheltering some of Tipu's men, who were using it to launch rocket attacks on the besieging force. As the Colonel and his soldiers approached the tope at dusk, they came under heavy fire and he lost his way. Consequently, the attack had to be aborted. However, the following morning, the Colonel was nowhere to be seen and it was widely assumed that he had lost his way in the dark and had been killed in the evening attack, somewhere or other. Consequently, the second attack had to go in without the Colonel, and this time it was successful. His disappearance and subsequent, perhaps somewhat sheepish, reappearance caused quite a stir at the time, but this aberration, as we know, did not affect his career in both the Indian and British armies, but the Indian guides at Seringapatam like to relate the story.

Following the capture of Seringapatam, Wellesley travelled down to Madras with Edmonstone, where they were received by the Governor, who was Clive's son. Wellesley did not think much of him and described him 'as a worthy, zealous, obedient, gentlemanly like fellow of excellent temper, but neither of talents, knowledge, habits of business or firmness of spirit equal to the present situation – how the Devil did he get here?' Wellesley and Edmonstone then travelled the long distance from Madras to Seringapatam and there he signed a Treaty installing the 3-year-old grandson of the Wadia Hindu family, which had been usurped by that illiterate Punjabi Muslim mercenary Haidar Ali in 1763, three years after Ensign, as he then was, William Baillie of the 89th Highland Regiment of Foot had arrived in Madras.

Chapter 12
Fort William College, Calcutta

Fort William College was established by Wellesley without the permission of the Directors of the Company, but this was a matter of little importance to the Governor General, bearing in mind, that a letter to London then took something like six months to get there and the response equally long, provided, of course, the East Indiaman carrying the mails did not sink on the voyage. Thus, the Governor Generals could, if they so wished, do their own 'thing'. However, there was the ultimate sanction of recall, which did, indeed, happen to Wellesley in the end, although it needs to be remembered that, by then, he had already submitted his resignation.

Wellesley was indeed an imperialist, and had minuted 'that the Company's servants must be prepared for their tasks as the judges, administrators and diplomats of a great Indian Empire by some regular course of instruction; that this instruction must be of a mixed nature; that its foundation must be judicially laid and the superstructure systematically completed in India'. Fort William College was to be where the Company's servants of all three Presidencies were to reside for three years following their arrival in India – not only to complete their general education, but also to study Indian Languages, Indian Law and Indian History so that, in this way, they would gain an intimate knowledge of Indian customs and culture in order to create a better understanding between the English and the Indians. Edmonstone wrote, 'Fort William College was a magnificent plan projected by the comprehensive mind of that distinguished nobleman.'

For this purpose, Wellesley purchased the first five houses in Garden Reach. Hickey was delighted with this purchase, because, one of these houses had been the property of a certain client of his, namely the late William Burke. He had been trying to sell this house for some time, but had been unable to sell it for anything close to the amount of the mortgage secured thereon. Curiously enough, Mr Burke had taken out this mortgage, when he was being hard-pressed for payment of a debt due to a well-known Jeweller, who had a shop on Ludgate Circus, close to St Paul's Cathedral in London. One does, of course, wonder for whom Mr Burke bought this very expensive item of jewellery, for which he had mortgaged his Calcutta home to the hilt and even beyond that. The eventual price, perhaps prompted by Mr Hickey, was 35,000 Sicca rupees, out of which could be paid the outstanding mortgage and interest to date of 32,000 Sicca rupees – the Sicca rupee was marginally more valuable than the Company rupee, containing 176 grams of pure silver as opposed to the Company Rupee with only 166 grams of pure silver. However, as it was to be some time before the College buildings could be erected and, as Wellesley was always in a hurry, he leased a large building, which had recently been constructed as a speculation by a certain Scottish dancing master by the name of Mr MacDonald, who had planned it to be a Public Exchange in the centre of Calcutta. However, this speculation had not worked out, so Mr MacDonald was no doubt delighted and, of course, highly relieved when the Governor General took a lease on it.

It is interesting to read Mr McDonald's advertisement to promote his dancing academy in 1795, which reads as follows: 'Advertisement. Mr McDonald presents his respects to the ladies and gentlemen amateurs of dancing and informs that he will instruct any lady or gentleman, who are in the habit of dancing, in the fashionable Scotch step and its application to country dancing, for Sicca rupees 100.'

Essentially, the College was dedicated to training British officers, both Military and Civil, in the languages of India and its customs. Wellesley devised the curriculum himself and, importantly, he ordered that the 'aspirant proconsuls' as he called them, were also to be instructed 'in the sound and correct principles of religion and Government, as preached by the Church of England and upheld by the Tory party'. Lecturers were instructed by the Governor General to instil a sense of moral duty in their students and to teach those, who were to fill important stations, that 'the great public duties, which they were called upon to exercise in India are not less of a sacred nature than those duties of a similar nature in their own country'.

Wellesley did, indeed, take a close interest in his College and the progress of the students. He regularly attended the graduation ceremonies and was most gratified to learn that the subject chosen for the Persian Disputation for the year 1802 was that 'the Natives of India under the British Government enjoy a far greater degree of tranquillity, security and happiness, than under any other former Government'. Thus, with thanks to Wellesley, ruling India was to become an elitist vocation, the I. C. S. the Indian Civil Service known as the 'Heaven Born' which, after India gained independence, became the I. A. S. the Indian Administrative Service with the same high standards as the I. C. S. As an aside, it could be noted that the standards of the British Sudan Political Service then ran a close second to the I. C. S. – now since independence they hardly exist at all.

In due course, the College developed as a Centre of Research and Scholarship, and what a galaxy of talented scholars emerged. The Persian Department was headed up by Edmonstone; the Department of Arabic Studies was headed up by Lieutenant John Baillie as he then was; the Urdu Department was led by the renowned Indian scholar John Borthwick Gilchrist; the equally renowned or even more renowned Henry Thomas Colebrooke headed up the Sanskrit and Hindu Law Department, as Honorary Professor at the College, while William Carey, a missionary and a specialist in Vernacular languages headed up that Department and served for no less than thirty-three years from 1801 to 1834.

Colebrooke deserves a full paragraph, given his importance. He was born in 1765, the third son of Sir George Colebrooke the 2nd Baronet and Chairman of the East India Company. He was appointed to a Writership with the Company and arrived in Calcutta, at just about the same time as Sir William Jones had arrived to take up his appointment as a Judge of the Supreme Court of Bengal and became, inter alia, the first great European Sanskrit scholar. Originally, Colebrooke did not initially show a great deal of interest in India, but his own particular interest in mathematics and astronomy led him to enquire how far the Hindus had progressed in these particular subjects. Then, his desire to possess a greater knowledge of Hindu Law led him to learn Sanskrit and consequently he was entrusted with the translation of the major Digest of Hindu Law, a monumental study of Hindu Law, which had been left unfinished by Sir William Jones. He also wrote his Sanskrit Grammar in 1805 and an *Essay on the Vedas*, the same year. In 1807, he was appointed to the Supreme Council and was elected President of the Asiatic Society of Calcutta. In 1823, he was a founder member of the Royal Asiatic Society in London, as were Baillie and Edmonstone.

Importantly, Sir William Jones also deserves a paragraph – in fact, more than a full paragraph. He was born to Welsh-speaking parents in London and by the time he was a teenager, he was fluent in Greek, Latin, Persian, Arabic and Hebrew – he could also write in Chinese. By the time of his very sad early death in 1794, when he was aged only 47, he had complete command of thirteen languages and could get by in another twenty-eight. In 1783, he was knighted and sent out as a Judge of the Supreme Court of Bengal. There, in Calcutta, he learnt several Indian languages and he also became fascinated by Sanskrit, which could be described as the classical liturgical language of both Hinduism and Buddhism. Here is what he wrote:

The Sanskrit language, whatever be its antiquity, is of a most wonderful structure, more perfect than the Greek, more copious than the Latin and more exquisitely refined than either, yet bearing to them both a stronger affinity, both in the roots of verbs and the form of grammar, than could have possibly been formed by accident, so strong indeed, that no philologer could examine all three, without believing them to have sprung from some common source, which perhaps no longer exists.

Even before he arrived in Calcutta, he wrote on his voyage out,

It gives me inexpressible pleasure to find myself almost encircled by the vast regions of Asia, which has ever been esteemed as the nurse of science, the inventress of delightful and useful arts, the scene of glorious actions, fertile in the production of human genius, abounding in natural wonders and infinitely diversified in the forms of religion and government, in the laws, manners, customs and languages as well as the features and complexions of men.

Jones was, indeed, inspired by a boundless curiosity in the civilization in which he was living, while his wide humanitarian interests helped him to make many friends among the Indians, and all this gave him a great affection for the country. He wrote that he considered himself to be the happiest man alive and Bengal a paradise of regions. Although he said he was no Hindu, yet he went on to say that 'I hold the doctrine of the Hindus concerning a future state to be considerably more rational, more pious, and more likely to deter men from vice than the horrid opinions inculcated by Christians on punishments without end'. And here he was echoing General Charles Hindoo Stuart.

But not the least of Jones's claims to attention was his founding of the Bengal Asiatic Society with Warren Hastings, which met for the first time on 15 January 1784. He died, as we have mentioned in 1794, shortly after Ensign John Baillie arrived in Calcutta and is buried in the South Park Street Cemetery, which is jointly maintained by the British Association for Cemeteries in South Asia (BACSA), mentioned earlier.

Clearly, such an assembly of talent at Fort William College could not be without its tensions and, indeed, there were some intense personal rivalries and one such included Lieutenant Baillie. When he was added to the faculty in 1801 to teach Arabic and Islamic Law, for which subjects he was more than qualified, a certain Francis Gladwin, who was a Professor of Persian and an old soldier diplomat, whom Warren Hastings had sent to Tibet in 1783, soon evidenced professional jealousy towards Baillie and a personality clash became inevitable. Edmonstone wrote to William Kirkpatrick,

I am sorry to have to inform you that the Persian Department of the College has, during the last term, been almost at a standstill. The whole burden of instruction was brought to bear on Gladwin, whose state of mind was ill adapted to bear so heavy a weight, nor perhaps could the individual exertions and abilities of any one man suffice for the instruction of 70 young men, the number in the Persian class. Gladwin was, therefore, extremely anxious for some assistance. I, therefore, proposed the expedient of uniting the Persian and Arabic Professorships. Mr Baillie's knowledge of Persian is very great and his proficiency in the Arabic language gives him an advantage that no other

European possesses. I was delighted with this notion for the relief of Gladwin, who, I concluded would be highly satisfied. But, Judge of my surprise when I found out that Gladwin absolutely refused to work with Baillie, not upon the plea of Mr Baillie's want of capacity, nor from any mistrust of his temper and disposition but declaredly because of Mr Baillie's superior qualifications. Gladwin interpreted the proposed arrangement as a 'degradation and a virtual dismission of himself' and, with that impression, he withdrew altogether in a state of mind that exceeds all description.

In the end and following a contretemps between him and the Provost, Gladwin resigned in a fit of temper.

Now, how was it possible for young Baillie to have become such a noted Arabist and Persian scholar at such an early age – that is to say in his middle and late twenties, and then be appointed as a Professor at the new College at Fort William? Of course, it was the case that he was highly intelligent, ambitious and persevering and it would appear that his Regimental duties in the 4th Native Infantry Battalion were not particularly demanding. The answer is that he recruited shortly after his arrival in Calcutta, a Munshi, a language teacher, who was somewhat older than he was, but who was very able and, indeed, remained with Baillie for most of his career. When Baillie was appointed Professor and Head of the Arabic Department, the Munshi, whose name was Ali Naqi Khan, was, in his turn, appointed as his Head Assistant.

Ali Naqi Khan was a Muslim, classically trained in Arabic and Persian and came from an elite service family in Oudh, which owned a small but apparently important area of land there. It would probably be true to say that he embodied, at that time, all those cultured and civilized traditions, which the Company wished to employ in their service. However, as we shall see later, he turned to venality when he returned home to Oudh from Calcutta, when Baillie was appointed the Resident at Lucknow in 1807. He lost his job at the College, when the Company decided to cut costs and merge the Arabic and Persian departments, as we have seen earlier – a not unfamiliar story and it also appears that he may well have lost some of his pension entitlements at the same time. However, going to Lucknow as Baillie's Mir Munshi was a significant promotion for him. Apart from anything else, it was a return to his homeland and to a very influential position, despite his monthly salary being reduced from 250 a month to 200 rupees. Ali Naqi Khan was able to use the apparent unwavering trust which Baillie placed in him for his own financial advantage and we shall see what happened to him later on.

Chapter 13

The Treaty of Bassein: The Second Anglo-Mahratta War

It was following his takeover of Mysore in 1799 that Wellesley was appointed an Irish Marquis, to his great disappointment – he had hoped for something better and had even dropped hints that he should be awarded Order of the Garter. However, he was presented by General Harris, who had commanded the Army at Seringapatam, with the Star and Badge of the Order of St Patrick, which had been made from some of Tipu's jewels, and this he wore all the time.

The only remaining power now to compete with the Company in India was the Mahratta Confederate Empire and we need here to provide some background to not only the Mahrattas but also to this Confederacy. The Mahratta Empire was a major Indian power that dominated most of the subcontinent in the mid-eighteenth century and, although originating from the west Deccan Plateau, now Maharashtra State, eventually stretched from the present State of Tamil Nadu all the way up to Peshawar now in Pakistan in the west and Bengal in the east. The Mahrattas did not or perhaps could not establish a central system of Government so that Madhavrao, the then Peshwa, turned it into a Confederacy. This Confederacy consisted of five Chieftains, namely, the Peshwa at Poona, the Gaekwar of Baroda, Scindia of Gwalior, Holkar of Indore and the Bhonsale of Nagpur. They were, however, quite bitterly divided and these divisions played into Wellesley's hands. The Peshwa, who was the Head of the Confederacy, had for many years, been advised and controlled by a certain Nana Farnavis, who was described as a man of strict veracity, humane, frugal, charitable but also Machiavellian. But then he died and, as it was put at the time by Colonel Close, the British Resident at Poona, with him died all the wisdom and moderation of the Mahratta Government.

Thus the then Peshwa Baji Rao II found himself very much under the thumb of Scindia and so, to offset this dependence, he approached the Company for a Subsidiary Force to protect him, something which Nana Farnavis had always tried to dissuade him from doing. The despatch of a Subsidiary Force to protect the Peshwa was something that Wellesley had always desired, as he felt confident that this would eventually lead to the Company's ascendancy over the Mahratta Confederacy. He, therefore, instructed Colonel Close to undertake the necessary negotiations to achieve this – however, Colonel Close reported that he, the Peshwa, was 'in the middle of personal peril and lowest debasement so that he viewed the admission of a permanent support from the Company with deep aversion'.

Negotiations did, however, continue somewhat desultorily until, in 1803, Holkar decided to attack Poona and there he defeated the combined armies of the Peshwa and Scindia. One should, nevertheless, bear in mind that one of the particular reasons for this attack, if not the main reason, was that the Peshwa had ordered that one of Holkar's brothers should be tied to the foot of an elephant and dragged through the streets of Poona to his death. The result was that, after his defeat, he fled to Bassein, which was not far from Bombay and there begged Wellesley to assist him in regaining his throne. Wellesley then dictated the terms of a Treaty, which the Peshwa perforce had to accept. Edmonstone writing to Colonel Close made the position clear by stating, 'You will, therefore, understand that the principal object to be accomplished by this Treaty of Bassein is the prevention of any hostile union of the Mahratta states against the British Government or its allies.'

There were eight terms to this Treaty and given their importance, we will spell them out: (1) was that a British force of some six thousand troops would be permanently stationed with the Peshwa; (2) was that any territorial districts, which had an income of 2.6 million rupees or more, then this income must be surrendered to the Company; (3) that the Peshwa was not allowed to enter into any other Treaty, without consulting the Company first; (4) that he was not allowed to declare war without consulting the Company; (5) that any territorial claims made by the Peshwa required the arbitration of the Company; (6) that the Peshwa had to renounce his claims over Surat and Baroda; (7) that the Peshwa must exclude all Europeans from his service; and (8) that he must conduct his foreign relations in consultation with the Company. All this was dictated by Wellesley and relayed forward by Edmonstone to the Peshwa via Colonel Close – all very much belt and braces and all bitterly resented.

The Peshwa was then escorted back to Poona by the Governor General's brother Arthur Wellesley and the Mahratta Holkar withdrew, understandably with a very bad grace. It was, indeed, the belief – it turned out to be a somewhat naïve belief on the part of Wellesley, although he had been warned – that the Mahratta chiefs would not attack the Company, but in that he was wrong and quite soon, Scindia, Bhonsla and Holkar formed an alliance against the Peshwa and the Company and this meant that what came to be called the Second Anglo-Mahratta War became inevitable. Arthur Wellesley – the brother of the

Governor General – was given command of the Deccan campaign against the combined armies of Scindia and Berar, while Gerard Lake was given command of the Hindustan campaign further north against Holkar, whose forces were largely trained and officered by the French with a sprinkling of British officer mercenaries, none of whom had counted on fighting the Company army. It was this campaign, which Baillie volunteered to join, thus relinquishing his academic Professorships at Fort William College, to which he had been seconded from his Regiment.

The Deccan campaign was successful, but as Baillie was not involved in it, we will just mention one battle, the famous Assaye battle. This battle was one, in which the author's Regiment, the Seaforth Highlanders, took part. They fought so brilliantly and bravely under Arthur Wellesley's command, that for ever after, their sporrans were adorned with the Assaye silver elephant. The Regiment in action was described by an observer as follows:

> every soldier of the 78th was a giant by Mahratta standards. The kilts were swinging in unison; their weapons and buckles were highly polished and their belts freshly whitened. Nobody who saw this magnificent Regiment deliver its first assault at Assaye would ever forget it. At 60 yards from the enemy guns and there were about a hundred of them and these guns continued to fire, they halted as if on parade, presented their muskets, fired, recovered and then reloaded. Then they went on again with their bayonets gleaming.

Casualties were very high on both sides – Wellesley lost about a quarter of his men, while the Mahrattas also lost heavily. The future Duke then went on to win a string of victories, won by the Company's Sepoy Regiments and his Scottish Highland Regiments, and these victories broke the armies of Scindia and Berar.

General Gerard Lake, who commanded the Company army was an Irishman born in 1744. He entered the Foot Guards in 1758 as an Ensign and, from thereon, went up the ladder. He had served in Germany and then in America, where he took part in the battle of Yorktown in 1781. It was during this battle or rather siege, when he had been pounded senseless by days of heavy French bombardment, that he decided that he could not take any more and led a spirited counter-attack on the French positions. As he put it at the time, 'there is no substitute for going on the offensive, when an infantryman's morale is sagging under the weight of siege induced inactivity'. He was then appointed an Equerry to the Prince of Wales, later King George 1V, but although he served him for no less than four years, the Prince never paid him, so that when he left, he became yet another of the innumerable creditors of the bankrupt Prince.

He then was promoted to Major General, when he commanded the Guards Brigade in the Duke of York's Army in Flanders during the Napoleonic Wars. He was then promoted to Lieutenant General.

In 1798, another Irish Rebellion broke out, assisted as usual by the French and he was appointed to command the Army that year and was able to suppress the rebellion with a certain amount of difficulty, after General Hely-Hutchison, his second-in-command, with his force of some six thousand militia, had been defeated at the battle of Castlebar. Readers will recall that Colonel John Baillie of Dunain, who was commanding his Inverness Regiment of Fencibles, a militia Regiment, died of a heart attack, while marching to reinforce General Lake's troops. Two years later General Lake was appointed Commander-in-Chief of the Indian Army. Thus, one Irishman in charge of the Deccan campaign; one Irishman in charge of the Hindustan campaign; and one Irishman in charge of everything – namely the Governor General, supported by his Scottish Assistants.

Although Baillie, now promoted to Captain, did not join the Hindustan campaign until the siege of Agra, we need to put this campaign into some form of perspective – apart from anything else, this Hindustan campaign has not received as much attention as the Deccan campaign, which the future Duke of Wellington commanded. Lake had, relatively speaking, a small force to fight the large disciplined Mahratta Army, which had been created for Scindia by mainly two French officers, namely General Count de Boigne and later General Perron, in what Wellesley called 'the French State' and by that, he meant the Doab, a large fertile territory lying between the rivers Ganges and Jumna. This territory had been handed over successively to these two French generals, for the payment and equipment of the Mahratta Army and also, of course, for their salaries. De Boigne, a most interesting man, had left India in 1795; Perron succeeded him and he was now not only the Commander-in-Chief of Scindia's Army but also, to all intents and purposes, a sort of dictator of the territories of the King of Delhi, wielding the propaganda power that still attached itself to the person of the Moghul Emperor. Perron had a large well-equipped Army based in Delhi, Agra and Aligarh, where his main arsenal was based.

Against this formidable force, Lake did not have much more than some ten thousand men, and when he took the field in a hurry in order to launch a surprise attack on the Mahrattas, he did not have more than half that number. He had a formidable task ahead of him because, not only did he need to capture the three locations just mentioned, but he also had the task of imposing the British will on the Emperor Shah Alam and establishing a British Resident there in Delhi. For this task, he was given full Military and political powers by Wellesley, who had now positioned himself at Cawnpore to watch the progress of the campaign as it unfolded.

Lake left Cawnpore at the head of his small Army on 7 August 1803 in the sweltering heat of an Indian summer. However, it was not until the end of that month that he received his official instructions from the Governor General to commence operations. These were to take over the Doab; take the Moghul Emperor into British protective custody from the protective custody of the Mahrattas; to form an alliance with the Rajputs and finally to occupy Bundelkhand. This occupation of Bundelkhand, for which Captain Baillie was ordered to act as Political Agent, on the recommendation of Edmonstone, was, indeed, a main thrust of Wellesley's grand strategy of containment, as Bundelkhand lay astride one of the main Mahratta invasion corridors to the east. Furthermore, the Deccan, Hindustan, Bengal corridor through Malwar needed to be controlled if complete containment was to be achieved and it was this Bundelkhand containment, which Baillie personally and successfully achieved, when he was aged only 30.

For this immensely important assignment, Edmonstone ensured that Baillie had been given a glowing recommendation to General Lake by drafting a letter for Wellesley's signature, which stated, 'Lieutenant Baillie's intimate acquaintance with the language and with the habits and disposition of the natives of India, and the judgement of abilities which that Officer possesses, qualify him in a peculiar degree to aid your Excellency in the conduct of any political negotiations.' Edmonstone did, indeed, want someone whom he could trust, because Bundelkhand was vital to any plans to divide the Mahratta Confederation. Its lands bisected the great Mahratta holdings, guaranteeing that, if British soldiers could be stationed there in force, there would be little likelihood of a union of the chiefs, which would, therefore, make manoeuvres much more difficult for them.

Edmonstone had indeed laid the groundwork for British aggrandisement in Bundelkhand even before the war began, instructing Graeme Mercer, the Political Agent there before Baillie, to encourage the Rajahs to make subsidiary alliances with the Company in order to undermine Scindia's and Bhonsla's authority. Mercer had also been instructed to assure the Rajahs that the Company had no interest in controlling their internal administrations, and to do whatever else he felt necessary, including the use of bribery, to create allies for the Company. Baillie was somewhat more subtle in his efforts as we shall see and acting under Edmonstone's instructions, he obtained a supplemental Treaty with the Peshwa, ceding most of Bundelkhand to the Company, as one of the requirements for continued British support for his cause.

General Lake was a skilful tactician, a good organizer and enormously popular with his troops – he always led from the front – and was a superb fighting general. He was then aged 60 and he remained a stickler for propriety, always appearing in full uniform, with all his buttons done up and a perfectly powdered wig in place, even when a march began at 2 am, which they generally did, in order to avoid the heat of the day. The march now was towards the immensely strong Fortress of Aligarh, which was commanded by a rather hopeless Frenchman, by the name of Colonel Pedron. He had been told by General Perron to make a determined defence, promising to return as soon as he could with the entire Mahratta Army. He even wrote him a letter:

Remember that you are a Frenchman and let no action of yours tarnish the character of our nation. I hope to send back the English gentlemen faster than they came. Make yourself perfectly easy on this subject; Do your duty and defend the fort while one stone remains upon another. Once again, remember your nation. The eyes of millions are fixed on you.

The trouble was that the Frenchman, Colonel Pedron, had no particular desire to fight a Company army, so he declared that he would surrender Aligarh, the moment the Company troops arrived. At this point, his Mahratta second-in-command, a Rajput, promptly arrested him and threw him into one of the Fortress's dungeons. All this meant that the assault was going to be a very 'sanguinary affair' as a Company officer put it, and it was. There was no time for a siege as such, due to the imminence of the arrival of a Mahratta relief force, and this meant that the assault had to be undertaken more or less immediately. Lake had been told by an Irishman like himself, called Lucan – a deserter from the Mahratta camp, that the Fortress was protected by an intricate series of inner gates designed by the French and that he would need to get his men over the causeway, across the ditch and then through the main gateway and then once through that, there would be another three gateways to get through, where his troops would find a series of mazes inside the bastions, which had deadly flanking loopholes – one would think it an almost impossible task. To everyone's surprise Lucan volunteered to lead the assault party – more or less a death sentence – but at least he knew what he was doing and where he was going. As it happens, he lived to tell the tale and we will meet him again on another occasion, where, unfortunately, he did not live to tell the tale.

In the very early morning, after a minor earthquake, the attack went in. It took twenty minutes or so for the assault force cannons to blast open the main gateway and there were heavy casualties. After an hour of intensive fighting, it was all over. Lake came up to see these casualties, which distressed him greatly. Monsieur Le Colonel Pedron was released from his dungeon, and it was reported that he emerged looking 'a very tired old man in his green jacket with gold lace and epaulettes'.

Delhi was the next stop and on 7 September, Lake set off once more. At this point in time, he received a letter from the Commander-in-Chief of the Mahratta Army, namely the French General Perron, stating that he had given up the service of Scindia and that he was now asking for permission to take refuge under British protection at Lucknow – in other words, he was deserting Scindia. What had happened was, like his predecessor the French General de Boigne, he was known by Scindia to be opposed to the war and he, therefore, no longer trusted him. It seems that everyone in the Mahratta and French camp knew this and it was, therefore, a question not whether, but when, he would desert. As a result, all those French officers loyal to Perron were confined to barracks and a particularly unpleasant Frenchman by the name of General Bourquin was appointed to succeed him, who also eventually deserted.

On 11 September 1803, as usual at two o'clock in the morning, Lake started his march towards Delhi, having captured the fort of Khurja on the way, which had been commanded by the son of Colonel Pedron and who, like his father, preferred not to fight the Company. In the early afternoon, the Army settled down for a picnic – the temperature was exceedingly hot and the soldiers were weary from their ten-hour march and there had been a lot of sunstroke casualties. At that moment, it was reported that the Mahratta cavalry were approaching. Lake, therefore, rode out with three regiments of cavalry, which is all he had, to see what was going on. The elephant grass, through which they were riding, was very high and masked a Mahratta ambush and they came under heavy fire.

Lake slowly withdrew, feigning a more significant retreat with the result that the Mahrattas left their ambush positions and advanced forward with some light artillery, thinking that they were winning the battle. As Lake's cavalry slowly retreated towards the Company artillery and infantry, who had now got themselves into position, Lake wheeled his cavalry to the left and the right, thus exposing the advancing Mahrattas to the waiting British infantry line – only a single line, as his battalions were very much under strength. Lake now came forward at the head of his Army to lead the attack against the enemy. His infantry marched forward with their muskets on their shoulders, showing extraordinary discipline and courage under heavy fire. They were then ordered into their firing positions only a hundred yards from the Mahrattas. They fired a single volley and then went in with the bayonets. The Mahratta line broke and the British infantry formed up to allow the galloper guns through to the river Jumna, beyond which was Delhi. The French General Bourquin, as we have mentioned, now followed Perron and deserted along with his French officers to General Lake.

After the battle was over, Lake moved his Army nearer to the river and pitched camp outside the Delhi walls. Although the battle for Delhi had been ferocious, nevertheless it was politically important in the sense that Lake was now able to have access to the blind and ageing Emperor, in whose name Scindia controlled the Doab. Thus, Wellesley was about to achieve his objective of 'freeing' the Emperor from the protective custody of the Mahrattas and take him under the protection of the British. On 16 September, Lake entered the city and formally presented himself to the blind, powerless Emperor poet, now over 80 years old. The Emperor received the General 'under a small tattered canopy, the only remnant of his imperial state and with every appearance of the misery of his condition'. The Emperor, when told who he was, greeted him with the words 'My Friend and my Deliverer'. He had been held a prisoner ever since Scindia had become Regent in 1784 and had then been blinded by that dreadful Afghan adventurer Gulam Kadir four years later, when he refused to tell him the location of the secret storerooms, where his treasure lay hidden. Gulam

Kadir then performed the operation of blinding him by inserting needles into one of his eyes and then, on the following day, he carved the remaining eye out of its socket.

Following this appalling Afghan atrocity, Scindia then recaptured Delhi and in the process took Gulam Kadir prisoner. The now blinded Emperor then instructed Scindia to remove Gulam's eyes, and these were sent in a small casket to the Emperor, although, of course, he could not see them. Moving on, the Emperor bestowed on Lake the second highest title of the Moghul Empire, while apologizing that he could not give him the highest, as he had just given that to Scindia. The title was as follows: Sword of the State; Hero of the Land; Lord of the Age and Victorious in War, all this being addressed in Persian, to the General. He now exercised his undoubted Irish charm on the Emperor and it was reported that he showed him every kindness, telling him that he would do anything to make him feel comfortable, as well as enabling him to retain his dignity.

On 30 September 1803, Wellesley wrote a long and effusive letter to Lake in the following terms:

My dear Sir,

I avail myself of the first moment of my recovery from sickness to offer you my most sincere congratulations on the glorious victory of the 11th and on its decisive and propitious consequences. An event more honourable to the British arms never occurred in any part of the world, and in India, the conduct and result of your action stands without parallel. Much as I feel indebted to the merits of your army, justice, universal consent of all parties and the plain evidence of indisputable fact concur to point my principal attention to your matchless energy, ability and valour.

You have formed the army to this illustrious and extraordinary achievement, and to your personal exertion must be attributed the promptitude, skill and irresistible intrepidity, which marked your exertions on that memorable day. The result must be the utter extinction of the last vestige of French influence in India, the defeat of the ambitious and rapacious views of the Mahratta confederates and a speedy peace with ample indemnity and security to the allies. You are entitled to the highest honours and rewards which your country and king can bestow; from me as the representative of both in India, you will receive every testimony, which I can afford in my public capacity, of my admiration of your conduct and of the high value and consideration, which I attach to your eminent services. My private gratitude cannot be expressed, nor is it possible to form a hope of discharging such a debt according to my estimation to its extent.

My life, however, protracted could not furnish the means of satisfying my sentiments on this occasion; but whatever can be expected from the most cordial, firm and zealous respect, affection and attachment, must ever be commanded by you from me and from every person connected with me.

Ever, my dear Sir, yours most faithfully and affectionately, with the most cordial esteem and attachment.

Wellesley

Chapter 14
The story of General De Boigne

Readers will have noticed the extent to which the Mahrattas were commanded by French officers and to a lesser extent also by British officers. Readers will also have noticed that one of the main reasons for the defeat of the Mahrattas in this Hindustan campaign was the widespread, if not total, desertion of these French officers during this War, which enfeebled the Mahrattas at a critical time during the campaign. Indeed, we have mentioned the desertion of General Perron, who had succeeded General de Boigne as the Commander-in-Chief of the Mahratta Army, followed by the desertion of the next Commander-in-Chief General Bourquin. All these French officers had Indian ladies, like Baillie and Edmonstone, but the private life of General de Boigne is more interesting than most, and will be related now in the context of European and Indian relationships at that time.

Benoit Leborgne, his original name, was born in 1751 in Lyon, France, the son of a furrier. He began his career as a soldier in the Irish Regiment of the French King, Louis the Fifteenth, but after a time, he went to St Petersburg with an introduction to the famous Fvodor Orlov, one of the lovers of the Empress Catherine. Prince Orlov was then in course of raising a Greek Russian Regiment for the Empress and, although de Boigne was French, he succeeded in persuading him to join it and, as a result, he took part in the Russo-Turkish War of 1768 to 1774, when he was only 17. Unfortunately for him, he was captured by the Turks during the campaign, was enslaved and put to work in a galley. Fortunately for him, he was able to speak some English and, unexpectedly, he came to the attention of one Lord Algernon Percy, who was visiting Constantinople at that time. Somehow or other again, he bought him out of slavery and, inexplicably yet again, he gave him letters of introduction and recommendation to Warren Hastings the Governor General in Calcutta and to Lord Macartney the Governor in Madras and off he went there and joined the 6th Native Regiment of the Madras Army.

Always a man to move on, he travelled to Lucknow, where he lodged with Colonel Antoine Polier, another Frenchman there, and who has not seen that wonderful conversation piece by the artist Zoffany in Lucknow of the Colonel, Claude Martin and Mr John Wombwell, the Lucknow Assay Master with Zoffany looking at the artist, that is to say himself, now in the Victoria Memorial Hall, Calcutta. In due course and to cut a very long story short, he ended up as the Commander-in-Chief of the Mahratta Army under Scindia, as mentioned. Not only that, he became the Governor of the conquered provinces, which entitled him to a share of the tax revenue or tribute of these conquered provinces, and all this made him enormously rich. However, he suffered badly from recurrent attacks of malaria and he, therefore, sold off his bodyguard – an unusual transaction – and then took ship for England not France and there he landed at Deal in Kent with his Indian wife and two children – in other words, he did not leave his Indian lady behind like Baillie and Edmonstone.

While he was in India, he had fallen in love with this woman by the name of Halima Noor Begum, who was the daughter of the Colonel of the Emperor's Persian Guard. She had been born in 1772, the same year as John Baillie – and had been married at a very young age to the Nawab of Pundri, west of Delhi – however, he died before the marriage was consummated. During a visit to Delhi in 1788, she met de Boigne, who had been placed in charge of the Red Fort after its capture by Scindia. So smitten and impulsive and, we suppose, infatuated was de Boigne that, on that very first day he met her, he requested the Colonel's permission to marry her, which he gave, despite de Boigne's refusal to convert to the Muslim faith. There were two very grand weddings – one in Delhi and one in Lucknow – and they had a daughter, who was given both an Indian name Banoo and an English name Anne. On her marriage, Halima took the name of Helen Benoit, but that was changed when she arrived in England to Helena Bennett. A second child, a son, came along, whose name started off as Ali Baksh but was changed in England to Charles Alexander Benoit de Boigne. De Boigne then became a naturalized British subject in 1798 and they lived in a grand house in Great Portland Street, which, in those days, overlooked the English countryside.

However, the story does not end there, because de Boigne, shortly after they had arrived in London, met a beautiful but precocious girl by the name of Adele, who was the daughter of an aristocrat the Marquis d'Osmond, who had fallen on hard times, probably as the result of the French revolution. De Boigne fell madly in love with this girl and despite the disparity in age – something like thirty years – asked her to marry him, despite the fact that he was already married to Helena and had two children with her. All this required a divorce, which placed Helena in a terrible position – a divorced upper-class Indian woman, deserted, alone and friendless in a foreign country. She went to live in Enfield with her two children, who went to school with the fees being paid by de Boigne.

Again, however, the story does not end there, because within a year, de Boigne and Adele, somewhat unsurprisingly, separated and although there were various reconciliations, they never got together again. It is interesting to note that when they got engaged, Adele told him she did not love him and would only marry him for his money to enable her parents to live in the style to which they were accustomed before the Revolution. Surprisingly, de Boigne agreed to this, so anxious was he to marry her but the mésalliance was there, she, from an impoverished aristocratic family – he, from a lower-class family from Lyon, but now extremely wealthy. There is, however, a surviving letter from de Boigne to Helena in which, inter alia, he writes, 'I have seen you to be a good daughter to your mother, an affectionate wife to me and a tender mother to our two offspring. God will reward you – believe me with most sincere affection, for ever your friend.' Later another letter was written to her in 1801, saying that 'he was a little happier than I have been these past three years, but I am afraid it will not turn out a lasting happiness', and it did not.

De Boigne purchased two chateaux, one for himself and one for Adele. Anne his daughter came over from England to be with them. Tragically, she died when she was 15 years old from a fever. De Boigne wrote, 'She was of an extremely good colour although born to an Indian mother, who mourns her loss just as much as I do.' After Anne died, her mother moved to a small village called Lower Beeding, near Horsham in Sussex, and that was where she became known as the 'Black Princess'. We do not know how dark she was, and it may be that she was called that because she was Indian and came from an upper-class family – after all, she was the daughter of the Colonel of the Emperor's Persian Guard. She converted to Catholicism, regularly attended Mass and was a generous benefactor to the poor of the village. We have one last sad description of her: 'She was of sallow complexion with strange dark eyes – she would sometimes stay in bed until mid-day and often kept her nightcap on when she got up. She took no trouble about her dress but did wear magnificent rings. She smoked long pipes and lost her temper easily and could not be bothered about anything.' In other words, she was a very lonely old divorced Indian lady, living alone in a foreign country. She died in 1854 and was buried in the local cemetery – her grave being the only one facing north, not east, as she did not want her tomb facing Mecca. As for de Boigne, he lived alone in his magnificent chateau, tormented by his dysentery, for which he took opium, and died in 1830 – twenty-four years before Helena. Alexander inherited his immense wealth.

Chapter 15

The capture of Agra: The Second Anglo-Mahratta War continued

On 23 September 1803, Lake said goodbye to the Emperor and on the following day the Army set forth along the left bank of the River Jumna in the direction of Agra, with the heavy guns captured at Delhi, being ferried down the river for use in the likely forthcoming siege of Agra. They stopped for a day, while the Hindu Sepoys went off to worship at the sacred city of Bindraban. On 4 October, they arrived near Agra with its great Fortress built by Akbar standing on the banks of the Jumna. This was commanded by two British officers as it happens – namely, Colonel Hugh Sutherland and Colonel George William Hessing. Lake called on them to surrender, which they did, but the Mahrattas under their command did not, and like Colonel Pedron at Aligarh, they were imprisoned in the Fortress.

Outside the Fortress, there was a Mahratta force of some seven thousand men, while inside the fort there was a garrison of some four thousand men. Lake decided to attack the town and the force outside the town but not the fort itself. Thus, on the morning of 10 October, the attack went in, with three battalions of Native Infantry now joined by Captain Baillie of the 4th Native Infantry. The ravines close to the fort were cleared and the infantry then went on to try and capture the guns on the glacis, but this was a failure and heavy casualties were incurred. By that evening, the Mahrattas had been driven from the town and twenty-six of their guns had been captured. Three days later, about 2,500 Mahrattas surrendered and then, on the following day, Lake began constructing the batteries with the intention of effecting a breach in the walls.

While all this was happening, the imprisoned Colonels warned the Mahrattas that, if the storming was successful, then they would be put to the sword and this encouraged them to ask the Colonels to negotiate terms. A certain Captain Salkeld was sent in, but he could not obtain an answer, so the siege batteries opened fire and it soon became apparent that a breach had been effected. The Mahrattas then decided to abandon the defence and the garrison numbering between five and six thousand marched out and the British marched in, and that was that. The capture of Agra resulted in another effusive letter of thanks from Wellesley to Lake, which ended, 'Ever, my dear General, yours affectionately and with sincere respect and confidence, Wellesley.'

It is interesting to note that these two British Colonels Sutherland and Hessing, who were commanding Agra for Scindia, were good friends of Ochterlony, now the British Resident at Delhi. All of them had Indian wives or lady friends, and they all entertained each other in their Agra homes. As it happens, Colonel Hessing was the brother-in-law of the French General Perron, while his daughter was married to the son of Colonel Sutherland, namely Captain Robert Sutherland. Many of these mercenaries were related by marriage and many of them were Scottish as well as French.

However, they were becoming increasingly concerned about the future of their Scottish Indian daughters, particularly if they stayed on, given the increasingly racial climate emanating out of Calcutta. At that time, these European mercenaries and their Indian wives all lived quite openly in the cosmopolitan society that was Agra, and this was regarded as being particularly healthy for the children, who did not have any hang-ups and concerns about colour and race. Ochterlony called it the 'Agra System' and it worked there. However, it had not been working for some time in Calcutta, where such relationships were beginning to be frowned upon and we have seen that, on the Baptismal Certificates, the Indian mothers' names were always either left blank or the word 'unknown' inserted. However, in no sense were they unknown, they were all known but not recorded. It is interesting to note that when the Scottish Indian children of Baillie and Edmonstone were being brought up at Leys Castle by Margaret Baillie, the darker complexioned ones appear to have been partly boarded out in Inverness, where they were less conspicuous than on the rural Leys Castle Estate.

The capture of Aligarh, Delhi and now Agra meant that Lake had suffered heavy casualties, but he had also now to garrison these three cities. He was, therefore, in urgent need of reinforcements, and meanwhile a Mahratta force of some seventeen battalions with a considerable number of guns was positioning itself only 30 miles from Agra. For some reason, it remained there, while Lake was about to batter away at the walls of Agra. The thought occurred to Lake that this force might be thinking in terms of recapturing Delhi, with its inadequate garrison, rather than in attacking him. He, therefore, decided to march in their direction with no more than ten battalions and his three cavalry brigades. In order to get there as quickly as possible, he left his heavy guns and baggage behind under the escort of two battalions and made a night march with his remaining battalions and cavalry Regiments riding ahead, in order to catch the enemy by surprise and bring on an immediate action. This resulted in the battle of Laswari, one of the most bitterly contested battles ever fought and won by the Company army in India.

This night march of some 24 miles brought him to the Mahrattas at dawn and he managed to take them by surprise. They were at full strength with no less than seventy-two guns and somewhere between 4,000 and 5,000 cavalry against Lake's now much diminished force, while his infantry were still plodding along, some distance behind him and his cavalry. The Mahrattas were positioned similarly to the position they had adopted in front of Delhi. There was a huge amount of dust in the air, which obscured Lake's vision and which made him believe that the Mahratta commander, Abaji Inglia, was retiring, but he was not. Lake now launched his cavalry into action, hoping to keep them engaged, while his infantry was coming up, which they did, shortly before midday. The Mahrattas fought with exceptional bravery, but seeing that Lake's infantry had now arrived, they sent word to Lake that they might be willing to surrender their guns on certain conditions, whereupon Lake gave them an hour to sort themselves out. Far from surrendering their guns, the Mahratta used this hour in taking up a new and more formidable position and a violent battle now ensued.

Lake, at the front as usual, led his cavalry forward, but his horse was shot from under him, whereupon his son Major Lake came forward and offered him his, but, as he did so, he was severely wounded and had to be left behind. The situation was critical for some time and defeat looked possible. However, the Mahratta cavalry did not perform as well as they should have done and were easily repulsed. The 29th Light Dragoons did perform well and supported by the 76th Regiment, which had disgraced itself at Delhi, charged through the Mahratta lines and broke them. The Native Infantry Regiments now came up and also broke through the Mahratta lines. It was a fearful battle, which continued most of the day and when it had all ended, Lake was effusive in his praise for the heroic bravery of the Mahrattas. It would be true to say that at Laswari, General Lake showed himself much more than a fighting general – he showed his calmness in the face of danger, his self-reliance, his power of commanding the confidence of his men and above all, his dedication to his duty when he left behind him his severely wounded son, not knowing whether he would live or die. Lake was, indeed, was one of the finest generals, this country – in his case Ireland – has ever produced – very much on a par with Wellington, another Irishman.

We have mentioned his son George. He did survive the battle of Laswari, although badly wounded as stated, but, how sad to relate, he was killed by the French, while storming the Heights of Columbeira during the Peninsula War. What happened was that in August 1805, when he was the Colonel commanding the 29th Regiment of Foot, he was ordered by General Arthur Wellesley to lead the attack on the Heights and led the way, as his father always did. Despite coming under heavy fire from the French on all three sides, he managed to reach the top, before being pushed back by the French during a counter-attack and was killed. If you go there and you might, you will see a Memorial to him, and on it are inscribed the words, 'Sacred to the Memory of the Hon. Lieut-Colonel G. A. F. Lake, who fell in driving the enemy from the Heights of Columbeira on the 17th August 1808. This Monument is erected by his Brother Officers as a Token of their High Regard and Esteem.'

Towards the end of the campaign against Scindia, it had become apparent that Holkar was unlikely to stand back and refrain from hostilities. Throughout, Holkar had been swayed by two conflicting motives – one was his wish to defeat the Company, whose power he increasingly resented and which would have pushed him in the direction of supporting Scindia, and one was his fear of assisting Scindia, whom he did not trust, as this would have enabled the latter to become the major power in India. There is little doubt that, if he had indeed assisted Scindia, which he did not, then the combined forces of Scindia and Holkar would have been too much for the Company. One of his first acts of hostility was to decapitate three Anglo-Indian officers, who, as it happens, had served him well, but had now refused to serve against their countrymen. When this occurred, Wellesley was outraged. At the same time, Lake, who had now been ennobled and was trying hard to establish some sort of order and control over the Company's newly acquired territories, felt that it would be necessary, sooner rather than later, to stand up to Holkar. He wrote to Wellesley, stating,

> I never was so plagued with this devil – he hardly ever keeps within the letter of the law and, as a result, is remaining in the field at enormous expense and if we retire, he will instantly come to Jeypoor, where he will get at least a crore of rupees, besides immense plunder, which will enable him to pay his army and thus become an even more formidable threat than he has been.

By 16 April 1804, Wellesley had had enough and instructed his generals to commence hostilities against him, even although he was acutely aware that this was the last thing the Directors in London wanted, bearing in mind the ever-increasing costs of these apparently endless wars. The Company was by now almost bankrupt and the price of its shares had fallen by more than 30 per cent since the start of this Second Anglo-Mahratta War. Wellesley was castigated for incurring these huge debts and Lord Castlereagh, the new Head of the Board of Control, said that it had all been an unnecessary expense. There was a big problem on the ground, however, and this was that the two armies, the Deccan and the Hindustan armies, were widely separated and it was the case that Arthur Wellesley was unable to move as there was a severe famine where he was situated and, as a result, he was unable to move until the monsoon arrived and there was sufficient fodder available for his thousands and thousands of bullocks. There was, however, one column of his Army consisting of four Sepoy and two European battalions in Gujarat, some 70 miles north of Baroda under the command of a certain Colonel Murray and he was, therefore, instructed to advance from Gujarat and liaise with Colonel Monson, despite the very considerable distance between them. Colonel Murray, who was described as a man of unreliable character by his contemporaries, was not particularly enthusiastic about this instruction and only advanced a short distance and then seems to have stopped, unfortunately just when his support was most needed.

There now commenced a series of manoeuvres, which are too numerous to set out in this book – however, we will describe the more important ones. Colonel Monson, whom you will recall, together with Lieutenant Lucan, had led the assault on Aligarh and had recovered from the wound, which he received there, was despatched by Lake together with three battalions of infantry to defend Jaipur, which was now being threatened by Holkar. He, Holkar, had retired rapidly south to Kotah, through which the River Chambal flows. On 27 April, Lake advanced towards Tonk, which has an interesting history, for those who can find the time to read it. It was, of course, the case that the timing of this campaign was extremely infelicitous, inasmuch as the hot weather had started, and the Company's troops suffered greatly through sunstroke. But the monsoon was only a month or so away and Lake, therefore, decided to sit it out until Arthur Wellesley could join him and therefore effect a combined operation after the rains had ceased. Consequently, he withdrew his main Army to Agra and Cawnpore, where he stationed his Regiments in the cantonment.

He did, however, remain concerned about Holkar and decided to increase the strength of Colonel Monson's column to five battalions, while he requested Scindia to provide him with cavalry – his thinking being that Monson should be able to hold his own against Holkar until the rains ceased and the main Army was ready to take the field again. Unfortunately, Colonel Monson, although brave and enterprising, does not appear to have been really up for the job in hand, and what happened now was calamitous. Prima facie, he commanded a column of quite considerable strength, but his weak spot was his Irregular Horse, which, although numbering some three thousand, were of doubtful quality and this Irregular Horse was commanded by Lieutenant Lucan, who had deserted from the Mahrattas, and who had successfully led the assault on the Fortress of Aligarh.

Monson, who had been instructed to hold the well-known Bundi and Lakheri passes south of Tonk and north of Kotah, seemed to be quite confident at this stage. However, instead of carrying out Lake's instruction, he crossed the River Chambal into Holkar territory and marched south to the Mokandwara Pass, which he told Lake was just as suitable for holding back Holkar's return. Lake agreed with some reluctance to his southward advance, but Monson continued to march further south – another 50 miles or so, thinking that he might soon link up with Colonel Murray marching north.

By now, the monsoon was starting, movement was becoming difficult and supplies were running short. Monson then heard that Colonel Murray instead of advancing towards him had, in fact, started to retreat, when he, in his turn, had heard that Holkar was advancing to attack him. He then heard that Holkar was not advancing to attack him, so he again advanced towards Monson, but Monson, thinking that Murray was retreating rather than advancing, also started to retreat and left Lucan behind with instructions to command the rear guard which consisted of some three thousand Irregular Horse. Communications were difficult in those days.

Lucan was, of course, very keen to show off his mettle, having recently deserted from the Mahratta camp at Aligarh and joined the Company army. When Holkar's advance guard showed up, he decided to attack it – unfortunately, a significant number of his men did what he did at Aligarh and went over to the enemy and, although he put up a very brave resistance, Holkar, who knew who he was, decapitated him.

Monson continued to retreat and the monsoon continued to pour down. The ground became increasingly boggy, so much so that some elephants and camels became so embedded in the mud, that they were unable to move. The River Chambal was crossed with difficulty – it is a wide river even without the increase due to the monsoon rains – and then Monson had to spike his guns and leave them behind for Holkar, who was able to unspike some of them. By now, there was no food and desertion became common. In the end, Colonel Monson limped into Agra, having lost the major part of his column – it was the worst defeat since Colonel William Baillie's defeat at the battle of Pollilur near Conjeveram in September 1780.

This Military disaster finished off the Directors, and they instructed that all fighting must come to an end – Wellesley was recalled. As it happens, he knew this would be the case and had intimated once or twice in the recent past that he was willing to retire, but the Directors had asked him to stay on. Edmonstone wrote, 'I here obey the restless impulse of my feelings in acknowledging a most grateful sense of the favour and kindness which I have uniformly experienced at his Lordship's hands and the unbounded confidence with which he favoured me, while thus ministerially employed under his immediate order throughout that most interesting and eventful period of the history of British India.'

Many years later, Wellesley put pen to paper and wrote a Testimonial for Edmonstone and, although it is quite long, it is worth reading. It reads as follows:

Following my arrival at Fort William in 1798, until my departure in 1805, Mr Edmonstone was constantly in my unreserved confidence – he was not only my advisor and intimate Counsellor in all my political transactions but also my faithful and active instrument in the execution of all my political arrangements and plans. The success, which attended my measures, is in a very great way to be ascribed to Mr Edmonstone's judgement in advising me and to his diligence, skill and discretion in executing them. This Testimony is quite general and given without limitation. It will be confirmed by a perusal of all my Official Proceedings lately published and still further by a minute examination of the Records of my Government preserved at India House.

Mr Edmonstone was scarcely for a moment absent from me during the whole of my eventful career in India. He accompanied me to Fort George and remained in my house at that Presidency, during the whole of the War in Mysore and during the Settlement of that Kingdom after its conquest. He returned with me to Fort William and afterwards accompanied me in my voyage up the Ganges and in my visit to Oude. He was intimately concerned in all the transactions before, during and after the War with those States. He was eminently useful in all my Regulations and the study of the Customs, Laws and Manners of our native subjects and he was one of my Chief Associates in the foundation of the College of Fort William. He presided over the Governor-General's Office, which has produced so many eminent men in the service of the Company, who have been, for the last thirty years, the principal ornaments of our Indian Empire.

He himself is one of the principal ornaments of the Company's Civil Service. After long and general experience, I cannot justly place my name above his, either for integrity, judgement, diligent knowledge, ability, discretion or temper – there is only one fault I could discover in him and that is that he was entirely ignorant of his own merits and extensive attainments. To this defect, I ascribe his present intention of withdrawing from public business to which no man is more equal. For the interests of the glory of our Empire in India, in which without vanity I may claim a deep concern, I implore my highly respected and beloved Friend, Mr Edmonstone not to deprive a Country, so justly dear to him and me, of those services, which as they have contributed so essentially to raise our fame and power, and to augment our prosperity and the happiness of our subjects, may still be employed to preserve our noble acquisitions in welfare and honour and to perpetuate the proud posterity and proud achievements of the present age.

Wellesley

Chapter 16
Bundelkhand Affairs

Readers will recall that one of the instructions to Lake from Wellesley was to occupy Bundelkhand and to try to effect this without bloodshed. It may well be the case that a number of readers may not be familiar with Bundelkhand and that is understandable, given that it has to all intents and purposes disappeared from the map – having been incorporated into the State of Madhya Pradesh in North India. At that time when Captain Baillie was appointed Political Agent for the territory in succession to Mr Graeme Mercer, with instructions to pacify it, it extended to a large area and maintained a population of some 2.5 million people. It was, therefore, a substantial responsibility for a young Captain of the 4th Native Infantry – aged only 30 – to undertake. The territory had a long complex history being fought over regularly by the Moghuls and the Mahrattas, but in 1792, following Anupgiri's successful defeat of Arjun Singh, the pride of the Bundela Pamar Rajputs at the Fortress citadel of Ajaigarh, the Mahrattas were acknowledged to be the Lords of Bundelkhand – eleven years before Captain Baillie was appointed the Political Agent there.

Going back in history to the time before Captain Baillie was posted there, it might be recalled that, at the time of the Mahratta Confederacy, one of their objectives was to invade British territory by way of Bundelkhand and, at that time again, at Poona, Shamshere Bahadur, who had been confirmed in his father's rights, was chosen to carry out this invasion. Letters were therefore sent out to Himmat Bahadur, whose real name was Anupgiri, and other adherents of Ali Bahadur requiring them to assist in this invasion. However, Himmat Bahadur, sensing that this invasion might precipitate his downfall, or thinking perhaps that he might be able to make better terms with the Company, decided to abandon the Mahrattas and, accordingly, made overtures to the British Government with the idea of transferring Bundelkhand to them. This would mean that Bundelkhand would be occupied by Company troops and the British Government accordingly accepted his proposal.

At this point, we will bring Captain Baillie more fully in the picture, and to enable us to put his successful Bundelkhand career into some sort of better perspective, we will jump the gun, so to speak, and see a long letter from the Hon. the Governor General in Council to the Hon. the Court of Directors in London dated 1 May 1807:

> Your Hon. Court will observe, that on this occasion, the Governor-General deemed it his duty to record the high sense, which he entertained of the distinguished merits and exertions of Captain Baillie, in the execution of the arduous duties committed to his charge during two missions to Bundelcund, and to propose that the public thanks of this Government should be given to Captain Baillie for the great and important services which he had rendered, and for the zeal and ability which he had exerted in the successful accomplishment of the views of the British Government in Bundelcund, suggesting at the same time that our opinion of Captain Baillie's merits and claims should be stated to your Hon. Court, with a recommendation that such reward be granted to that deserving public officer, as on a review of his important services your Hon. Court might consider him to merit.
>
> Concurring entirely in the justice of this honourable testimony of applause and approbation, and in the propriety of the Governor-General's suggestion, we consider it to be our duty to enable the Hon. Court justly to appreciate the value of Captain Baillie's services by a succinct review of his conduct in the execution of the arduous duties committed to his charge, although the general nature of them, as recorded in the proceeds of the Government, and from time to time reported in our despatches to your Hon. Court or to the Secret Committee, must have already attracted your attention.
>
> With a degree of public spirit, highly honourable to his character as an Officer, Captain Baillie, soon after the commencement of the war with the confederated Mahratta chieftains, although engaged in the duties of Professor of Arabic and Persian languages in the College of Fort William, offered his services as a volunteer in the field and then proceeded to join the army then employed in the siege of Agra. At the time, the precarious situation of affairs in the province of Bundelcund required the superintendence of an officer qualified by talents and abilities to conduct the various important and difficult negotiations, on which depended the establishment of British authority in that province. His Excellency the Commander-in-Chief with the approbation of Government selected Captain Baillie for the conduct of that arduous duty.

The original object of the British Government, as connected with the general operations of the war, was to establish its authority in the name of the Peshwa, over that portion of the province of Bundelcund, the command of which was necessary for the protection of our own territories against the hostile attempts of the enemy, who, at an early period of time, projected the invasion of our western provinces, by the aid of the chieftains possessing military power in Bundelcund.

The prosecution of this object placed the Nabob Shumshere Bahadur, who, under a commission issued by Amrut Rao, when seated on the Musnud of Poona by Jeswant Rao Holkar, to proceed to occupy the province of Bundelcund in a state of enmity to the British power. The cause of Shumshere Bahadur was supported by the Ranee of Culpee and other chieftains of the province, whilst, with a view to counteract this combination, the descendants of the ancient chieftains of Bundelcund were encouraged to employ their exertions in recovering the possessions wrested from them by the arms of Alee Bahadur, the father and predecessor of Shumshere Bahadur.

The latter chieftain had been defeated but not subdued and it was therefore deemed expedient, with a view to the accomplishment of our political objectives in Bundelcund to establish the influence of the British Government by conciliation rather than by hostility. The transfer of a large proportion of the Peshwa's nominal possessions in Bundelcund, which occurred shortly after Captain Baillie's mission, gave us a more direct interest in the province and rendered necessary the occupation of most of the territories, which the Bundelah chiefs had been encouraged to seize.

To combine with the establishment of our authority over the lands ceded by the Peshwa, the conciliation of the chiefs who were to be deprived of them, at a time when the British Government was engaged in a contest with the Mahratta power and when the province of Bundelcund was menaced with foreign invasion and disturbed by internal commotion, became a duty of the most arduous and difficult nature, requiring the exertion of eminent talents, firmness, temper and address. It was connected also with the duty of superintending and directing the operations of troops of the British Government, and of the auxiliaries of Rajah Himmat Bahadur, for the support of which, lands of the estimated produce of twenty lacks of rupees per annum had been assigned. It embraced the reduction of the power and influence of Himmat Bahadur and the Native Chiefs of Bundelcund, without weakening their attachment or hazarding their revolt, and the establishment of the British civil power and the collection of revenue in the province, under all the disadvantages of impending invasion and the desultory operations of numerous bands of predatory troops.

Within the space of three months, these objectives were achieved by the zeal and ability of Captain Baillie and we have reason to believe that in the months of May and June 1804, when the regular forces retreated following the invasion of the province by Amir Khan and when the utmost disorder was apprehended in consequence of the decease of Himmat Bahadur, the British authority in Bundelcund was alone preserved by the fortitude, ability and influence of Captain Baillie.

Even at that crisis of distress and danger, Captain Baillie was enabled to frame an arrangement with regard to the lands granted in Jaidad (a revenue assignment specifically earmarked for the maintenance of troops) for the support of the late Himmat Bahadur's troops, which laid their foundation of their ultimate transfer to the possessions of the British Government. Ample testimony to the merits and services of Captain Baillie on this occasion is borne by the Supreme Government in its despatch to the Hon. the Secret Committee of the 15th June 1804. The record of Captain Baillie's correspondence, however, testifies more demonstratively than the preceding statement, the arduous and responsible nature of the duties committed to his charge, the zeal and ability with which he fulfilled them and the importance of his services to the interests of the Company during the eventful period of the last war.

The services of Captain Baillie were subsequently continued in his capacity as a member of the Commission appointed in July 1804 for the administration of the affairs of Bundelcund; and the introduction of the regular civil and judicial system into that portion of the province, which had been subjected to the British authority, principally by the means of Captain Baillie's ability and exertions, admitted to his return to the Presidency in the month of July 1805.

Notwithstanding, however, the various arrangements concluded by Captain Baillie with the Nabob Shumshere Bahadur and other chieftains of rank and power in Bundlecund, by which their interests were connected with those of the British Government, much remained to be accomplished for the complete establishment of our rights and interests in that province. Of the territory ceded to us by the Peshwa, under the additional articles of the Treaty of Bassein, to the extent of 3,616,00 Rupees annual produce, lands only to the value of 12 Lacs of Rupees had been acquired. The Jaidad of the late Himmat Bahadur yet remained to be resumed. The situation of the numerous chieftains in Bundlecund relative to the British Government, their claims and pretensions, together with various other important questions connected with the establishment of British authority in the province, remained unadjusted.

The objects to be accomplished are accurately detailed in Captain Baillie's able report of the affairs of Bundelcund, to which we have had frequent occasion to refer in our despatches to the Hon. the Secret Committee. These objects were, in our judgement, alone susceptible of attainment by the aid of

Captain Baillie's personal exertions, influence and abilities; and this conviction occasioned Captain Baillie's second mission to Bundlecund in December 1805; the arduous duties of which, Captain Baillie with his characteristic spirit of public zeal undertook, without the prospect of any other immediate profit than that which was annexed to his actual situation in the College of Fort William.

Our successive despatches to the Hon. the Secret Committee and to your Hon. Court, commencing with the month of March 1806, contain a regular narrative of Captain Baillie's proceedings during his second mission, under the instructions issued from time to time for the guidance of his conduct. The first success of his exertions was manifested in the peaceable dismission of the turbulent and ferocious body of Nangahs, the continuance of which in the service of Government opposed a material obstacle to every salutary arrangement. The next and most important object accomplished by Captain Baillie was the complete resumption of the Jaidad lands of the late Himmat Bahadur, without the slightest commotion, although opposed by the powerful influence of the family and a numerous body of chieftains, in command of large bodies of troops and in possession of numerous forts; thus affecting the peaceable transfer to the British dominions yielding an annual revenue of eighteen lacks of Rupees, with the sacrifice of little more than one lack of Rupees.

The services of Captain Baillie were further enhanced on this occasion, by the successful manner in which he resisted the extensive claims of the manager of the Jaidad for arrears of pay to the troops and balance of revenue. These objects were not accomplished by the presence of troops, but by the personal influence and address of Captain Baillie, which enabled him to control the impulse of the strongest interest supported by local power and to subvert the efforts of combination and intrigue, by which the progress of his measures in the establishment of the British authority within the Jaidad, in the occupation of the forts, the discharge of the troops and the final settlement of the lands, were embarrassed and impeded.

Captain Baillie's arduous exertions, in the completion of these important arrangements, were not restrained by the repeated reports of external and internal confederacies. The same firmness of character and maturity of judgement, which had formerly distinguished his conduct amidst scenes of turbulence, disorder and rapine, enabled Captain Baillie to resist the influence of these interested reports and to prosecute to a successful issue the important objects committed to his charge.

With a spirit of zeal and energy, aided by the exertion of his political talents and address, Captain Baillie succeeded in accomplishing those arrangements with the principal chieftains in Bundelcund, which were proscribed by our instructions and which have produced a degree of tranquillity and security, hitherto unknown in this turbulent province; and has finally placed the authority and relations of the British Government in Bundelcund in a condition to admit our conducting the affairs of the province under the ordinary system of administration established in other parts of the Hon. Company's dominions. These services have been rendered peculiarly important and meritorious by the extraordinary local and incidental difficulties, which opposed the execution of them, as well as by the advantages, political, territorial and pecuniary, which the Government has derived from them.

Under such circumstances, we cannot but doubt your Honourable Court's concurrence in our opinion that Captain Baillie has established a peculiar claim to distinguished reward.

We then see an extract of a letter from the Hon. Court of Directors to the Governor General in Council to the Political Department dated 14 September 1808:

With respect to the strong recommendation contained in your last mentioned despatch, that an adequate reward might be conferred on Captain Baillie for the services rendered by that officer whilst he acted as Political Agent to the Governor-General in the province of Bundelcund, we observe by your letter that your Government has itself had an opportunity of rewarding those services, of the importance of which we are fully sensible, by the appointment of Captain Baillie to the Office of Resident of Lucknow, on the demise of Colonel Collins, which appointment, for the reasons stated in Sir George Barlow's minute of the 22nd June 1807, we hereby confirm.

We now need to introduce you more certainly to Himmat Bahadur, whose real name was Anupgiri, because it was he, together with Captain Baillie and Colonel Mieselback, who, one could say, engineered the transfer of Bundelkhand to the Company. He was born in the year 1734 into a Brahmin family but, shortly afterwards, his father died, leaving his mother destitute. She had no alternative but to sell her two sons Anupgiri and Umraogiri to a certain Rajendragiri – a Gosain, who adopted the two boys. Apart from the fact that we know from Captain Baillie that Anupgiri enjoyed playing with toy soldiers, we know little more except that this Rajendragiri had, apparently, been a respectable banker in Jhansi, but had 'as a result of some disturbances which had arisen between the people of Rajindegeer and certain turbulent persons' abandoned his property and moved east to the village and Fortress of Moth. There, he was able to rebuild his fortifications, but he had then started to intrude on land owned by Naru Shankar, who ruled Jhansi on behalf of the Peshwa. All this was too much for Naru Shankar, who threw him out, whereupon he crossed the river and took service with the Nawab of Oudh, who was then Shuja-ud-Daulah, together with his brother. This service of Anupgiri and his brother Umraogiri provided them both with the opportunity of meeting some of the players in the then North Indian game, including, so we are told, the Governor General.

However, given their humble origin, they seem to have been reviled by more or less everybody with whom they came into contact and this applied particularly to their unorthodox soldiers, who wore no clothes and thus went about generally naked. In the famous battle of Panipat in 1761, Anupgiri, then aged 27, fought on the side of the Emperor, the Nawab and the Afghans against the Mahrattas. Shuja-ud-Daulah's main ally, the Afghan Ahmand Shah Abdali was so shocked by their unclothed appearance that 'he lectured Shuja on the impropriety of unrestrained Kaffirs, naked both in front and behind, parading in front of his Muslims and ordered them to be removed out of sight of his Camp'. Anupgiri was present with the Oudh and Mahratta armies when he fought the Company's army, commanded by Sir Hector Munro at the famous battle of Buxar in 1765, where he was apparently wounded in the thigh, while protecting and helping Shuja to escape after his defeat; he was instrumental in the downfall of Bharatpur and the rise of Najaf Khan, the Persian adventurer, at Delhi in the 1770s; he engineered Scindia's foray into Delhi in the 1780s; he was the force behind Ali Bahadur's conquest of Bundelkhand in the name of the Peshwa in the 1790s. Ali Bahadur himself was the fifth son of Baji Rao, the Peshwa, while his mother was Mastani, a Muslim, so naturally there was a scandal when he tried to bring her into the 'Royal Household'. His last act was to enable the Mahrattas to be defeated by the British in Bundlekhand and the Doab in 1803 and, thereby, assist enable the British to capture Delhi, an event which, as we have reported, catapulted the British into the role of the paramount power in southern Asia. At the end of the day, Anupgiri, Himmat Bahadur, which means a man of great courage, was both amoral and immoral, but, nevertheless, he was, arguably, the most successful Military entrepreneur in late-eighteenth-century India with the exception of the East India Company, to whom, in the end, he allied himself, knowing that he could not defeat it.

As the star of Anupgiri had risen round and about Delhi, it had correspondingly fallen in Oudh, where the British officials reviled the naked Gosains – the warrior ascetics – and tried to keep them away from the Nawab for fairly obvious reasons. He was spied on by the British and we see a letter dated 4 June 1804 from a certain Thomas Brooke, the second Judge of the Appeal Court at Benares, who wrote to Edmonstone, 'Himmat Bahadur is not to be trusted; by the inhabitants of every class he is detested and while he stays we can never prosper in Bundlecund.' An Indian reported that 'he likes to fish in troubled waters'.

From 1789 to 1802, as we have mentioned, Anupgiri was allied to the Mahratta adventurer Ali Bahadur, when the latter died somewhat mysteriously during the siege of the Fortress of Kalinjar/Calinger (illustrated) – it was reported that the cause was dropsy. They had devoted their time together to the conquest of Bundelkhand. During the latter part of the eighteenth century, the fighting between the various Rajput and Mahratta clans turned it into the most violent province of the subcontinent. This fighting was so bad that it deprived the province of most of its fighting men, thus creating a sort of male vacuum. Anupgiri's re-entry into Bundelkhand was successful and in 1792. He defeated the chief of the Bundelas, Arjun Singh, and actually decapitated him personally, presenting his head to Ali Bahadur. All this rather went to his own head and he began to think of himself as some sort of Maharajah and he paid a large sum of money to a poet to compose a long laudatory poem in his honour, which started off as follows: 'Himmat Bahadur is a great king, incomparable in his excellent benevolence; he is generous, brave and compassionate but to his enemies he is death'. All this was somewhat over the top, because, whereas Arjun Singh had been a true Kshatriya, Himmat Bahadur or Anupgiri was the son of a Sanadhya beggar and the disciple of a thieving Gosain: 'a man constantly engaged in trickery and deceit, which, as it was put, was for a man of supposed honour and courage, a great sin'.

Now that Himmat Bahadur had acquired for himself the revenues of most of Bundelkhand, he began to make some alterations in his armed forces and, in order to enable him to do this, he engaged the services of a certain European adventurer by the name of Colonel Mieselback, who was probably of Danish origin because, when he died, the Danish flag at Serampore, whither he had retired, was hung at half-mast. Mieselback, who had been one of Ambaji Inglia's battalion commanders, signed on with Anupgiri shortly after the latter's defeat of Arjun Singh and then stayed with him until 1804, when Anupgiri somewhat mysteriously died, with Captain Baillie holding his hand, as he did so. Anupgiri had a considerable Army together with 'three battalions of infantry disciplined and armed in the European manner under the command of Colonel Mieselback'. The then Political Agent Mr Graeme Mercer was of the opinion that these troops constituted the most effective force in Bundelkhand. Here, you will recall that it was Mr Mercer, who accompanied Edmonstone's youngest son Frederick Elmore from Calcutta to London to that school of Mr Shepherd in East London, where he died from tuberculosis.

This Colonel Mieselback was and had been a spy for the British Government and had been able to provide that Government with some extremely useful intelligence; he had also, at the same time, managed to endear himself to Anupgiri and, indeed had become his closest political advisor and not only that, he had also been appointed Head of his Personal Bodyguard – a particularly important position. He was, thus, a key figure in the Bundelkhand imbroglio. His minder in British Intelligence was a certain Mr Richard Ahmuty, the Collector at Allahabad, who reported to Henry Wellesley, the Lieutenant Governor of the Ceded Provinces and who, in his turn, reported to his brother the Governor General, as did his other brother Arthur Wellesley. During 1802, Anupgiri was very much preoccupied with the chaos at Poona, as the war could have gone either way and he wanted to hedge his bets. Aware of this, Ahmuty applied pressure on Colonel Mieselback to apply pressure in his turn on Anupgiri to agree to a Subsidiary Treaty Alliance with the British. This was not, as it happens, initially successful but what did happen was that Colonel Mieselback became even closer to Anupgiri, which assisted British Intelligence even more in their designs to annex Bundelkhand and he therefore remained in situ with Anupgiri.

This gamble to allow Colonel Mieselback to remain with Anupgiri paid off and as Holkar and Bhonsla committed themselves to war with the British, Anupgiri sensing that, if the Confederates were successful, he would lose out, he granted the Colonel full Treaty negotiating powers with the British and, on 4 September 1803, he travelled to meet Mr Ahmuty and his then associate Mr Graeme Mercer. The Colonel then quite openly admitted that he had received a counter offer from Shamshere Bahadur and a bribe if he would defect to his cause, but he had declined the offer. Using his prearranged authority from Anupgiri, he then arranged a provisional Treaty with the British inviting them to occupy Bundelkhand, which naturally they did and Mr Ahmuty then fired off a thirteen gun salute when Anupgiri arrived. As some sort of douceur, Anupgiri was to receive a Jaidad revenue of 20 lakhs. At the end of the day and this day was now 16 September 1803, Colonel Powell linked up with Colonel Mieselback's troops and went off to defeat the forces of Shamshere Bahadur after what was described as 'feeble resistance'. Thus, this Colonel Mieselback had initiated, managed and delivered a political and Military victory to the British.

Mr Ahmuty then fell rather mysteriously sick – there were various theories as to why – perhaps he had been poisoned – the usual theory; or perhaps it was even Anupgiri's apparent occult powers at work; or perhaps he had been colluding with Anupgiri in some sort of manner and that he was, therefore, departing the province under the cover of sickness, before Colonel Powell could find out what he was up to, if he was; or, perhaps his illness was indeed genuine. As it happens, he did recover but two years later in 1806, he returned to Ireland where he died. His departure meant that there was a vacancy, which was filled by Mr Mercer, which, in its turn, meant that Captain Baillie could succeed him as Political Agent in Bundelkhand. Captain Baillie, therefore, took post with instructions to report to both the Governor General and to the Commander-in-Chief Lord Lake – a significant responsibility for a 30-year-old Captain of the 4th Native Infantry.

Chapter 17

The Jhansi Treaty and Anupgiri's death

It appears that before Baillie had to deal with Anupgiri himself, one of his first negotiations, with which he was tasked, was a proposed Treaty of Peace and Alliance with the Subadar of Jhansi, remembering that Jhansi was situated in Bundelkhand and this he was able to have signed, sealed and delivered on 6 February 1804. This Treaty is not particularly long, but given its importance and interest and also to demonstrate what Baillie was up to, we have set it out as follows:

Whereas a firm Treaty of Friendship and Alliance subsists between the British Government and His Highness the Peshwa and Shere Rao Bhoo, Subadar of Jansee, which is a Tributary of His Highness the Peshwa and whereas Shere Rao Bhoo, understanding a just sense of the Obligations imposed upon him by the said Treaty of Friendship and Alliance between the British Government and His Highness the Peshwa, shortly after the arrival of a Detachment of the British Army in Bundelcund, transmitted to His Excellency General Lake, the Commander-in-Chief through Captain John Baillie, Political Agent on the part of His Excellency in Bundelcund, a Paper of Requests, expressive of his Submission and Attachment to the Views and Interests of the British Government, and containing seven distinct Articles or Requests, all of which have been acceded to by His Excellency the Commander-in-Chief and whereas certain Requests and Engagements on the part of Shere Rao Bhoo were not included in the said Document and are now necessary to be added, the following Articles are now agreed on for the purpose of affording additional Security and Confidence to Shere Rao Bhoo and of including an additional Pledge of his Fidelity and Attachment to the British Government.

Article 1. The Bhoo professing his entire Submission and sincere Attachment to the British Government and to His Highness the Peshwa hereby engages to consider the Friends of both Governments as his Friends and their Enemies his Enemies – that is to say, he promises not to molest any Chief or State, who shall be obedient to the British Government or His Highness the Peshwa, and considering all such as may be rebellious or disaffected to the Government as his Enemies, he engages to give no protection in his Country to such Persons or their Families, to hold no Intercourse or Correspondence of any native or with them, and to use every means in his power to seize and deliver them to the Government against which they offend.

Article 2. If at any time a dispute or differences arise between the Bhoo and any neighbouring State or Chieftain professing disobedience to the British Government, the Bhoo engages to communicate such Disputes or Differences to the British Government, that they may have an opportunity of investigating the matter in dispute and of adjusting it to the mutual satisfaction of the Parties or of punishing the Party who shall be refractory.

Article 3. Whereas a Detachment of the British Forces shall be employed in punishing the disaffected in the Countries to the possessions of Shere Rao Bhoo, the Bhoo engages on every such occasion to join the British forces with his Army, and to assist in the accomplishment of their aims; and, if at any time, a Detachment of the British forces shall march into the Bhoo's country for the purposes of quelling disturbances, the whole expense of such Detachment shall be defrayed by the Bhoo; on the other hand, if the assistance of the Bhoo's troops be demanded at any time for the purposes of quelling disturbances in the British territory, the expenses of such troops shall be borne by the British Government.

Article 4. If the Bhoo is in reality the Commander of his own Troops, it is hereby agreed that on every occasion when they may be acting with the British Forces, the general Command of the whole shall be vested in the Commanding Officer of the British Troops, and in the event of Peace being concluded, a due attention will be paid to the Bhoo.

Article 5. Shere Rao Bhoo engages never to take or retain in his Service any British Subject or European of any Nation or description, without the consent of the British Government.

Article 6. Whatever Tribute has hitherto been paid to His Highness the Peshwa by the Bhoo shall continue to be paid to His Highness; the British Government do not demand any tribute for themselves.

Article 7. If Rajah Ambaji Inglia at any time molests the Possessions of the Bhoo, the British Government shall interfere to prevent him.

Article 8. Accusations of disaffection or disobedience, if adduced by any Person against the Bhoo shall not be attended to by the British Government unless the Truth of them shall be proved.

Article 9. Shere Rao Bhoo possesses a house in the City of Benares – if any Children, Brothers or other Relations of the Bhoo hereafter reside in that City, they shall enjoy the Protection of the British Government and shall not suffer any molestation.

This Agreement containing nine Articles signed and sealed by Captain John Baillie, Political Agent on the part of His Excellency General Lake Commander-in-Chief and Shere Rao Bhoo Subadar of Jhansee in Camp at Hatra on the 6th Day of February 1804, is delivered to Shere Rao Bhoo and another of the same date, tenor and contents, signed and sealed by the Parties on the same day, is delivered to Captain John Baillie. Whenever the ratification of this Agreement under the Seal and Signature of His Excellency General Lake or of His Excellency the Most Noble the Governor-General in Council shall be delivered to Shere Rao Bhoo and the Bhoo engages to return this Agreement.

A fine Copy and Translation into Persian and Hindoo of the Agreement signed and sealed by Me Captain John Baillie and the Subadar of Jhansee.

Signed John Baillie

We also see an extract of a letter from the Governor General in Council to the Secret Committee dated 15 June 1804, shortly after the Agreement with the Bhoo was signed. It reads as follows:

At this period of time Captain John Baillie who, as stated in our despatch to your Honourable Committee of 12th April conducted on the part of His Excellency. the Commander-in-Chief, all Political and Civil duties in Bundelcund, resided at Banda a place situated to the southward of the River Betwa and nearly in the centre of that part of the Province of Bundelcund, in which the British Authority had been established. The Force with Captain Baillie consisted only of a small contingent of Cavalry belonging to Shrimshire Bahadur, about 200 Cavalry belonging to the Rajah Himmat Bahadur and 1000 Sepoys under the command of a European Officer in the service of the latter Chieftain. Notwithstanding the consternation which had spread throughout the Province of Bundelcund on the incursion of the Predatory Horse, whose number had been greatly exaggerated, Captain Baillie deemed it to be his duty to maintain his situation at all hazards, and the Governor-General in Council is satisfied that the preservation of tranquillity in the Districts in our possession south of the River Betwa is to be ascribed entirely to the confidence inspired and the subordination maintained throughout those Districts by the firmness, manly prudence and fortitude manifested by Captain Baillie on that occasion.

The Bundela succession following his death

During this time, Anupgiri took the opportunity to reduce his armed forces – the number of which he reduced to about three thousand or four thousand cavalry and between one thousand and two thousand of infantry as a result – a very far cry from the twelve thousand troops said to be attending the Gosain two months previously. Baillie wrote to Mercer just after the death of the Gosain, which we will come to shortly:

> I could never induce him to submit a muster roll of his forces, nor could form a correct view of their numbers, from the circumstances of a large portion of them being constantly employed in the collection of the revenue of his Jaidad, but I now have every reason to be convinced that the number of his cavalry has never exceeded two and a half thousand and that these, with the three battalions commanded by Colonel Mieselback and occasional levies of matchlockmen employed in the Jaidad collection, have uniformly constituted the whole of the Rajah's force.

All these calculations and accusations stemmed from the disagreements over the exact revenue value of the Jaidad. Baillie said it was 22 lakhs of rupees; Anupgiri said before he died that it was 18 lakhs of rupees. However, now Baillie discovered that Anupgiri was squeezing 24 lakhs of rupees out of his Jaidad and that the 'districts which he set apart for the Company could never be collected without the entire force in the country being employed in it'. Baillie went further and charged that Anupgiri was putting up a façade of enmity and aggression against the Bundela Rajputs, while actually colluding with them secretly, so as to prolong the Military operations in the province, which thereby extended the term of his Jaidad collections.'

Baillie kept in close touch with Mercer and via him with the Commander-in-Chief and we see various letters in which Baillie states that 'Anupgiri's conduct to his entire conviction, will not secure us the benefits, which might have been justly expected from him, given the favourable terms which were originally granted to him.'

There are more letters and we see Baillie stating that Anupgiri was adding insult to injury, as he continued to collect money from the districts which had been assigned to the British Government. Baillie then goes on to state that

Plate 1 A portrait of Colonel John Baillie in his East Indian Company uniform when he was the British Resident at Lucknow.

Plate 2 Neil Benjamin Edmonstone, Peter Harrington Ltd.

Plate 3 Dr George Baillie, 1795–1852, and his wife Harriet Nee Garford. He was the eldest son of Colonel John Baillie by his Indian lady. They had six sons and six daughters.

Plate 4 Margaret Baillie, 1761–1831, the eldest sister of Colonel John Baillie. She was the Chatelaine of Leys Castle, Inverness on behalf of her brother. She oversaw the education and upbringing of the 7 children of her brother and 2 sons of Neil Edmonstone, whose surnames he changed to Elmore.

Plate 5 A portrait of Mary Martin, the European mistress of Colonel Baillie when he was the British Resident at Lucknow. She was the mother of 3 of his children namely Anne, John Wilson and Henrietta.

Plate 6 A portrait of Anne, John Wilson and Henrietta, the children of John Baillie and Mary Martin. Courtesy of Alexander Baillie of Dochfour.

Plate 7 Leys Castle, Inverness, Scotland – the home of John Baillie. A recent photograph.

DUNTREATH CASTLE STRATHBLANE WHERE THE LATE KING STAYED SEPT. 1909.

Plate 8 Duntreath castle, Strathblane, Scotland – the home of the Edmonstone family. Photograph taken in 1909.

Plate 9 A portrait of Sir Archibold Edmonstone, the father of Neil Benjamin Edmonstone.

Plate 10 Ghazi-Ud-Din Haidar, the Nawab Vizier of Oudh who succeeded his father
Saadat Ali Khan. Courtesy of Alexander Baillie of Dochfour.

Plate 11 The Baillie Memorial erected at Seringapatam near Mysore by Colonel John Baillie for his uncle Colonel William Baillie in 1816.

Plate 12 A portrait of Colonel John Baillie and Mary Martin in Durbar at the Oudh Court at Lucknow. By an Indian artist.

Plate 13 A picture of the Gosain Anupgiri also known as Himmat Bahadur, courtesy of Professor William Pinch.

Plate 14 A painting of the East Indiaman the *Bridgewater* on which John Baillie sailed to Calcutta in 1791. The painting depicts the Bridgewater by the American privateer Hampden.

THE BENGAL LEVEE.

Plate 15 The Bengal Levee by Gillray. This shows Lord Cornwallis Governor General in the doorway, courtesy of National Portrait Gallery.

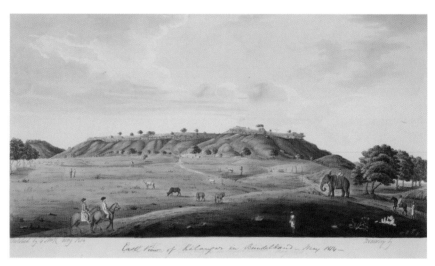

Plate 16 A view of the fortress of Kalinjar/Kalinger in Bundelkhand in 1814 by Colin Mackenzie 1754–1821. This fortress was captured by the company in 1812 and is frequently mentioned by Captain Baillie in his reports. Courtesy of the British Library Board, WD 706.

Plate 17 A portrait of Sir Richard Wellesley, Earl Mornington, as a young man later Governor General of India, 1798–1805, by Ozias Humphrey, 1783. Courtesy of National Portrait Gallery.

Plate 18 A Portrait of Gabriel Hyacinthe Roland in 1791, the French mistress, later wife of Sir Richard Wellesley, and later the Marchioness Wellesley by Elizabeth Vigee Le Brun, 1755–1842. Oil on Canvas, the Fine Arts Museums of San Francisco, museum purchase, Mildred Anna Williams Collection, Bequest Fund of Henry S. Williams in memory of H. K. S. Williams, 1991.

Colonel Mieselback had, as it happens, informed Mr Ahmuty of this, presumably before his illness intervened and that the latter had replied, 'We must please the Rajah until we get rid of the Nawab Shumshere Bahadur.' So perhaps it might have been true that Mr Ahmuty had been colluding with Anupgiri and that his illness was perhaps to some extent feigned – who knows?

It was then that Baillie was brought up short on 2 June 1804 by the news that Anupgiri's health was failing. Sensing that time now was very short, Baillie rushed to his bedside for a final interview. Later he recalled, 'The Gosain's faculties and powers of utterance were almost entirely exhausted. On the occasion of my visiting him this morning, he made an exertion for the purpose of requesting my protection of his infant son, which I thought would prove fatal.' It did prove fatal and he died the following day. The British thought that the cause of death was poison and that perhaps it had been administered by some woman, but nobody knows for certain to this day.

It was then that Baillie earned the approbation of His Excellency the Most Noble the Governor General. He, Baillie, describes the sequence of events thus:

> As the solemn declaration of the Rajah, on the day before his death, left me in no doubt of his intention of bequeathing all his property and rights to his only son, an infant now in camp and the avowed inclinations of the several Sirdars pointed to this boy as the only heir of his father's property and successor in command of the troops, whose rights they were disposed to acknowledge, I considered it indispensable to the important object of avoiding tumult and disorder in the Camp, to evince my acknowledgement of those rights by a formal Act and Declaration vesting the command of the Rosala (cavalry) on Rajah Nerinder Geer (Narindragir), the child, until the pleasure of the British Government be known. I proceeded accordingly to the camp of the late Rajah this morning and having summoned Rajah Omrao Geer (Umraogiri) and all the principal Sirdars to his tent, I there placed the boy upon his father's Musnud and directed all the chiefs of Bundelkhand to make the customary presents and acknowledgements of his authority, all of which were afforded unanimously and with the greatest readiness and satisfaction by all in my presence, excepting Rajah Omrao Geer, who departed from the tent with some appearance of displeasure.

Rajah Omrao Geer was Anupgiri's brother, who might legitimately have expected to inherit the Musnud:

> The general character of Rajah Omrao Geer and the limited influence which he possesses over the troops of his deceased brother, give me no grounds to apprehend any ill effect from his dissatisfaction at the measures, which I was induced to adopt and I have every reason that my endeavours to prevent

any commotion or disturbance in this country upon this critical and arduous occasion, will prove completely successful and that no material difficulty will occur in the accomplishment of any objects, which His Excellency the Commander-in-Chief or the Supreme Government may have in view respecting the Rajah's Jaidad.

He went on to write,

Whatever may have been the principles or motives by which the late Rajah was guided and the objects to which the services of his troops were directed during his life-time, I have not observed the slightest disaffection or disorder in his camp since his death and, on the contrary, the conduct and appearance of all his relations, principal Sirdars and troops have been such as to inspire me with their fullest confidence in their attachment to the British Government and in their ready submission and obedience to its will and commands.

Baillie then wrote a letter of condolence to the widow, to which she replied stating that 'his children, his relations, his servants and his troops, which have been supported during a period of sixty years by his money, are now the faithful servants of the British Government and are ready to obey its commandments'. And they did. Less than three weeks after his death, several of the Gosain's commanding officers intimated to Baillie 'their earnest desire of being admitted into the immediate service of the British Government on any terms which may be granted to them'.

We need here to return to the deathbed of Anupgiri, and the reason why his brother left the tent with such bitterness – he was the elder brother after all, or rather thought he was. At the time, the Gosain camp was situated at Bhuragarh near Banda and Umraogir, who was then at Shivapur near Cawnpore, rushed to Banda to take charge of the situation, only to be forestalled by Captain Baillie, who then proceeded to put the 5-year-old boy on the Musnud instead of himself. Let us see what he wrote in a Petition to the acting Governor General Sir George Barlow:

It is now two years since my brother Anupgiri sent for me in haste in his last illness and committing into my hands his ring and his chela Kanchangir, resigned his soul to his Creator. While I was engaged in mourning for the death of my late brother, the above mentioned chela in concert with the other officers of the Government availing himself of my absence, by various pretexts carried Captain Baillie to his house and persuaded him to place on the Musnud, a child of five years of age, born of a Muslim in my brother's family.

He had earlier written to the Governor General as follows:

The late Muha Rajah Anoop Geer Himmat Bahadur and I were full brothers. On the death in 1753 of Muha Rajah Rajinder Geer, my spiritual preceptor, I received from the late Nawab Sufdur Jung a Khellaut (a robe of honour) investing me with the Government and in concert with my brother and the adherents and dependants of my family, I proceeded to arrange and regulate the affairs of the Province. My brother in the spirit of our mutual harmony and friendship adopted my eldest son and for a period of some twenty years continued to conduct the administration of public affairs. I, being relieved thereby from the weight of all worldly concerns, passed my time on the banks of the Ganges in the full and undisturbed exercise of my religious duties. With these facts, all the Chiefs and Rajahs of Bundelcund are acquainted, but it is probable that Captain Baillie, who had the charge of the affairs of that Province, was not fully apprised of them.

He then went on to detail what he considered to be the conspiracy that led to the installation of the child Narndagiri in 1804 by Captain Baillie and Kanchangir and the wider political and Military circumstances, which forced him to acquiesce and leave the tent.

It could be mentioned here, as some sort of footnote, that Rajah Omrao Geer did not apparently spend all his full and undisturbed time on the exercise of his religious duties on the banks of the River Ganges, as he had gone off to support Wazir Ali, the Nawab of Oudh, who had been deposed by Sir John Shore and Edmonstone, in the murder of George Cherry at Benares and the insurrection there – previously mentioned. He was arrested and then held in confinement, first at Chunar and then at Lucknow, only to be released as a condition of the alliance formed between the British and Anupgiri in 1803 when Bundelkhand was ceded to the Company.

This successful cession and pacification of Bundelkhand conducted by Baillie, more or less entirely on his own, as the Political Agent, without hardly any Military support and with no bloodshed, earned him the coveted appointment as Resident of Lucknow in 1807 in succession to Colonel Collins who had died at his post and we shall see later the Governor General's comments on his appointment.

There is, however, a somewhat sad footnote to Baillie's pacification of Bundelkhand and this is that in May 1809, three years after the termination of the service of the Gosains under the British in Bundelkhand, Narindargiri, the young son of Anupgiri, who had been 'anointed' by Baillie after the death of his father, was settled in Rasadhan not far from Cawnpore with his Gosains and very extended family, who had been convinced by Baillie and his successors so to do. And there they stayed until 1841, when the Rasadhan estate, was, so to speak, reclaimed by the British or using the official terminology 'resumed', citing financial mismanagement and family illegitimacy. Consequently, the Gosains lost the land, which had been assigned to them and were now all penniless, except for some very small pensions. It is, therefore, not entirely surprising that all this was so bitterly resented that, sixteen years later in 1857, they took a leading part in that famous or rather infamous massacre at Cawnpore, when all the men, women and children from General Wheeler's detachment were massacred by these Gosains, as they tried to board the boats at that ghat.

The second footnote is that following the recall of Wellesley to London and the departure of Baillie to Lucknow, the province of Bundelkhand reverted to its usual state of anarchy. Many Military adventurers started ravaging the province for plunder again; the various chieftains started feuding with each other again; the inhabitants actively resented and disliked the British fiscal and administrative and judicial systems and took to violence again. General Lake told the Government in Calcutta that peace could not be assured without gaining control of the fortresses of these chieftains, but Sir George Barlow, then the acting Governor General told him that 'a certain extent of dominion, local power and revenue would be cheaply sacrificed for tranquillity and security within a more contracted circle'. The sacrifice was made but tranquillity and security became more distant than ever.

However, when Lord Minto, the successor Governor General arrived, he stated that 'it was essential, not only to the preservation of our political influence over the chiefs of Bundelkhand, but also to the dignity and reputation of the British Government to interfere for the suppression of internal disorder'. From there on things changed and the numerous Chieftains, who had increasingly viewed with contempt the British Commissioner, hastened now to make their submissions and agreed to refer their differences to British officers. Some did not, and Military operations were undertaken against them and tranquillity and security once more reappeared. Unfortunately, this did not last for long, when it appears that one of the Company's unscrupulous tax collectors came along and started to rack rent the province, thus blighting once again the prosperity there, but all this was long after Baillie had left.

Chapter 18

The return of Lord Cornwallis, Holkar, the Vellore Mutiny

During all this time, Edmonstone had kept in close touch with Baillie in Bundelkhand via the Governor General and the Commander-in-Chief and now in 1805, he was saying goodbye to Wellesley. His successor was Lord Cornwallis – his second time round – who should never have gone out to India again as he was an ill man. Edmonstone was horrified when he saw him get off the ship. This was the man, who had shown him so much kindness and who had, indeed, greatly advanced his career. He was now a shadow of his former self and looked like a very old man, which, indeed, he was. Lord Cornwallis was also horrified when he arrived to observe the opulence and splendour of the new Government House – now Raj Bhavan – and felt he was in some sort of prison, insisting that the sentries at his bedroom door should be dismissed, saying that 'if I showed myself outside a door, there was always a soldier with a musket with a fixed bayonet presenting himself to me'. On his arrival, he immediately appointed Edmonstone as his Private Secretary.

Cornwallis had had a bad voyage out to Calcutta but, ill as he was, he decided to go to the Upper Provinces and there to 'terminate by negotiation a contest in which the most brilliant success can afford us no solid benefit'. By this, he meant that both Holkar and Scindia remained a threat to the Company. He, therefore, embarked on the Governor General's barge to go upstream and upcountry and Edmonstone was with him all the time. However, it soon became obvious that his heart condition was worsening to the point where he could not even sign his name. Edmonstone wrote,

One of the symptons [sic] of his disease, which was gradually undermining him, was an almost constant and over-powering drowsiness, from which nothing seemed to rouse him, but for the claims of public business. Whenever I approached him for the purpose of reading despatches or drafts or letters or communicating with him on the business of my office, he did exert himself to the utmost of his faculties to attend and converse with me, until by degrees the power of his mind and body were exhausted and after a few days of insensibility and a wandering of mind, he sunk to death.

He died within two months of arriving in Calcutta and was mourned greatly by Edmonstone, who had watched over him as he lay dying and who had marvelled at his courage in the last days of his life. He was buried at Ghazipur and, if you go there, you can see his Memorial.

Cornwallis died before he could negotiate with Holkar, and this meant that Lake now had to undertake this, which he did successfully. That part of Bundelkhand, which he claimed to be his, was restored to him together with some areas north of the River Chambal. As it happens, unknown to Holkar, Lake had been in an extraordinarily weak negotiating position, as the Company had run out of money and the pay of his Army was five months in arrears. It had been agreed that the rest of Bundelkhand would go to the British, as has been related. Holkar was, of course, delighted because after defying the Company for almost two years, he had at last managed to emerge from defeat with impunity – it was certainly some sort of triumph for him. Unfortunately for Holkar, he was not able to enjoy the fruits of his victory for long – a nephew tried to take over his throne, whereupon Holkar had him and his half-brother murdered. Overcome with remorse, he started to take to the bottle, drinking vast quantities of cherry brandy. In the end, he went mad and had to be tied up with ropes and fed on milk. Three years later, he died.

Following the untimely death of Cornwallis, Sir George Barlow took office as acting Governor General and he appointed Edmonstone as his Private Secretary. Together, they went off to Allahabad and there they stayed in an old mosque, which had been converted into some form of accommodation and it was there that Edmonstone narrowly escaped assassination. He wrote,

For several weeks before our departure, a Mussulman fanatic had been hovering around, occasionally sending in petitions through me, soliciting employment and offering his services, engaging various propositions to accomplish the personal destruction of Holkar and seeking also to be admitted to the Governor-General, but he, being of a suspicious nature, met with no encouragement.

One morning when I happened to go out on foot and alone a short distance from the house, he came up behind me and touched me on the shoulder and, on my turning round, I saw that he was in the act of drawing a dagger from his belt. I instantly seized both his wrists until a sentry heard my voice and came to my relief. From the subsequent examination by the Magistrate, it appeared that his intention was to assassinate the Governor-General, but, fearing he might not have the opportunity before our departure, he resolved to have one victim and that victim was me. He represented that his motive was our profanation of the mosque, which had been converted in to a house by General Kyd, the former commandant of the station and had been occupied by him and others. He was placed in unlimited confinement.

We should remember that ever since Cherry's assassination at Benares, Edmonstone had always lived in mortal fear of a similar attack.

Sir George Barlow's short term of office was marred by the Mutiny at Vellore in July 1806, when Captain Baillie was still in Bundelkhand. This was when the Sepoys rose against their British officers which had resulted in over two hundred men being massacred, before the famous Rollo Gillespie rode to the rescue. It is worthwhile having a short look at this Mutiny, which caused the Governor General and Edmonstone to travel down to Madras to investigate the cause of it. Vellore lies not far from Madras and you can see the Fort from the railway line, as it curves around the town. Vellore was well known to Colonel William Baillie and he saw it in the distance for the last time in 1780 when he was being marched – possibly in chains – from Conjeveram to Seringapatam. He had hoped that word might have got through to the garrison there about his predicament and that he and companions might have been rescued. Sadly, that was not the case and two and a half years later, he died in his dungeon in Seringapatam.

At that time, Vellore was the Fortress in which the twelve sons and eight daughters of Tipu Sultan were rather loosely imprisoned, following his death in action in 1799 at Seringapatam. At the time of the Mutiny, there were only four companies of His Majesty's 69th Regiment and some invalid artillerymen stationed there. The British forces were vastly outnumbered by the native forces, which included the 1st, 2nd, and 23rd Regiments of the Madras Native Infantry – about 1,500 soldiers – not to mention the large number of Muslim followers of the Mysore princes totalling several thousands, who had taken up residence in and around the fort. As it happens, a Sepoy of the 1st Madras Native Infantry had warned his Commanding Officer, Colonel Forbes, of the plan to kill the British. Colonel Forbes did not believe him, however, but he did refer the matter to his senior native officers, but as they were the leaders of the forthcoming mutiny, they told him not to worry and that it was only a rumour.

The British officer responsible for the Mysore princes and their security and welfare was a certain Lieutenant Colonel Thomas Marriott, who despised his princely prisoners, claiming that they spent their days quarrelling with each other; engaging in fornication, sodomy and even incest with their mothers-in-law and generally frittering away their somewhat over generous allowances. In fairness, they had nothing much to do, if anything, except perhaps plot and their boredom was intense.

The Field Day was to be on 10 July 1806 for the 2nd and 23rd Madras Native Infantry Regiments and consequently, that night they drew their arms and slept with them by their cots. At three o'clock in the morning, they attacked the British and European officers and men, opening fire on the barracks and killing about a hundred and wounding many more. More than a dozen officers were killed as they emerged from their houses in their night clothes to see what was going on. It was fortunate, however, that a certain Major Coote, who might or might not have been a relation of the famous General Sir Eyre Coote, realized very quickly what was happening, jumped on his horse and rode as fast as he could to the garrison at Arcot, familiar to those who have studied the Anglo-Mysore Wars and which was only 16 miles away from Vellore. Arcot was where His Majesty's 19th Regiment of Dragoon Guards was stationed along with some 7th Madras Cavalry and they were commanded by the famous Colonel Rollo Gillespie. He, in his turn, immediately jumped on his horse and galloped off to Vellore with a squadron of Dragoon Guards followed a little later by some galloper guns – horse artillery. He, Rollo, arrived at Vellore about 8 am, where he found that the outer gates of the fort had been left open, although the inner gates had been shut. Gillespie was pulled up by a rope, which was held by some survivors on top of the wall overlooking the gate, and immediately assumed command, Two hours later, the galloper guns arrived, the closed inner gates were blown open and the 19th Dragoons poured into the fort, The Mutiny was then suppressed in only ten minutes, and during those ten minutes, four hundred mutineers were killed.

It could be said that the insensitivity of the Madras authorities was to blame for this ghastly episode. The Commander-in-Chief of the Madras Army Sir John Craddock had issued a new set of regulations designed to smarten up the appearance of the Sepoys – nothing very wrong with that – after all they were supposed to be regimental soldiers and, of course, they were paid accordingly. They were instructed to shave off their beards, to trim their moustaches, to give up wearing earrings, to cease displaying caste marks on their foreheads and so on. However, above all, and this seemed to be some sort of crunch point, a new turban designed to resemble a grenadier cap was ordered and there was a theory – only a theory – that this cap resembled a hat which Christian converts wore. This new hat had a feather in it with a cockade, made either of pigskin which offended the Muslims or cow leather which offended the Hindus. The introduction of this wretched hat meant that both Muslims and Hindus were affronted and believed that their religions were being attacked. They took the view that 'we shall be compelled to eat and drink with the outcast and infidel English, to give our daughters in marriage to the English' and so on. After the suppression of the Mutiny, these instructions were rescinded and so, we suppose, these Sepoys then reverted to their former motley appearance.

After the Governor General and Edmonstone returned from Madras, they issued an official statement that the underlying cause of the disaffection was a rumour that the Company intended to convert its soldiers by force to Christianity. However, Edmonstone privately considered that it was the sons of Tipu Sultan who, not having anything very much to do, if anything, were primarily to blame and he may well have been right, as there were no missionaries in either Arcot or Vellore at that time and only one or two in Madras. It also needs to be remembered in all this, is that, although their father Tipu was a hated figure in the eyes of the British, this was not the case with many of the Mysoreans and for this, one has only has to read the accounts of his State funeral in 1799, when the processional route to the Lal Bagh at Seringapatam was lined with thousands of weeping mourners.

Moving along a year or so later, Lord Minto, the Governor General, who had succeeded Sir George Barlow, visited Madras and said that he was even then very much struck 'by the mutual ignorance of each other's motives, intentions and actions, in which the Europeans and Indians seemed content to live – I do not believe that either Lord William Bentinck or Sir John Craddock had the slightest idea of the aversion that their measures would excite. I fully believe that their intentions were totally misapprehended by the natives'. He also felt that dismissing both the Governor and the Commander-in- Chief had been wrong. In the event Bentinck's dismissal did not have a long-term effect on his career, as he returned later to India as the Governor General.

Chapter 19

Sir George Barlow and the White Mutiny

One could say that there was nothing particularly novel about revolts and mutinies during the period of British rule in India. If you count them up, there were more than a hundred such events of various shapes and sizes between 1783 and 1900. Of course, by far the worst was the Indian Mutiny or Rebellion in 1857, for which there were a number of reasons. However, after the Vellore Mutiny, there was another one, three years later in Madras, when this time the European and British officers numbering some 1,900 refused to obey the orders of their Commanding Officers – a mutiny known as the White Mutiny – not the first time that this had happened and here we recall the earlier near mutiny of the British and European officers of the Bengal Army during the last year of the Governor Generalship of Sir John Shore in 1796.

The Governor of Madras at that time was Sir George Barlow, who had been acting Governor General. He was a member of the Bengal Civil Service and had served in India for twenty-eight years. He had assisted Lord Cornwallis with the introduction of the Permanent Settlement in Bengal and Sir John Shore had appointed him Chief Secretary to the Government of India when he was aged 33. It was Wellesley, who had appointed him a member of the Council and had made arrangements that, if any unforeseen vacancy should arise, then he, George Barlow should succeed him and he also arranged that he should be given a Baronetcy.

In 1805, as we have seen, Wellesley was recalled and when Lord Cornwallis died at Ghazipur, Sir George Barlow became acting Governor General, with Edmonstone as his Private Secretary. However, there was a snag and the snag was that, whereas the Directors of the Company were relatively relaxed about his appointment, the Ministry in London was not, as they had no desire that such an important appointment and its patronage should go to another Company employee. This almost certainly related back to Sir John Shore, who, as they say, 'had risen from the ranks'. Indeed, they had now laid down the principle that it needed to be someone who possessed 'Rank, Weight and Consideration in the Metropolitan country'. They then suggested the Earl of Lauderdale – however, he was not popular in Leadenhall Street, where he was considered not only a Jacobin but also a believer in free trade – anathema to the Directors, who wanted, above all else, to retain their East Indian monopoly. In the end, the Ministry retaliated by getting the King to cancel the proposed appointment of Sir George Barlow and the Earl was also persuaded to bow out gracefully.

In the event, the name of Gilbert Elliot the Earl of Minto, who was then the President of the Board of Control of India who was described as a quiet, sensible fellow emerged and he was, therefore, appointed to be the new Governor General of India. It was the case that, although he had never visited India, he was nevertheless no stranger to Indian affairs. He had taken a prominent part in the impeachment of Warren Hastings and Sir Elijah Impey, which had given rise to many mixed feelings and for the past twelve months, he had been President of the Board of Control of India as mentioned earlier.

Edmonstone went to meet Lord Minto at Diamond Harbour and it was with a huge relief to him, when he realized that the new Governor General was a kindred spirit as well as a fellow Scot, whose main concern was the consolidation of past gains. Minto had once written to Edmonstone that 'he felt like a sort of Griffinage of European notions about character and conduct', referring to the Company slang of a 'griffin' being a newcomer to India, whereas Edmonstone was 'an old Indian' who understood the nuances of India, which Minto could not hope to do. The new Governor General informed Edmonstone that he was anxious to compare 'my sentiments with yours, before any measure of consequence is taken'. It was a sentiment that would last through Minto's Governor Generalship, during which his respect for Edmonstone continued to grow.

Edmonstone's usefulness to Minto was reflected in his increasingly more important positions. In 1809, he became the Chief Secretary to the Government, overseeing all the other secretaries and on 30 October 1812, he was elevated to the Governor General's Supreme Council by a unanimous vote of the Court of Directors. Edmonstone, although now wishing to return home, had been persuaded to stay on, not only by the prospect of a further increase in his emoluments, but also because 'he entertained the ambition of closing his long and laborious service by obtaining the honourable distinction of an appointment to a seat in Council'. This he had now achieved, and it meant that he could now direct and manage the Company's entire Indian operations – in modern day parlance he was now the Chief Executive Officer of the Honourable East India Company – with the Governor General as his Chairman while the East India Company was becoming the first truly multinational company in the world.

Sir George Barlow, after being the acting Governor General, had been appointed the Governor of Madras, in succession to Sir William Bentinck. He arrived there on Christmas Eve in 1807 and took up the post – he was, as has been said, one of the most experienced officers in the Service and had been acting Governor General for nearly two years. However, whereas in his private life, he was regarded as being amiable and affectionate, in his public life he was not at all popular. Let us see a letter from Lord Minto to his wife:

Notwithstanding the awkward situation in which Sir George and I are placed with regard to each other, I find that no unpleasant circumstances flow from it. His good sense and some other neutral qualities in his character have enabled him to act the part, which he had chosen with dignity and with many real marks of magnanimity. His good properties are of a good class. A real attachment to his public duties and I have every reason to believe a naturally sincere and honourable character. A constitutional coldness and apathy of temper which has exposed him to the reproach of indifference to the interests of other men and has enabled him to carry out many harsh duties pretty inflexibly, seem as the same time to have kept his personal feelings in a temperate state and to render a second place less irksome and irritating than it would be to ninety men out of a hundred.

Going back to the White Mutiny, at the end of the day, the issue between the Government of Sir George Barlow in Madras and the British officers of the Madras Army was really quite simple – that is to say, the question was whether the civil government was supreme or whether the civil government could be overridden and overthrown by Military force. It might be supposed that there was only one answer to that question. However, in all the turmoil of an Indian empire being established, perhaps the answer was not entirely clear. However, in the particular circumstances of this White Mutiny, Sir George Barlow's firm and decisive handling of the crisis certainly averted the very real danger of a Military junta being formed.

So what did really happen to cause such a disturbance? It was not entirely due to the usual Army grievances – they did, of course, exist as they do in any Army, but not to the point of mutiny. It was not entirely due either to Sir George, although it is true that he was very unpopular and the word 'detested' was even used. What does seem to have happened is this; that there had been such an influx of young junior officers into the Madras Army, that the ratio of the junior to senior officers had become totally disproportionate. Out of a total of 1,450 officers, only 150 were above the rank of Captain, which meant that the rest numbered 1,300 – all of them young, mainly unmarried junior officers with nothing very much to do – garrison duties were hardly onerous and morning parades were finished almost before the sun was up, thus leaving the rest of the day empty. There was thus a lot of boredom – similar in a way to the Mysore princes. These junior officers seemed to have had a collective dislike bordering on hatred of Sir George Barlow. The famous Colonel Malcolm wrote that the 'officers seem to be under the influence of collective insanity'. However, once again, to cut a very long story short, it was the gradual realization on the part of these junior officers that their Sepoys had no wish to fight the British regular Army Regiments, which is what would have happened, so that, in the end, they came to their senses and the mutiny collapsed. Perhaps at the end of the day, it might just have been the case that these young, bored junior officers were just letting off steam, but it was a steam that went far too far – perhaps it really was a collective exuberant almost juvenile insanity.

Once again, Edmonstone travelled down to Madras with the Governor General, this time on the East Indiaman, the *Dover*, to assist in dealing with the mutiny and its consequences and there they stayed for eight long months while, as Edmonstone put it, 'they were re-establishing the completely subverted organisation of the Coast Army'.

Sir George Barlow came out of this debacle well – he had stood up to the mutineers, although, of course, he had no alternative but so to do. In 1812, he was recalled to London and retired to Surrey and died there in 1846 at the age of 83. Very sadly, although having no less than fifteen children, his marriage was terminated by Act of Parliament, when he discovered that he was not the father of one of them. And there we must leave Sir George; and we can see him in that portrait in the National Portrait Gallery, looking so sad and mournful. However, he did write a Testimonial for Edmonstone, which was found in his papers after his death:

Among the Public Officers of the aid of whose abilities I availed myself while I held the situation of Governor-General of India, Mr Edmonstone is more particularly entitled to my grateful acknowledgement.

That Gentleman was Secretary to the Government in the Secret, Political and Foreign Departments and Persian Secretary to the Government. During the course of his long service in these important Offices, he had acquired an intimate knowledge of the interests and policies of all the Native States and his established reputation and conciliatory manners invariably obtained for him the esteem and confidence of the Ministers deputed to them by the British Government. The ability and unwearied diligence with which he discharged such arduous duties of his Department has long been the subject of public applause and had marked him out as the most distinguished Diplomatic Officer of his time.

The high opinion which I had formed of his talents determined me to give him my unlimited confidence and the result fully justified my expectation. In the course of the political negotiations, which were depending on my succession to the Government, I derived the most essential information and sound judgement with Dowlat Rao Scindia and Jeswant Rao Holkar and the other Native Princes, who were parties in the War on which the British Government had long been engaged. It was indeed to his able and judicious advice that I chiefly attribute my having succeeded in reconciling the conflicting interests, which opposed the final adjustments of these treaties and ultimately in completing the pacification of India – nor was it only in this branch of the Public Affairs that I experienced the advantage of his powerful assistance. On all questions connected with the General Government of our Indian Dominions I ever found his opinions guided by the most enlightened view of policy.

To these and to his many other rare qualifications for the exercise of public authority, he united the most unshaken firmness and resolution in times of internal difficulty and danger. This valuable trait in his public character signally displayed itself in the discovery of the conspiracy formed at Vellore. His wise and steady counsel afforded me important aid and support in carrying into effect the measures necessary made by that alarming event, which threatened the most serious consequences to the securing of our power.

If great talents, inflexible integrity, a just and comprehensive view of the public interest and a long course of distinguished service had been deemed to be the sole qualification for presiding over the affairs of our Indian Empire, I cannot doubt that he would have been called to the discharge of that high trust, That it was not confided to him, I ascribe partly to other considerations having been allowed to operate in the selection for it, but chiefly due to that unwillingness which he invariably manifested to urging his well-grounded pretensions on public notice, a feeling so often the concomitant of transcendent merit and equally so the cause of it not meeting with its due reward,

G. H. Barlow

Edmonstone had for a number of years affirmed that 'he was averse to selecting Governor-Generals from among those who had belonged to the Service and that a person of eminence and distinction proceeding from England, if duly qualified by talent and character, carried with him a greater degree of influence and inspired more respect than an individual who had been known in a subordinate capacity'.

Chapter 20

Captain Baillie: Lucknow Resident

We now move back to Baillie, and we see an extract from the Bengal Political Consultations dated 25 June 1807:

On the 22nd June 1807, the Governor-General circulated the following Minutes the Sentiments in it being approved by the Collective Authority of Government, it is ordered to be here recorded together with the Orders, which were issued in consequence,

Governor-General's Minute Fort William 22nd June 1807.

The melancholy event of the Decease of Colonel John Collins late Resident at Lucknow impresses on me the Duty of stating to the Board my Sentiments with regard to the selection of a Successor to that able late lamented Officer.

Some degree of difficulty and embarrassment is involved in the determination of this question, arising principally from the contending obligations of Claims on the part of certain Military Officers founded on the duration or the magnitude of their Services in the Political branch of the Administration and the approved qualification for the vacant Offices and of attention to the recommendation of the Hon. the Court of Directors on the Subject of appointing in all practicable cases, Gentlemen in the Civil Service of the Company to Diplomatic Situations. Upon the general question of selecting for such situations, Officers in the Military or Civil line of the Service, it may be proper to state a few short observations.

It cannot be supposed to be the intention of the Hon. Court in recommending the above mentioned principle of selection that it should be pursued in a manner calculated to affect the Political Interests, the character and reputation of the Government, which are intimately concerned in the selection of its diplomatic

Agents. The Court of Directors have invariably permitted the Civil and Military Servants of every description to hold Political Situations and especially the situation of Residents or Ministers at the Courts of India and the records of Government for a long course of years, demonstrate that the Gentlemen, who have been appointed to these Situations, have been selected on a count of their peculiar habits, their possession of local experience and knowledge or on account of fortuitous circumstances, which have rendered their Services in those situations particularly useful and necessary at the time of their selection. Indeed, the successful conduct of the Interests entrusted to the management of the Persons employed in the principal Political Situations is of such high importance to the Public Welfare, that the ordinary rules of the Service with regard to Appointments have never been allowed to form obstacles to the Selection of the Persons deemed at the moment to be best qualified for such Situations.

If no superiority of Claim founded on experienced qualifications and services actually rendered in the Political line existed on the part of Military Officers, I should desire to recommend for the Residency at Lucknow some Civil Servant of the Company of suitable rank, although he should have been employed in the Political Duties of the Service. But the claims of certain Military Officers founded on duration of employment, which have demonstrated their possession of the requisite qualifications, press upon the attention of the Government.

I allude to Captains Bradshaw and Baillie. The former has held successively the Situations of Assistant to the Residents with Dowlat Rao Scindia and at Lucknow during a long course of years and has occasionally been left in charge of the Duties of the principal Office. The known conduct of Captain Bradshaw in those Situations, independently of the presumption justly founded on his long experience in the political line, leaves no room to doubt his entire qualifications for the Office of Resident at Lucknow, while the length of his Service and his actual situation of Assistant to the Resident justify his pretensions to the Succession. These pretensions must, in my judgement however, yield to the Claims of Captain Baillie, to whose exertions and abilities, successfully employed under circumstances of unprecedented difficulty, the Government is indebted for the possession of one of the most valuable portions of its Territorial Dominions. It is unnecessary on this occasion to trace the Political Services of Captain Baillie. They have been represented in the most forcible terms in a late General Letter to the Court of Directors and Government has acknowledged its obligations to Captain Baillie by a formal Note of Thanks for the eminent Services, which he has rendered to it.

Captain Baillie's nomination to a high Diplomatic Office appears to me justly and naturally to flow from an acknowledgement of public Obligation so honourable and so distinguished. But it is proper to observe as a circumstance, which adds peculiar force to his claims, that he was selected by Government to undertake the arduous Negociations and Arrangements in Bundelcund, which he has so ably and successfully concluded, as the only Officer deemed capable of carrying them into effect. That he had the merit of undertaking this arduous Duty without any augmentation of his Allowance and without any other corresponding advantages than that which arose from the Authority to charge his extra expenses to the Public Accounts, the intended reduction of his Salary as Translator and Compiler of Mohammedan Law being unknown to Captain Baillie at the time when he consented to proceed to Bundelcund. That the pecuniary benefits of his temporary Situation, therefore, could not be deemed an adequate compensation for labours as arduous and important as those, which he undertook and so successfully performed. That even the duration of those inconsiderable advantages was abridged by the rapid success of his zealous actions in the Public Service and that he was entitled to expect from Government, a permanent reward of his zeal and abilities in accomplishing the objects of his Mission – I cannot consider it to be consistent with the principles of equity or with the interests of the Government to neglect the present opportunity of rewarding an Officer, whose talents and excursions we have found it necessary to call into action for the attainment of a great political object, who has manifested by the most important Services, his peculiar qualifications for the duties of a diplomatic situation and whose success in the accomplishment of his temporary appointment has alone produced its revocation.

During the whole course of his Political Services in Bundelcund, Captain Baillie has practically displayed the qualities of temper, conciliation, judgement and firmness of character and intimate knowledge of the British Government in India and especially of the languages, habits, prejudices and customs of every Class, talents and address in negotiations, extensive information and experience and an animated spirit of public zeal – possessing these qualifications, the Interests of the British Government at the Court of Lucknow, may with perfect confidence be entrusted to the conduct of Captain Baillie.

I am anxious to regulate the selection of a Successor to the late Resident at Lucknow exclusively, according to the obligations of justice and the Interests of the Public Service. The claims of Captain Baillie founded on the circumstances of his employment in an arduous political and diplomatic situation and on the distinguished Services, which he has rendered in that situation appear to me to be beyond competitions, whilst the experience of his political abilities and qualifications justified the fullest confidence in the security of the Public Interests which in the capacity of Resident at Lucknow may be committed to his charge.

I accordingly propose that Captain Baillie be appointed to this situation.

Signed G. H. Barlow

G. Udny

J. Lumsden

To Captain John Baillie etc. etc. etc. at Cawnpore.

Sir,

I am directed to inform you that the Honble. The Governor-General in Council has this day been pleased to appoint you to be Resident at Lucknow in the room of the late Colonel Collins – you will accordingly be pleased to proceed to that City with the least practicable delay.

The Officer commanding the Station of Cawnpore is authorised, if necessary, to furnish you with an Escort of One Company of Sepoys from the Station at Lucknow.

The requisite Credentials of Appointment will be transmitted to you from the Persian Department.

I have, Sir etc signed

N. B. Edmonstone

Secretary to the Government

It is perhaps pertinent in all this to point out that the Honourable Company had always had an aversion to promoting officers in situ, particularly if they had been there for a long time, which Captain Bradshaw had. Another point against him was that the Nawab had requested the Company to promote him formally as Resident, but here again the Company had an aversion to promoting any Officer, whom a Ruler had requested should be so appointed. We see this in the following letter from His Excellency the Nabob Vizier to the Governor General dated 23 June 1807, which might be thought to be rather late in the day:

The melancholy news of the death of Colonel Collins has involved me in the greatest affliction and distress; and I am satisfied that this will occasion you sincere concern. But as these events are regulated by the dispensation of an all providing Providence, and as no human being in this perishable world is exempt from the same Fate, then there is no remedy but patience and resignation to his Divine Will and therefore it is our duty to submit with patience.

Be assured, however, that the interests of the State, which were committed to the charge of the late Colonel Collins will not experience any interruption since Captain Bradshaw possesses an intimate acquaintance with the views and sentiments of both Governments and is endowed with wisdom and discernment; and having been with Colonel Collins from the first, possesses the most perfect knowledge of all affairs. In my judgement, that knowledge would enable Captain Bradshaw successfully to execute the orders and promote the interests of the two Governments. For further particulars, I have the honour to refer you to the communications of Captain Bradshaw.

Believing me to be ever anxious for accounts of your Health, be pleased to gratify me by frequent communications of it.

A True Translation signed J. Monckton Personal Secretary to the Governor.

To this came the reply of the Government to the Nabob Vizier dated June 1807:

Your Excellency well knows the high degree of estimation, in which the character and talents of the late Colonel Collins was held by the Government. Your Excellency yourself, therefore, will judge of the deep regret and concern I received the melancholy intelligence of that lamented Officer's decease. I know that the sorrow of your Excellency's mind on this occasion can scarcely be inferior to mine for the late Colonel Collins, professing your cordial Esteem and truly meriting the honour of your friendship by the virtue of his character by his sincere attachment to your Person and Government, and by the zealous disposition, which he uniformly manifested to consult your wishes, and to prosecute your welfare and prosperity. But it is our duty to acquiesce with resignation in the dispensation of an over-ruling Providence and to encourage the nature of consolation rather than indulge in the dictates of distress.

In selecting a person to succeed the late Colonel Collins as the Representative of the British Government at your Excellency's Court, it is my duty to be guided exclusively by the principles of Justice and the Interests of the Public Service. Those principles require the selection of an officer, who has not only established the strongest claim to promotion but has also manifested in the course of his Service, all the qualifications necessary for that elevated situation and possesses the entire confidence of Government founded on a knowledge of his character and a full experience of his abilities.

These circumstances are applicable in a peculiar degree by Captain Baillie who has rendered the most important Services to Government by the exertion of all those Qualities, which should be united in the person selected for a situation so distinguished as that of Resident at your Excellency's Court and I have accordingly deemed it my duty to elect that officer to succeed the late Colonel Collins at your Court as Resident at Lucknow.

Your Excellency may be assured that in discharging the duties of that situation, Captain Baillie will sedulously cultivate your Excellency's esteem and regard and will endeavour to acquire your Excellency's confidence to the same degree in which he possesses mine.

Captain Baillie is fully apprised of my solicitude to promote your Excellency's satisfaction and will both in his private and public conduct devote his attention to this object; and by his agency I am confident that the harmony and friendship so happily subsisting between your Excellency and the British Government will be maintained and augmented.

I entertain a high opinion of Captain Bradshaw's merits; and should have been happy to acquiesce in your Excellency's recommendation in his favour if, consistently with the principles of Justice and the Public Duty of my Station, it had been practicable to appoint that officer to the situation of Resident at Lucknow. But, although I concur entirely on the recommendations which your Excellency has bestowed on Captain Bradshaw, I am apprehensive that, independently of the claims of Captain Baillie, circumstances, which have no reference to Captain Bradshaw's qualifications, have imposed insuperable obstacles to his nomination.

I have directed Captain Baillie to proceed to Lucknow with the least practicable delay.

A true copy (signed) J. Monckton
Persian Translator to Government

To His Excellency
The Nabob Vizier. Written 24th June 1807.

This Letter will be delivered to your Excellency by Captain Baillie the Officer whom I have appointed to succeed the Resident at your Excellency's Court in the room of the late Colonel Collins and whose character and qualifications have been made known to You by the letter which I had the honour to address your Excellency under date the 22nd instant.

I request your Excellency will consider Captain Baillie to be vested with the same powers and authority as were exercised by the late Resident and that you will manifest towards Captain Baillie the considerations which are due to the accredited on the part of the Honourable Company.

Captain Baillie will express to your Excellency on my part my earnest solicitude for the maintenance and improvement of the relations of Harmony and Friendship between the two States and the sentiments of personal regard and esteem which I entertain towards your Excellency.

A True Copy
Signed J.Monckton
Persian Translator to Government

Chapter 21
Lucknow

Captain Baillie, having resigned his Professorships at Fort William College, left Calcutta for Lucknow in the late summer of 1807. By then, his four children had been put on the boat for Scotland, while their mother was left behind in Calcutta. It was a long journey to Lucknow – some 700 miles – and it took an equally long time. The journey usually began by water up river and against the current – this part of the journey was disconcerting for European travellers, as the boatmen had a habit of drawing a white circle around their camp fires, when they stopped for the night – this was in order to prevent the Europeans venturing too close to their preparations for their evening meal (which would be immediately thrown out, if the circle was broken). Further on at Secrole and Benares, the journey was equally disconcerting, when they saw the large number of ash-covered naked ascetics with their wildly matted hair and foot-long finger nails, rolling river mud and rice into small balls for sale as offerings to Mother Ganga. Away from the river, Captain Baillie would have continued over land to Lucknow by Dak. Dak or Dawk meant staged travel by palanquin or horse – usually the former. Finally, he would have arrived at Lucknow as the new Resident in succession to the late Colonel Collins, who had always been regarded as a somewhat eccentric figure in his old-fashioned Military coat and large highly powdered wig, but who was, nevertheless, highly intelligent, shrewd and very able.

When he arrived at Lucknow, escorted by his company of Sepoys, he entered the grounds of the Residency, of which he was now in charge. The area, which extended to some 33 acres, was originally owned by the Sheikzada family, but sometime during the late 1770s Claude Martin bought some of the land there, with the remaining land being bought by the Nawabs. It rested on a hill, quite high above the River Gomti on the north side, while on the south-western side, it sloped down to mingle with the streets and houses round the Chattar Manzil, formerly the Farhad Baksh Palace, which was developed and constructed, shortly before Captain Baillie arrived.

Not much is known about the site and its buildings until quite a lot later –
perhaps the documents, if there were any, did not survive the famous Siege of
the Residency during the 1857 Mutiny – however, we do know that it was never
a clearly defined area made over to the British to be laid out in a formal style
compatible with the status of the Resident at a Native Court– in fact, it was all
rather a muddle, with Muslim buildings and shrines interspersed among the trees,
British bungalows and then three or four fairly distinguished and substantial brick
built British two-storeyed Residency buildings, in one of which Captain Baillie
presumably lived and resided, as had his predecessor Colonel Collins.

The term 'Resident' does require a certain amount of explanation for those,
who are, perhaps, not entirely familiar with the term in its Indian context; what the
appointment entailed and for that matter, how the term arose in the first place.
The Company used the title Resident to designate their Agent of indirect rule
and what was indirect rule was, in effect, the exercise of political control over a
nominally sovereign State – a state of affairs, which required to be recognized
by both sides, provided, of course, that this control was both exercised and
controlled and exerted. It also needed to be exercised with discretion, given that
the Nawab regarded himself, despite the presence of a British Resident, as the
Head of the State, which indeed he was.

The Residency system was also relatively inexpensive for the Company –
for instance in the case of Oudh and Lucknow, when Captain Baillie was the
Resident and, therefore, indirectly responsible for controlling the whole of the
State, he was assisted generally but not always by an Assistant – one of whom
later on was his half-brother George Baillie. He would have had an Accountant; a
Superintendent of the Military Arsenal; a Surgeon to the Civil Establishment; a
Surgeon to the Military Establishment, an Auditor and a Postmaster and a few
Assistants and that was more or less that. It was these few Company officers,
who indirectly ruled the State of Oudh, which then had a population of some
ten million people similar to the present population of London. However, the
Residency did employ a huge number of servants – something like 146, when
Captain Baillie was the Resident. These servants including the camel and
elephant keepers, gardeners and blacksmiths as well as the domestic servants,
were all paid for by the Nawab. Later on, the number was reduced to something
like 65, when these had to be paid for by Calcutta. All this did, however, mean
that Captain Baillie had a very regal way of life and indeed, in all forms of etiquette
at the Court, he was treated as an equal of the Nawab. Thus, he was allowed
the shade of an umbrella, the traditional symbol of authority in the presence of
the Nawab and he also smoked his hookah as of right before him. Furthermore,
Baillie and the Nawab sat in each other's presence and even travelled together
on the same State Elephant.

However, there was something else and that was the important ability of
the Resident to exert and exercise control by being in a position to call in the

Military for support in the event of any difficulty. This Military was known as the Subsidiary Force, which was stationed nearby and which had the advantage, from the Company's point of view, in being funded once again by the Nawab, as it also provided security for the Nawab himself. Edmonstone wrote 'that the Subsidiary Force was the most effective and apparently the only mode of counteracting the weakness in this system of indirect rule and this weakness demonstrates the importance of obtaining generally a corps in the pay of the allied state under the control of British officers'.

Indeed, the Resident was told to keep always closely in touch with the officers of the Subsidiary Force. The Government in Calcutta explained to Baillie,

> He must be prepared to entertain in frequent rotation the officers belonging to the Subsidiary Force, as well as officers joining or departing from that Corps; officers visiting the Residency or cantonment on their route to and from the Headquarters of the Subsidiary Force, or the neighbouring military stations. All these guests and strangers visiting the Station for business or for pleasure must be entertained by the Resident in a manner superior to or at least equal to that of the generality or gentlemen filling public stations.

As it happens, the Company never really had any single or consistent set of policies in Oudh, but it did have three overall major objectives: (1)was the control of Oudh's Military power; (2) was the extraction of Oudh's resources for the Company; (3) the manipulation of Oudh for the political purposes of the Company. Otherwise, within these three major objectives, the day-to-day duties of the Resident were not particularly onerous, at least at first and what duties there were, depended to a considerable extent on the energy and or interest or both, of the individual Resident. Baillie was, of course, both young, energetic and interested, so much so, that he tended to become somewhat authoritarian and interfering and that may have reflected his Presbyterian upbringing – he was described as pompous.

In 1808, shortly after his arrival, he fell ill and we see a letter which Captain Baillie wrote to Edmonstone dated 15 January, in which he refers to his severe and dangerous indisposition which commenced on the 7th Ultimo, from which he had not entirely recovered till the beginning of the present month. The Surgeon Robert Wilson was awarded the sum of 5,000 rupees by the Nawab Vizier Saadat Ali Khan for his attendance on Captain Baillie during his illness and when he recovered, he was given a splendid entertainment by the Nawab to celebrate his recovery.

There were, however, several particularly sore points between the Resident and the Nawab – there were many others – and one was this question of the 'guaranteed families', which does require some explanation. These families were pensioners – wasikadars – whose pensions were paid directly by the Resident from the interest on sums invested in Company loans and whose persons and property were protected by the Government in Calcutta. The making of these loans, with such conditions attached, was a favourite expedient of the Nawabs, since it was a method of making provisions for relatives and proteges, which would, hopefully, be unaffected by future political difficulties and could also be a method of getting round the Muslim prohibition of usury. It appears that this method was first proposed by Bahu Begum, the wife of the Nawab Shuja-ud-Daula, who was exceedingly well off and was now under British protection – a protection which she herself had purchased.

It was in 1808, the year after Baillie had arrived in Lucknow, that she made a Will under the terms of which she left the bulk of her very large fortune to the British Government on condition that a certain amount would be invested in bonds and that the interest thereon should be paid partly as pensions to a number of listed beneficiaries and partly for the upkeep of her Mausoleum at Faizabad. When she died, the Government renounced her request and made over the capital to her son, while insisting that the sum of £500,000 – a very large sum – should be lent to the Company at an interest rate of 6 per cent per annum, which would thus enable the Company to provide for the large number of bequests willed by her.

During the first year of operation, so to speak, there were 120 pensioners, whose pensions were paid from this source. When a pensioner died, the interest attributable to that pensioner, was paid to reduce the loan, but, as was generally the case, there were heirs, then the pension was divided and then subdivided until, by the Indian Rebellion of 1857, nearly a million rupees was being paid out annually to something like 965 beneficiaries with the number exponentially rising all the time, so that as a result the pensions got smaller and smaller and eventually minimal. It seems that these by now minimal pensions continued until 1947, the year of Indian independence.

Now the point of all this, is that it was the Resident, as Agent, who was responsible for the payment of these pensions, so that in due course, the pensioners looked to the Resident and not to the Nawab and, in so doing, began to regard him, the Resident, as the only person truly worthy of their trust and loyalty. Thus, the Resident became a sort of second ruler and, indeed, it was the case that until 1831, the Resident actually held his own Durbar, to which the various pensioned princes and princesses, nobles and favourites sent their vakils to present their grievances and pay their respects to the Resident with all the punctiliousness of an Oriental Court.

Naturally, all this led to considerable friction between the Nawab and the Resident – the former seeing his own wishes and, indeed, his own Courts of Justice being set aside by a privileged group, who invoked the authority of the Resident in cases relating to internal administration and even in private domestic matters. It seems that Captain Baillie was a particular offender in this respect, and it was reported that his interference could go to humiliating extremes. Bahu Begum, who was the mother of Saadat-Ali-Khan, who was the Nawab during most of the time Captain Baillie was the Resident at Lucknow and was a protégé of the Company, got into the habit of referring all her problems and complaints, which were, needless to say, many, to the Resident and not to the Nawab.

As an example of this, there was one spectacular occasion, when the Nawab dismissed Tehsin Ali Khan, the Eunuch, whom we have met before, in connection with the deposition of Wazir Ali and who had, for many years, as we know, managed the Khurd Mahal of his father's establishment at Faizabad. Prompted by Bahu Begum, Captain Baillie invoked all the weight of his considerable authority to press the Nawab into reinstalling the Eunuch. As it happens, this move on the part of Captain Baillie provoked a revolt on the part of the ladies of the Khurd Mahal, who, not only disliked the Bahu Begum, but also the Eunuch, who, they said, cheated them. They then staged a march on Lucknow from Faizabad and implored the Nawab to get rid of the Eunuch. They then staged a sit-in or rather a sit-out, outside the Nawab's palace, while Captain Baillie continued to insist that it was the Nawab who had fomented the ladies' strike in order to confute the Begum. This sit-out lasted for four months, while the Nawab, embittered and hideously embarrassed, stood by helplessly, until the Khurd Mahal ladies, very reluctantly, gave up their sit-out and went back to Faizabad.

This Residency system arose from the great increase in the Company's business from about the middle of the eighteenth century. This increasing business began to require a political element for the control and success of this business and its protection. As it happens, it took the Company quite a long time to decide on the title Resident for its Political Agents and this was after what was described as an exhausting debate. Advice was sought from all quarters but, in the end, the Company decided that, its Political Agents for that is what they were, and were sent to reside at the Courts of the Native Rulers, should be called just that 'Residents'. The first Resident was sent to Murshidabad, north of Calcutta, the seat of the Court of the Nawab of Bengal; the second to the Nizam of Hyderabad and the third, eventually, to the Nawab of Oudh.

Initially, Calcutta did not consider establishing any permanent sort of line of communication with the Nawab – rather, it was the other way round. The Nawab, as Head of State, had sent Vakils to the Emperor in Delhi – the Prince of Persia as he was called, as the family came from Persia. He also sent Vakils to the Punjab and Afghanistan and he also sent a Vakil to Calcutta to represent him as Head of the State of Oudh. However, the then Governor General asked the Vakil to be withdrawn, as he said he preferred the intermediary of an Army officer. The Nawab in 1772, the year of Baillie's birth, had written to the Company protesting against a rumoured decision that the Company had apparently taken to assign 'an English gentleman' to reside at his Court, without consulting him. He then went on to request, however, that a certain Captain Harper, who was currently acting as an informal liaison officer, should be formally appointed to his Court. Unfortunately, it turned out that it was Captain Harper himself, who had started the rumour, as he wanted the job for himself, if indeed there was going to be one. Calcutta had, however, made up their minds that, as he was recommended by the Nawab, it was not to be the case. As has been noted, it was a firm rule of the Company not to allow a Ruler to choose his own Resident and there were fairly obvious reasons for this. Captain Harper was, therefore, ordered to return to his Military duties.

However, it was not long afterwards that the then Governor General Warren Hastings personally raised this matter of a possible Resident with the then Nawab at a private meeting with him:

> I took the occasion to ask him whether it would be agreeable to him that a person in whom I could confide should be appointed by me to reside near his Person for the sake of perpetuating and strengthening the good understanding so happily begun, as well as for the transaction of such ordinary affairs as might not suit the formality of a correspondence by letter.

Put like this, the Ruler, after some consultation, accepted the offer, and that year 1772 a Resident, Mr Middleton, was shortly thereafter appointed.

Chapter 22
A very short history of Oudh

We now need to introduce you more fully to Oudh in 1807, when Captain Baillie took post as the Resident at Lucknow. There have, of course, been countless books written about the Nawabs, Lucknow and the Indian Rebellion in 1857 and the famous siege of the Lucknow Residency, which almost certainly only survived, because Captain Baillie had constructed what became known as the Baillie Guard Gate during his last year as Resident in 1815. It is interesting to note that during the long siege, the mutinous Sepoy Military bands continued to play outside the fortifications every evening, as they had prior to the siege, and always ended up by playing 'God Save the Queen', and this always cheered the besieged. Nevertheless, Captain Baillie's tenure as Resident at Lucknow does need some sort of background.

Oudh was a large State – it covered something like 25,000 square miles and its then population amounted to some ten million people. During his time, most of the population lived off the land in mud huts and hovels. There were around seventy thousand of these villages or hamlets, surrounded by fields – entirely distinct and separate from the rich, literate and civilized living in the two main cities, namely Lucknow and Faizabad, whither went all the tax money from these impoverished villages and hamlets.

This rural population was divided in to four main groups: the religious classes; the non-cultivating landholders, as they were called; the cultivating peasants; and lastly, the very poor landless labourers. The Brahmins, who numbered around 1.5 million, did no work for reasons of religious purity. At the bottom of the pile were these poor landless labourers, who were destined to fight a losing battle with hunger and destitution and who often sold themselves into slavery to avoid starvation. The most powerful group were, of course, the landowners, who were mainly Rajputs, and although they only represented something like 5 per cent of the population, nevertheless they controlled more than half of the land in Oudh.

It is interesting to note how the State of Oudh arose in the first place. It had its origin in Persia, where a man by the name of Mohammed Amin was born in the town of Nishapur in Khorasan, although this man was more generally known by his Moghul name Saadat Khan. At that time the Safavid Empire was collapsing, so in the year 1708, when he was still a young man, he followed his father and his elder brother to India and like them, began to seek his fortune there. As a Sayyid, meaning that he was a descendant of the Prophet – there were many such descendants, including Captain Baillie's Munshi. He held the most respected genealogy in Islam and, as a Sayyid and also an Irani nobleman, he was the sort of person, whom the Moghul Court in Delhi highly valued. As it happens, the Iranis did represent a large number of the foreign-born nobles at the Delhi Court and something like one-fifth of all the high officials holding the Mansab rank. Thus, Saadat Khan was able to use his Irani background, heritage and training at the Court and all this brought him to the attention of and then later on the approbation of the Court authorities.

Following the death of the unlamented Emperor Aurangzeb in 1707, the last of the 'great Moghuls' – no less than fourteen Emperors were enthroned between that year and 1757. During this period of upheaval and instability, Saadat Khan managed to survive and rose steadily through the ranks, eventually emerging as a member of the Moghul elite. He was appointed not only the Commander of the Imperial Household Cavalry, but also the Subadar of Agra and all this only thirteen years after he had arrived in India. Subsequently, he was demoted from Agra to Oudh, which was then a less important province, but he still had high ambitions.

Saadat did not have a son; thus there was a conflict between his brother's son and his sister's son, whose father was Safdar Jung and he it was, through the usual Byzantine manoeuvring, was able to outwit his cousin, thus obtaining the major part of Saadat's titles, honours and territories, which were in the gift of the Emperor and thus it was that he also obtained the title of Wazir and Minister of the Empire. However, things went downhill with him thereafter and to cut a long story short, he died in 1754, whereupon his son Shuja-al-Daula took over, while his father's nephew was created the Subadar of Allahabad and later given the title of Wazir – a title which would remain hereditary to the family. This nephew was imprisoned by Shuja, who then took over his title.

Shuja then set about trying to restore the unity of the Empire, but all this came adrift when his armies were defeated by the Company and here we come back to the famous battle of Buxar in 1765, when Major Hector Munro of the 89th Highland Regiment of Foot, having brutally suppressed a Bengal Army mutiny in the then novel way of blowing the mutineers from the guns, went on to defeat the combined armies of Oudh, the Emperor and the Subadar of Bengal. It was after this battle that the now penniless Shuja entered the Company's encampment alone at night and threw himself on the mercy of the Company.

So vast were the territories which the Company had acquired that the Directors came to the conclusion that it was incapable of administering them. It, therefore, returned most of them to the Emperor and Shuja-al Daula. In the case of the latter, Oudh was firmly bound by a Treaty, which provided for the mutual defence paid for naturally by Oudh; free trade for the Company in the Nawab's territories and lastly a payment of 5 million rupees, which, to everybody's astonishment, the Nawab paid immediately, thus creating the impression in the minds of the Company that there was a lot more money there than they had thought and there was. Once his territories had been restored to him, Shuja transformed Oudh into one of the Company's most valuable allies and, in a sense, provided the Company with a buffer protecting its territories until it had consolidated them, thus putting itself into the position where it could come back for more in due course of time.

Moving on to the year 1801, we arrive at the Treaty between the Nawab and the Governor General Sir Richard Wellesley, which established the basis of the relationship between the Nawabs and the Company, which would exist until 1857. It was grossly unfair to the Nawab. It defined the political context within which the Nawabs were compelled to function. Prior to that, the Nawab, Saadat Ali Khan, who died during Captain Baillie's tenure as Resident, had written wrote to the Governor General in the following terms:

> That the proposition of the Governor-General was so repugnant to his feelings and departed so widely in the most essential ways from the principles on which he wished to relinquish the Government and would, were he to accept, bring upon him such indelible disgrace and odium that he could never voluntarily subscribe to it. The Sovereignty of these Dominions had been in the family for nearly a hundred years and the transfer of it under the stipulations proposed by Your Lordship would in fact be a sale of it for money and jewels, that every sentiment of respect for the name of his ancestors and every consideration for his posterity combined to preclude him from assenting to so great a sacrifice.

But he did – he was in effect forced to assent.

From then on, the Resident was the de facto ruler of Oudh and the young, and one has to say arrogant, Captain Baillie, appointed in 1807, adopted this position without any particular regard for the de jure ruler.

Chapter 23

Captain Baillie's Lucknow family

Once he had arrived in Lucknow, Captain Baillie, almost immediately, took the opportunity to take up with a European lady by the name of Mary Martin, who had been adopted by a certain Mr and Mrs Martin. He may possibly have married her, but this seems unlikely, as no church in Lucknow records such a marriage – also there is no mention of her in his Will nor is she mentioned in any of his few surviving letters. He refers to her as both Martin and Baillie. He proceeded to have three children with her and, like his Calcutta children, they were all sent back to Leys Castle to be brought up by his sister Margaret Baillie, who was also at the same time, as we know, bringing up the two Elmore sons of Edmonstone, as well as the four Baillie children by his Calcutta lady.

The first child to be born in Lucknow was Ann Baillie on 10 August 1809, and she appears to have been baptized in 1811 by the Reverend Mr Martyn, who was then the Chaplain at Cawnpore and had come over to Lucknow. On 29 July 1835, Ann married John Frederick Baillie, the second son of Peter Baillie of Dochfour near Inverness. It must have been a very grand wedding as it took place at St George's Church, Hanover Square in central London, which was and still seems to be very much a high society church. She and John had two children. Ann died quite young on 5 October 1847, at Clifton near Bristol, where the Baillie family were entrepreneurs.

There were two more children – a boy and a girl. The boy was born in 1810 and was baptized John Wilson Baillie by the Reverend David Corrie at Lucknow in 1811, while the daughter, Henrietta, was born in 1811 and was baptized on the same day as her brother. Both were sent back to Leys Castle, where Henrietta died on 10 September 1822, when she was only 10 years old.

John Wilson Baillie joined the East India Company, sponsored by his father, but died on his first voyage to China in 1829 when he was only 19 years old. It was reported that he was a young man who showed great promise and ability and there should be and perhaps still is a Memorial to him in the old High Church in Inverness. It was thought that he was his father's favourite child and the Leys Castle Estate was left to him in his father's will, but when he died, the Colonel left it to his daughter Ann.

In all this, there lies a mystery and that is that the Baillies seem to have convinced themselves that his Lucknow lady was a Princess of Oudh and, as such, she appears on the family tree. We have found nothing to substantiate this; what we have found, however, is a sworn Affidavit to the Directors of the Company in 1827 by the Colonel, which he then was, that he, John Baillie, declared 'that John Wilson Baillie is my son and this was my only inducement' – this was when John Wilson Baillie was applying to join the Company as a Writer. On 18 June 1827, the Colonel again swore on oath: 'I, John Baillie, do make oath and swear that Mary Martin or Baillie, the mother of my son John Wilson Baillie, was the offspring of European parents to the best of my knowledge and belief and was so believed and declared to me by her Adoptive Parents in India.'

We do not know who this Mary Martin was – we do find a Baptism recorded in the Mission Church in Calcutta for a Mary Martin dated 12 November 1781, when she was 7 years old, but that is all and whether that is her and she had already been adopted, we do not know, but it remains a possibility. What seems to be almost impossible is that she was a Princess of Oudh – nowhere in the files is it mentioned that Captain Baillie carried off, so to speak, a Princess of the Oudh Royal family, shortly after he arrived in Lucknow. In any case, the Nawab would have almost certainly forced him to adopt the Muslim faith as a precondition of him marrying into the Royal blood of Oudh. Equally, there can be no doubt that the Calcutta authorities would not have allowed him, the Resident, to marry a Muslim Oudh Princess and, if he had, then they would almost certainly have withdrawn his appointment as Resident, because of the resultant conflict of interest. It is also the case that the portrait of these three charming children shows no sign of mixed blood. The only pointer is that there is a portrait of the Nawab Vizier Ali in the same house in Scotland and it has been reported that the reason for the portrait was that he was Captain Baillie's father-in-law. But there is nothing in the Oudh Archives to support this theory. We do know that Baillie regarded his Lucknow family as his legitimate family, possibly or probably because the children were European, unlike his Indian Calcutta family, all of whom, with the exception of George, returned to India. It, therefore, remains a mystery as to why a Princess of Oudh appears in the Baillie Family Tree as the wife of Colonel John Baillie, when there is no evidence at all for such a supposition and one wonders very much how it arose in the first place.

Chapter 24
Two downfalls

We now need to return to the affairs of Oudh after our foray into Captain Baillie's affair with his European mistress Mary, who had been adopted by the Martin family, and his three Lucknow children. In a sense, one could say that we are now back to the Nawab Saadat Ali Khan, who was placed on the throne by the British, following their deposition of Wazir Ali and all this has been recounted earlier in this book. It is not possible in a book such as this to give a detailed account of the activities of Captain Baillie during his eight years as Resident at Lucknow. We have recounted the story of the revolt of the ladies of the Khurd Mahal, the history of the Wasikadars and Captain Baillie's weekly durbars so bitterly resented by the Nawab. However, there are other matters of significance such as the attempt by Captain Baillie to persuade the Nawab to reform his Revenue Department – this was on the premise that 'the origin of the evil was the vicious system of His Excellency's Administration'. What the Resident Captain Baillie wanted to do was to abolish the system of revenue farming and all the misery which flows from it and, in its place, introduce salaried managers who were, accordingly, accountable and who were known as Amins. This had not been the first time that it had been tried – it had been attempted by Lord Cornwallis, but it had never got very far.

In 1810, Captain Baillie, three years after his appointment, did manage to get certain districts placed under Amins, whose instructions had been drawn up by him and the following year, he submitted a comprehensive plan for the reform of the administration. This plan prescribed the territory being divided up into four or five large Zillahs (large districts), which, in their turn, were to be divided up into smaller districts. Each district was to be under the charge of 'an upright and intelligent Amin', who was to receive a fixed salary and conduct triennial surveys, on the basis of which a fair rent could be achieved. This attempt on the part of Captain Baillie, sensible as it was, failed because the Nawab deeply resented this degree of British interference and control in what he considered to be his private affairs. He did, as it happens, agree with the appointment of a few Amins in 1810, but he refused to accept that these Amins needed to be appointed after consultation with the Resident. He also refused to accept that the Proclamation, announcing these new Amin appointments, used the expression 'that it was adopted with the advice and consent of the British Government'. The Nawab maintained that this was a contravention of the 1801 Treaty which had been negotiated by Wellesley, and his point was accepted – it was, indeed, a contravention and the proposal was therefore withdrawn.

Both the Nawab and the Resident now started to get on each other's nerves, with the Nawab telling the Resident, 'I continue to apprehend the subversion of my authority, the retirement and disaffection of my subjects and general disorder in the country and other injurious effects, from the ignorance of the Amins and the want of a proper measurement of the lands.' He went on to complain that all this amounted to placing himself and his subjects in the relation of defendant and plaintiff. Later on, well after Captain Baillie had retired and gone home and died, when Mohammed Ali Shah was the Nawab, his attitude to the then Resident was also one of nervous prostration: 'The idea so hurt the old man's feelings that it had an immediate effect on his disease by producing an instant attack of spasms in the toes of both his feet, which put him in such pain at the time and from which he did not entirely recover for twenty four hours.'

There was another occasion, and as I have mentioned there were many such occasions, when there was a particularly painful interview between the Nawab and Captain Baillie regarding the unauthorized movement of Company troops across the former's boundaries in pursuit of bandits. Captain Baillie subsequently reported,

His Excellency suddenly replied that he was helpless or words to that effect and when I signalled that the meeting was over, we got up and moved towards the door. The Nawab then commenced another pitiful complaint and deplored in a manner most unmanly and unbecoming with tears in his eyes, the unhappy situation in which he was placed, unwilling, as well as unable, to contend with His Lordship the Governor General on any point and yet incapable of reconciling to his feelings the arrangement which His Lordship had proposed.

And you will almost immediately notice that it was Baillie, who signalled the end of the meeting and not the Nawab, as was his right. And even when negotiations were broken off due to the illness of the Nawab, Captain Baillie attended at his bedside, bringing along with him a British doctor seemingly to emphasize his incapacity and weakness.

In the end, the tension between the two got so bad that the Nawab, who was by then old and frail, became so irritated by Captain Baillie that 'he retired from his palace for a time, withdrawing all attention to his business, suspending all discussions of reforms, expressing distaste for the exercise of sovereign authority and expressing the desire to go on pilgrimage' – the classic renunciation. Lord Minto was just as insistent as Captain Baillie and wrote to the Nawab as follows:

However desirous Your Excellency may be to evade the performance of your engagements, the British Government will not cease to require you to fulfil them, and no lapse of time and no change of circumstances will induce the British Government to relinquish a measure which it considers to be so essential to the welfare and happiness of your Excellency's subjects and to the reputation and interest of both Governments.

It was, indeed, necessary for Captain Baillie to obtain the cooperation of the Nawab, because it was only thereby that his policy of interference could be reconciled with the 1801 Treaty and, here it does need to be borne in mind that this Treaty negotiated by Wellesley did restrict the Company to providing advice only with regard to the Nawab's domestic affairs. Eventually, when the new Governor General Lord Moira, whom we will introduce shortly, dropped Captain Baillie's plans for reform and also at the same time the whole policy of Lord Minto, Lord Moira wrote to the Directors in London,

It is evident from the whole tenor of the 1801 Treaty, that an uninterrupted exercise of the Nawab's own authority within the reserved dominions was assured to him, in order to qualify the very strong step, which we took in appropriating for ourselves so large a portion of his territories. The Nawab is consequently to be treated in all public observances as an independent Prince. The Resident should consider himself as the Ambassador of the British Government to an acknowledged Sovereign; a respectful urbanity and a strict fulfilment of established ceremonials should thence be preserved by the Resident towards His Excellency.

It is probably true to say that Lord Moira doubted from the beginning that his new policy would be implemented by Major Baillie, in whom he noted 'a captious disposition and a domineering tone, of themselves highly calculated to excite irritation in a prince, whose situation would naturally render him acutely jealous of his independence'. These impressions were confirmed when a certain Captain McLeod arrived in Calcutta from Lucknow, late in 1813. The Nawab Saadat Ali Khan unburdened himself to this Captain, who was an officer in his own service, concerning Major Baillie's harassment and indeed his bullying and it was this Captain, who had access to Government House, by virtue of his family's association with the wife of the Governor General, reported all this to Lord Moira.

The removal of Major Baillie was then apparently discussed but postponed pending the visit of the Governor General to Lucknow and the death of Saadat-Ali-Khan in 1814. This visit to Lucknow convinced Lord Moira that the new Nawab Ghazi-ud-din was just as unhappy with the Major Baillie, as he now was, as his father had been, but, inhibited by fear of the Major and the fear of the then Governor General Lord Minto, he had kept quiet. Indeed, the new Nawab did make some complaints and associated with these complaints were four Europeans in Lucknow – that is to say Dr John Law, James Henry Clarke, Captain Duncan Macleod and Antoine De L'Etang, but when Baillie heard about this, he ordered them to leave Lucknow. Thus, positive grounds for removing him were wanting, but the Major, when he heard of the Governor General's subsequent meetings with Captain McLeod, had a rush of blood to the head, so that he then publicly accused Lord Moira, not only of plotting his removal, but also of sabotaging his plans for reform. As a result, the Governor General, who was only there as a protégé of the Prince Regent and who had asked the Company to remove Lord Minto, so that he could take his place, thereupon removed the Major. Richard Strachey, who was then at Gwalior, was summoned to take the Major's place as Resident at Lucknow. However, the Major decided to get his own back later on Lord Moira, now the Marquess of Hastings, by suing him and it is these charges, which he brought in evidence before the appropriate Committee of the House of Commons and also before the Directors of the Company at India House, which we will examine shortly.

There was yet another casus belli before Baillie left Lucknow and this was that he failed to attend the funeral of Saadat Ali Khan. The new Nawab Ghazi-ud-din-Haidar wrote on 31 October 1814,

On the day of my late Father's decease, neither the Resident nor anyone of the English Gentlemen attended the Funeral. When my Grandmother died, the Resident attended the Funeral in person. My late Father was desirous to such a degree to manifest respect to the British Government that he went with all the respectable persons of his Court to attend the funeral of a female who had lived in the Resident's House. Several English Gentlemen were also present. It is a matter of regret, therefore, that the Resident should not have gone in person, nor to have sent any of the English Gentlemen to attend the Funeral of so great a Vizier and so old a Friend of the British etc.

So why did Major Baillie not attend the funeral of the Head of State of Oudh?

Before we return to the dismissal of the Major as the Resident at Lucknow, we need to revert to his Munshi, Ali Naqi Khan, and find out what happened to him when he returned to Lucknow, as the then Captain's Munshi. On his return, the Munshi began to use his special relationship with the Captain to his own advantage. As did all Company employees native to Oudh, he, the Munshi, held the right to petition the Nawab through the Resident. As the Munshi at the Lucknow Residency, he assessed all such petitions, including, of course, his own. As the trusted Chief of Staff at the Residency, he drafted covering letters for the Resident to sign and then presented both the petition and the Resident's letter drafted by himself, to the Nawab for satisfaction.

In the end, his alleged victims and the Company's own enquiries, as to what he was up to, ended his career. What he had been up to, inter alia, was that he had been using his position as Munshi to ask the Captain to recommend to the Nawab, that his son be appointed Tahsildar – District Revenue Collector – over an area known as Sumirpur and Hamirpur. However, his son was only 10 years old at that time, although he insisted that he was 15, so Ali Naqi Khan appointed his own brother-in-law and nephew as Deputies to carry out the Tahsildar duties, as clearly his son could not, as he was still at school. It was the case that the income of the Tahsildar was derived from the difference between the actual amount collected in taxes and the amount which was handed over to the Oudh Treasury – therefore, the greater the difference, the more they received – revenue farming in other words – something which Baillie wanted to reform. The landowners began to accuse Ali Naqi Khan of coercing them into paying more than they should, but he denied this and when he was asked what he was doing in these districts at the time, he replied that he was visiting a famous courtesan there!

Ali Naqi Khan also involved himself in acquiring land rights in a certain district called Sandi to some fifty villages and the attached hereditary office of Chowdry (headman), by compelling the young heiress, through a highly questionable line of inheritance, to marry his son. The Nawab, unusually for him, put up a show of resistance to the will of the Captain, as represented by his Munshi and delayed complying with the Munshi's claims for no less than two and a half years. This resistance on the part of the Nawab seemed only to confirm the Captain's low opinion of what he called 'the unhappy and vicious judiciary of Oudh'. He then demanded in apparently very strong terms, that his Munshi be put in control of the disputed lands immediately and this prior to any judgement in the Court. When even this failed to work, he requested the Governor General to write 'enducing [sic] His Excellency the Vizier to confirm immediately on the Munshi without any further investigation, the claims of that old servant, who had long been in the confidential employment of the Company'.

The Nawab countered, complaining to the Governor General about the unjust pressure placed on him by the Resident and his 'faithless' Munshi. He then offered the Munshi a large salary if he would leave the Company's service and join that of Oudh. Naturally, the Governor General reacted to all this and ordered a full Inquiry. As a result, Ali Naqi Khan lost his job and the Captain now Major was censured for using 'Irregular Influence', since he had already been 'fully apprised of the dissatisfaction with which His Lordship the Governor-General viewed the practice of the Major, exercising a despotic authority over the Sovereign of Oudh'. Thus the Munshi, who had been with the Major for some thirty years or so, now disappears from view.

Chapter 25

The capture of Bourbon, Mauritius, Amboyna, the Dutch Spice Islands and Java

We now need to revert to Lord Minto once more, before continuing with the unravelling of this Lucknow saga. We have mentioned earlier that Lord Minto and Edmonstone had sailed down the coast to Madras to deal with the White Mutiny and had stayed there no less than eight months, sorting out what they called 'the mess' of the Madras Army. It was while they were there that they began to make arrangements for an attack on what were called 'the French Islands'. The first French Island was Bourbon, and here Lord Minto acted on his own initiative without any sort of authority from London to go ahead and capture the island. Later, he sent another expedition, manned by a force recruited from all three Presidencies, to capture the Isle of France – namely Mauritius. Both these islands were captured without difficulty and should have been captured years before, as Wellesley had desired, bearing in mind the constant attacks on British shipping in the Indian Ocean and the Bay of Bengal by French privateers and French frigates based on these islands.

Meanwhile the Company's financial position continued to improve and with the temporary end of the usual French aggression, Minto came to the conclusion that he should send a small naval force, with some troops on board, to capture Amboyna and the rest of the Dutch Spice Islands. This was carried out and the territory accordingly annexed. The next year, which was 1811, a much larger expedition was organized to go off to capture Java, where the French had recently arrived.

We need to put this invasion of Java into some sort of context. What had happened was that, after the Netherlands had been absorbed into the French Empire, Napoleon quickly grabbed hold of the Dutch possessions in the East Indies, sending out a strong French force to garrison the country. The British

Government in London then instructed Lord Minto to capture these former Dutch possessions from the French and thus an invasion force of some twelve thousand soldiers, commanded by General Sir Samuel Auchmuty and consisting of both European and Sepoy Regiments, set sail 'across the black water' – an expression, which was full of religious connotations for the men of the Hindu Sepoy Regiments – for Java. They captured without difficulty the capital Batavia – now Jakarta – but 8 miles away stood the formidable Fortress of Cornelius, which had been significantly strengthened by the French and was now garrisoned by some seventeen thousand soldiers. An immediate assault was decided upon – there was no time for a siege – and this was led with such determination and vigour by the famous Colonel Rollo Gillespie of Vellore fame that this huge and immensely strong Fortress was captured within a few hours and the French surrendered. If you go to Barrackpore outside Calcutta, the country seat of the Governor of Bengal, you will see a most wonderful Memorial to all those who fell in this Batavian campaign. It had been the intention of the London Government that, following the capture of the islands, Java should be handed back to the Javanese rulers. However, Lord Minto decided otherwise and took Java under British control.

Edmonstone wrote,

Lord Minto deemed it necessary to proceed himself with the Armament destined for the conquest of the island of Java, rightly judging that the presence of the Supreme Authority in India would be required for the settlement of the administration, when the island should have fallen in to our hands, This very important successful expedition as well as that which followed against the Dutch possessions in the Archipelago, was projected and undertaken by Lord Minto on his own responsibility. Almost all the arrangements connected with the plan and the voluminous and extensive correspondence of these important expeditions appertained to my Office.

Edmonstone had been very gratified when a grateful Lord Minto dictated and recorded in the Minutes of the Secret Department dated 25 February 1811 that

he was prevented from requesting the attendance of Mr Edmonstone on this occasion because the whole business of the Political, Foreign and Secret Departments, as well as the more general and extensive duties of the Office of the Chief Secretary, must be transacted at Fort William. Nothing can more forcibly evince my own sense of the extreme importance attached to the residence of Mr Edmonstone at the Seat of Government during my approaching absence, than my announcing on this occasion his invaluable advice as well as assistance of which I experienced so signally the public benefit and personal consolation last year at Fort George.

Edmonstone went on to say that 'Lord Minto's administration was characterised by transactions, undertakings and proceedings of a highly important nature, which imposed on the Departments under my superintendence, duties only inferior in labour, anxiety and responsibility to those which appertained to the more eventful and momentous period of Lord Wellesley's Government'. And he then went on to list all those transactions, undertakings and proceedings such as the affairs of Hyderabad, the invasion of Nagpore by Ameer Khan, the administration of Oudh accomplished through what he described as the able agency of Major Baillie, then Resident at Lucknow, Sind, Persia, Kandahar, the Punjab and the expedition to Java where, as we have seen, Edmonstone was left behind to 'conduct the business of the Secret, Political and Foreign Departments at Fort William'.

Lord Minto was still the Governor General when, in October 1812, Edmonstone took his seat as a member of the Supreme Council of India under the provisional appointment spontaneously conferred on him by the Court of Directors. However, shortly after what he describes as 'the most harmonious association and confidential intercourse with the excellent and highly gifted nobleman, under whose authority I had served for five years', Edmonstone's association with Lord Minto, whom he so greatly admired and respected, came to an abrupt end. It was in that year the Directors decided, at the request or perhaps demand of the Prince Regent, to relieve him of his appointment, not because he was doing a bad job, but because the Prince Regent wanted this plum appointment for one of his cronies, Lord Moira, later the Marquess of Hastings and there is an unattractive story behind the machinations of the Prince Regent. So, Lord Minto went home and died the following year.

Chapter 26

Lord Moira, Governor General, and the Oudh loans

Lord Moira was an experienced man of the world – by now aged 59 – a soldier by profession, who, as a young man, had fought with distinction in America and afterwards had been promoted to be a General. Following the assassination of the Prime Minister Perceval, Moira attempted, at the request of the Prince Regent, to form a coalition Government with his friends participating therein. This did not work out, but as a douceur for his efforts, the Prince Regent considered that he should have some acknowledgement and this was not only the appointment as Governor General of India but also his appointment as the Commander-in-Chief of India. He was almost entirely responsible for what could be described as the unnecessary wars against the Nepalese and the Mahrattas, which were the main feature of his nine-year-long term of office.

He was tall, good-looking and rather vain. He was apparently open to flattery, not particularly good with money and he left for India, trailing considerable debts behind him. He was fond of ceremony and he brought out with him his wife Flora Campbell, who was the Countess of Loudon in her own right. She had borne him six children. In Calcutta, he reverted to the ostentatious days of Wellesley and, at his first Reception at Government House the ladies were all told 'to wear full court dress with ostrich feathers and long trains'. Lady Moira's train was supported by two pages in regimental uniform.

Lord Moira regarded it as his responsibility to finish the job which Wellesley had begun. He, therefore, brought the rest of India south of Delhi under British control and increased the control of the Company over the allied states. The fact that the first required years of warfare to achieve and that the second caused years of dangerous resentment, were not matters that particularly concerned him – the point for him was that his actions were designed to win him recognition in Britain, which they did – he was made a Marquis.

However, his ideas were diametrically opposed to those of Edmonstone, who disliked wars and only went along with Wellesley's wars, because he considered them a necessary evil. Those of Lord Moira he deemed an unnecessary evil, because the British did now have effective control of India. As Edmonstone would recall, 'it was my misfortune to differ with Lord Hastings on various subjects of great political importance, while associated with him in the Government of India – this difference of opinion led to numerous elaborate discussions in Minutes recorded in the Secret Department – on subjects which I am not at liberty to disclose'. He viewed with great concern, if not horror, the wars into which his pacified India had been plunged and now openly opposed the Governor General. The Directors of the Company, who never wanted him in the first place and also the three members of the Supreme Council in Calcutta, namely Edmonstone, Seton and Dowdeswell openly came out against the Nepalese War but, given Lord Moira's royal support in England, their objections were brushed aside.

Lord Moira did not like assuming any responsibility for the internal administration of the Indian states. His idea was to leave them 'possessed of perfect internal sovereignty'. If a Ruler oppressed their subjects, this was not, as he later somewhat cynically explained, the concern of the British. His dislike of meddling with the internal affairs of the India rulers seems to have originated with what was going on in Oudh – indeed within a few months of his arrival he wrote that the Nawab had been 'driven to desperation' by the interference of the Resident Major Baillie. Indeed, he wrote, with some accuracy, that 'we recognise them as independent sovereigns. We then send them a Resident to their Courts. Instead of acting as an ambassador, he assumes the functions of a dictator; interferes in their private concerns; countenances refractory subjects against them; and makes the most ostentatious exhibition of this exercise of authority,' and in this he was almost certainly correct. All this seemed to be a warning that the Major's position as Resident at Lucknow was in some sort of danger. However, the Major still had his uses, in that he was able to 'persuade' the Nawab to lend the Company the money, which Lord Moira required to finance his war against the Gurkhas, before dismissing him in 1815.

Saadat Ali Khan was immensely relieved when the Major's pressure on him eased, but he died shortly afterwards in 1814, leaving a vast sum of money, which the old miser had accumulated over the years – no less than £18 million in the value of money at that time. This meant that when his eldest son inherited the title there was no shortage of money. In fact, his smooth accession to power was considerably facilitated by the Major, who believed in primogeniture and who also managed to persuade the second and favourite son to retire to Benares, to live comfortably on a pension guaranteed by the Company.

At first, Ghazi-ud-din Haidar was grateful to the Major for his assistance in endorsing him as the successor to his father and, more or less, allowed the Major to do what he wanted. He even agreed to institute the tax reforms, which the Major had proposed but which had been resisted by his father. Later on, however, he began to resent the Resident's constant interference and what seemed to be to him his dictatorial attitude towards him. He then began to complain to the Governor General and then almost simultaneously withdraw his complaints. However, one has to admit having read some of the papers, that there is little doubt that the Major was over-officious and patronising, so much so that the Nawab began to change his mind to the extent of trying to get rid of him.

In all this, one has to ask the question as to why Major Baillie went so far down this route to the point at putting his job at risk and then ultimately losing it. He had probably overstayed his welcome – in any case his eight years as Resident at Oudh from 1807 to 1815 was quite long for such a position – most terms were shorter, so perhaps it was time for him to leave, but not in the circumstances he did. He had had the confidence of previous Governor Generals and the support of Edmonstone but not that of Lord Moira. He was still a young man, when he went to Lucknow – only 35 years old – perhaps he was overconfident; perhaps this overconfidence led to his being impatient; perhaps he, as a Presbyterian Scot, did not like what he saw in Lucknow and Oudh and wanted to change it – 'make an impact' is the modern expression. Who really knows at this distance in time; his antennae could not have been very sharp, unless he ignored them; what we do know is that he did fall foul of Lord Moira, as did Edmonstone and when he got back to London – aged only 44, he categorically refused to go back to India, while Lord Moira remained as Governor General and it all ended up in Court. However, despite all this, he was appointed a Director of the Company, relatively shortly after his return, although not quite so quickly as Edmonstone. There was a report that he had only been appointed a Director of the Company to silence him, and there just possibly might have been a grain of truth in this. In any case, as we have pointed out, the Directors had not wanted Lord Moira as Governor General and only reluctantly agreed to his appointment because of the 'undue' influence of the Prince Regent and his coterie.

Before Lord Moira dismissed the Major from his appointment, he was instructed by his Lordship to 'request' the Nawab to dip into his pocket for yet another loan to the Company to finance his war against the Nepalese. This so-called 'request' increased the Nawab's dislike of the Resident, although the latter was only acting under orders and intensely disliked what he was being instructed to do. In the end the Nawab did hand over, with the utmost reluctance, yet another crore of rupees (a crore is ten million rupees – for many years the exact equivalent of one million pounds sterling) – a lot of money.

Let us now examine the case which the now Colonel Baillie – he was promoted to Colonel when he left Lucknow – brought against Lord Hastings in respect of these Oudh loans and other related matters – a case which he brought before the relevant Committee of the House of Commons and before the Directors of the Company at India House, although by now he was a Director of that Company! By contrast, Lord Hastings was later demoted from being the Governor General and Commander-in-Chief of India to being Governor of a small island in the Mediterranean, called Malta, and died shortly thereafter.

Baillie's charges were as follows:

1. That Lord Hastings had falsely stated that the Nawab of Oudh had, during the Nepal War, voluntarily offered a loan of more than two crores of rupees, as the price of his release from the subjection in which he felt he was held by the Resident.
2. That Lord Hastings had falsely stated that there was an understanding between the late and present Nawabs on this subject.
3. That Lord Hastings had falsely stated that the present Nawab had made a spontaneous offer of a crore of rupees or any sum.

Firstly, Baillie stated that the Nawab was 'reluctant to give any loan at all;
Secondly, he asserted that he was compelled by Lord Hastings to press for the loans;
Thirdly, the loans were given with 'great reluctance, for voluntary it was not;'
Fourthly, as he Baillie alleged 'the financial difficulties of the Company's Government were made known to me by the Governor-General in person'. Baillie then stated that it was the Governor-General himself, who took the initiative in suggesting the practicability of loans from the Nawab.
Fifthly, that the Nawab knew nothing about the Nepal Wars. 'He could have known nothing of them', he claimed.
Sixthly, that he Baillie stated that a Muslim, who cannot charge interest, will not think of granting a loan.
Seventhly, that the first loan may have been given willingly, but the second loan was 'forced' out of him.
Eightly, that he Baillie alleged that Lord Hastings had made gross misstatements in defence of the loans.
Ninthly and lastly, that all the negotiations, which he had with the Nawab, were 'in point of fact most arduous and vexatious'.

Lord Hastings defended himself to the Court as follows:

His Excellency the Vizier, at a Conference which I held with His Excellency, tendered to me as a proof of his friendship, and of the cordial interest which he feels in the prosperity of the affairs of the Honourable Company, an accommodation of one crore of rupees in the way of a loan. I deemed it to be my duty, in consideration of the actual state of the public finances and the public demands, arising out of the prosecution of the hostilities with the Nepalese, and the eventual necessity of supporting by military preparation, our political views with relation to Saugor and Bhopaul, to accept his offer.

This response entirely failed to mention the second loan, which was the one that caused Baillie all the trouble and to all intents and purposes had been extorted from the Nawab by Baillie, who, in so doing, had been greatly embarrassed. There is, indeed, no dearth of evidence to show that this was the case and that it had certainly not been provided 'in a free and friendly spirit' as Lord Hastings maintained.

There was no doubt that the second loan had indeed been extorted from the Nawab and Baillie averred that 'so far as the Vizier from coming forward spontaneously with an offer of this second loan, that I may make so bold as to state that he never even dreamt of such a demand being made on him'.

At the end of the day, these Oudh loans had no justification, moral, legal or otherwise. The war with Nepal was unnecessary and was only undertaken by Lord Hastings, whose abiding wish seemed to be to make more and more conquests for the Company and emulate Wellesley. Edmonstone's advice that this ambition should be achieved through diplomacy, rather than warfare with its inevitable loss of life and ruinous expense, was ignored. Indeed, when Edmonstone asked how this war could be afforded, Lord Hastings rather airily replied that he had already funded it by taking loans from the Nawab, on which no interest would be paid, on the basis that the Nawab as a Muslim could not act against the dictates of the Quran by accepting interest.

Perhaps, it really was the case that the Nawab had struck a tacit deal with the Governor General in that, although the second loan was indeed forced out of him, there was a sine qua non to the effect that, in return for this loan, the Governor General would dismiss the Major, although there is no firm evidence for this. However, it could just be the case, because we see a letter from the Major to Edmonstone, when he writes,

Shall I tell you anything of my trip to Cawnpore to meet the Governor-General, I had better not, I believe; for I have nothing pleasant to communicate. I was desired to propose to the Nawab that he, His Excellency, should propose to Lord Moira for him to make a voluntary loan to the Company of a crore of rupees; His Excellency did so accordingly and his proposal was graciously received. To reconcile a proposal like this with all my original disinterestedness, was an effort of diplomatic effrontery, you must admit, but mark the sequel and admire. His Excellency has proposed that, in return, Lord Moira should propose to His Excellency to put a stop to the system of reform.

This was tantamount to requesting Lord Moira to dismiss the Major, who was the author of such reforms and, if the reforms were not stopped, then the initiator of such reforms must go, otherwise, he would be placed in an intolerable position.

In the end, the manifest complicity of Lord Moira in these extractions of cash from the Nawab was not censured by the Company. It was agreed that the loans had not been provided as a result of extortion, although they might have been obtained by 'persuasion'. The Noble Lord 'came out of these transactions free from blame'. It was now suggested that, even if these loans had been extorted from the Nawab, he Lord Moira had done so 'from patriotic motives and for the advantage of his country'. And there, I think, we must leave the noble Marquess and the Major, who was now promoted to command his Regiment in Calcutta, before leaving for England. Despite everything, he was honoured by the Nawab – but whether it was Saadat-Ali-Khan or his successor we do not know – with four very high sounding Persian titles: Amal-al-Daula, Afdal-al-Mulk, Wafadar Khan and Arsalan-I-Jung, which being interpreted are the Pillar of the State, Most Favoured of Kings, the Faithful Governor and the Lion of War. Perhaps all this did go somewhat to the head of the youthful Captain.

Chapter 27

Edmonstone leaves Calcutta: A summary of his Indian career

Colonel Baillie was not the only one to fall out with Lord Hastings – Edmonstone in Calcutta had likewise. Although he had been appointed Vice President of the Supreme Council of India, his views were markedly different to those of the new Governor General, whose main concern, as we have mentioned, seemed to be to emulate Wellesley in making yet more conquests for the Company. Edmonstone, in contrast, believed that his ambitions might be the more readily achieved by diplomacy rather than by war, but he was ignored. Indeed, he wrote, 'It was my misfortune to differ with Lord Hastings on various matters of great political importance, during the time I was associated with him in the Government of India; this difference of opinion led to numerous elaborate discussions in Minutes recorded in the Secret Department – on subjects which I am therefore not at liberty to disclose.'

This was putting it all rather diplomatically. Edmonstone was so opposed to the actions of the Governor General that he drafted several dissenting Minutes. These became public documents that, although carefully worded, nevertheless expressed open resistance to the Governor General's policies and were, indeed, communicated to the Directors. The first of these came in 1815, after the commencement of that unnecessary war with Nepal, which started as a territorial dispute and only ended after eighteen months of war with a British victory, which brought some territory in the foothills of the Himalayas under the control of the Company and also brought about the death in action of the famous Colonel Rollo Gillespie at the siege of Kalunga.

Although Edmonstone did not expressly say so, it was clear that he viewed the Governor General as being too unfamiliar with India to judge what constituted a real menace to the Company. The latter did take this on board for he sarcastically replied to Edmonstone's opposition with the words, 'If the reasoning of Mr Edmonstone be valid, I must have, with unaccountable imbecility, presented to myself imaginary dangers and must have culpably expended large sums of the Company's money in providing against fancied Enemies.' Of course, it was the case that it was not the Company's money, but that of the Nawab of Oudh, from whom the reluctant and unwilling Major Baillie had been forced to extort from him. Although the entire Council was opposed to Lord Moira's actions, Edmonstone was singled out for castigation.

Edmonstone viewed the wars into which India was now plunged with horror and he had, for the first time, openly opposed the Governor General. Unfortunately, despite the fact that the other members of the Council supported him, the opposition to the Governor General failed. Even the Directors in London supported him, but they could not in the end go against Lord Moira, because behind him lurked the malevolent influence of the Prince Regent.

He remained a Vice President of the Council and Deputy Governor of Bengal until 1818, when, at last, he achieved his long-deferred ambition to leave India, which he had served without a break for many years, and return home. He was now 51 years of age in a country, where the lifespan of the average European was less than 50, and at that time – late 1817 – there was a particularly virulent outbreak of cholera in Calcutta, which carried off a large number of Europeans as well as, of course, a large number of Indians. Thus, on 22 January 1818, with a salute from the guns of Fort William, the East Indiaman, the Carnatic, with Edmonstone and his European family on board set sail for England.

Perhaps, despite everything, he left Calcutta with mixed feelings. His brother William and his best friend George Cherry lay in Indian graves – his Indian lady and his now married daughter Eliza, who would produce five grandchildren for him, remained behind and it was reported that they were at the dockside to wave goodbye to him and his English family and one wonders what his and their feelings were as they did so, bearing in mind that it was unlikely they would never see each other again and they did not. But, before he left Calcutta, there was a whirlwind of parties and receptions and one wonders whether Eliza and her mother were invited to these – again probably not. Mrs Edmonstone gave a 'brilliant fashionable party' in October and Edmonstone, perhaps somewhat surprisingly, hosted a 'Grand Dinner' on the Prince Regent's Birthday, to which all the senior officers and company men of the Settlement were invited, whilst the Company responded with a lavish ball and supper commencing at 1 am which featured 'every delicacy that the season affords and the champagne was unusually sparkling'.

On 8 January 1818, there was a Meeting of some three hundred British inhabitants of Calcutta, with the proceedings being reported in the Calcutta Gazette two days later. Mr Udny was in the Chair. He gave a long eulogy and ended with these words:

In offering to you this tribute of our respect for your public character, we must be permitted to give expression to a sentiment, which still more intimately comes home to us at the moment of separation. This society, which has so long graced by the accomplishments of your mind and charmed with the kindness and suavity of your manner, cannot contemplate your departure, without feeling most strongly, how painful is the necessity, which, in this country, occasions the abrupt dissolution of friendly and social intercourse. Our regret can only be alleviated by the hope and assurance, that in your native land, and in the bosom of your family, the remainder of your life with be passed in the enjoyment of the fullest prosperity and happiness'.

Signed by the Committee and 300 of the Civil and Military Service and other inhabitants of Calcutta.

To this Edmonstone made a very lengthy response, of which the last paragraph runs as follows:

Gentlemen, I would, if possible, express in adequate terms the grateful sense which I entertain of the kind and flattering terms in which you have been pleased to advert to my departure, and to convey to me your benevolent wishes; when I look around me, and see the number of those respectable members of this community, by whose friendship I have been honoured, by whose kindness I have been benefitted, by whose society I have been delighted and informed, I painfully feel the force of the affecting observation, with which you have closed your address. The pressure of this feeling is aggravated by the accumulated marks of distinction and attention, which I have had the honour to experience on the occasion of my approaching departure. It is my consolation and pride that I have been thought deserving of these great and unexpected honours. It is my prayer that Providence may bestow upon you, who have conferred them, collectively and individually, every happiness and success, both public and private.

And now, Gentleman, with a deep and lasting impression of obligation, attachment and regret, I bid you – Farewell.

The Carnatic stopped briefly at the Cape and the Island of St Helena, where he was greeted with receptions and 'public honours'. At St Helena, they stayed with the Governor Sir Hudson Lowe who, as Governor, was also responsible for guarding Napoleon Bonaparte, who, by then, had become a tourist attraction. Napoleon, by then, had had enough of gawking tourists and so Edmonstone did not meet him. In London, he bought a six-storey mansion in Portland Place, near Regent's Park, where he lived surrounded by his large library which, inter alia, included a number of rare Persian books, some of which had once belonged to Tipu Sultan at Seringapatam and these he bequeathed to the Royal Asiatic Society, as none of his sons had any interest in his Oriental matters.

In 1820, he was appointed a Director of the Company and became a Member of Parliament in the time-honoured way. He had earned and had saved up a lot of money in India and some of this fortune went to his nephew, the young Sir Archibald Edmonstone, to assist him rebuild the then largely ruinous family home Duntreath Castle – a rebuilding which was not completed until 1863.

Of his and Charlotte's children, their eldest son William Archibald went back to India, where he died aged only 22 at Nusseerabad, apparently trying to rescue his spaniel from drowning. Nusseerabad was the cantonment for Ajmer and had only been constructed nine years previously by Sir David Ochterlony. At Nusseerabad, there is or was a Memorial to him with the following inscription:

Here lies interred the Body of William Archibald Edmonstone Esquire, who died at Nusseerabad on the 19th July 1827.

Distinguished by Simplicity and Friendly of Heart by his Virtues of filial, fraternal and social affection, by benevolence of mind and gentleness of disposition, he conciliated the esteem and attachment with all whom he associated and terminated a promising career of public service and a life of private worth and goodness at the early age of 22 years and 9 months.

To the Memory of this, their Firstborn, his afflicted Parents, lamenting in him the loss of a Son endeared to them not more by the ties of Nature than by the excellence of character have caused this Tablet to be erected over his Remains.

In 1827, his second son, another Neil Benjamin Edmonstone, went out to India, made some money there and then returned to England on grounds of ill-health. The third son Charles became a clergyman and on 24 June 1847, we see a cutting from the local Devizes paper as follows:

'Marlboro'. On the 19th Inst the Church Wardens of St. Mary's Marlboro' presented on behalf of the parish to the Revd Chas. W. Edmonstone, the vicar, a Silver Breakfast Service as a Memorial of the Esteem entertained for him by his parishioners of gratitude for his past labours. It is impossible to overstate the feeling of regret existing in St. Mary's at the removal of Mr Edmonstone, who has accepted the benefice of Holloway near London – and, although the more substantial mark of regret proceeded, of course, from the more opulent class, yet the smaller contributions were not wanting; and the demonstrations of deep regret by the poor as well as the rich on the conclusion of Mr Edmonstone's officiating for the last time on Sunday Evensong; in him the poor have lost a friend.

To which he accordingly replied with a long letter, which ended as follows:

I shall entertain a most grateful remembrance of the universal kindness and goodwill and good, which I have met from my parishioners and also from others in the town. It is my sincere prayer that the Divine Blessing may rest upon you all and be multiplied towards you. Believe me, my dear Friends, Yours Faithfully and Affectionately C. W. Edmonstone.

His fourth son, George Frederick, named after George Cherry, had a long and illustrious career in India – inter alia – overseeing the annexation of Oudh. He had served initially as the Commissioner and Superintendent of the Cis-Sutlej States, then in the Secret, Foreign and Political Department during the Indian War of Rebellion also known as the Mutiny and later as Lieutenant Governor of the North-West Provinces 1859–1863. He was then knighted in 1863 for his work in creating the Government of the Central Provinces. Sadly, his fifth son James died in 1834 aged only 14. His Elmore sons were not allowed to return to India and they both regretted this.

Of his daughters, the eldest four all married, while the two youngest seemed to have remained single and stayed with their parents, as was not unusual at that time. Charlotte, his wife, died in 1838 after a long illness, while Neil himself on 30 April 1841 was caught in a sudden downpour of rain in an open carriage, while driving to a Company Board Meeting in Leadenhall Street. Soaked to the skin, he returned home, but by then, he had caught a chill and died sadly from pneumonia five days later. He lies buried adjacent to Charlotte in All Souls Cemetery at Kensal Green and on his grave, you will see the following inscription:

His zeal, ability and perseverance in the discharge of his public duties during upwards of half a century . . . secured for him universal esteem and admiration.

Sometime before his death at the age of 76, he summed up his career in India as follows:

I may venture to assert that the arduous character and extended duration of the duties, which devolved on me in my capacity as Persian Translator and Secretary of the Secret, Political and Foreign Departments of the Government of India, more especially during those great measures and achievements, which was perhaps the most perilous and critical times of Indian History, saved the British Empire in the East from destruction and laid the foundation of its present supremacy, have not had their parallel in the career of any other Civil Servant of the Company; calculating only from the commencement of the Marquess Wellesley's administration, until I took my seat as a Member of Council (although the duties of this situation were no less arduous and responsible) the period of time in which I had to maintain this burden of official labour was fourteen years, in the course of which time I never once had leave of absence nor was my attention to the duties of my office suspended even by indisposition, neither was I one day absent from duty, while I continued in the situation of a member of the Government. The same remark applies to the whole time of my fulfilling the duties of the office of Persian Translator and Persian Secretary – an office in the then conditions of the Native States of an extremely laborious and responsible nature antecedent to my appointment to the higher situation of Secretary in the Secret, Political and Foreign Departments, a period of seven years, embracing altogether a term of 26 years of official duty (the daily application of which I may venture to average about 8 hours) without any intermission.

At the end of the day, it would be true to say that it would be difficult to find another man, whose influence in India was so pervasive and continued for so long. In all, Edmonstone devoted fifty-seven of his seventy-six years to the Honourable East India Company. He formed its policy and continually worked for its enlargement. His is not a well-known name in history, mainly because his methods were those of the boardroom and not the battlefield. His lifelong battle to support and promote British Imperialism in India was more effective than any single conflict could have been. Through his patient and single-minded diplomacy, he helped not only to impose British control over the subcontinent of India but also to ensure its relative stability for some considerable time to come.

Chapter 28
Colonel Baillie leaves India; His Early Death

Colonel Baillie left Lucknow in 1815 for Calcutta, and then from there left for England at the turn of the year. He landed at Brighton on 30 June and arrived in London two days later. He left Mary Martin behind either in Lucknow or in Calcutta and we have to wonder what happened to her. After all, she had been the lady of the Resident, she had given him three children and we see paintings of them together at various Durbars and receptions – one would not call her a beauty but obviously she was attractive and had three lovely children judging by their portraits. Surely, he could not have jettisoned her just like that. Perhaps she would have found herself in a difficult position in Lucknow, if she had remained there, as the lady of a dismissed Resident and perhaps she did return to Calcutta with him– she may have even married again – women were in short supply there, as everywhere else in India. She is not mentioned in his Will, so what did become of her – it is all a mystery and an uncomfortable mystery.

One also wonders when he returned to Calcutta from Lucknow, before proceeding to England, whether he met up with the Indian mother of his four Calcutta children, assuming she was still alive. As we know, three of these children went back to India from Scotland and married there, so it stands to reason that they could have met up with her, again assuming she was still alive, when they arrived back in Calcutta. What we do know, is that he made no provision for her in his Will, which must mean that he would have or should have settled some money on her before he left Calcutta. He was not short of money and apart from anything else, he had been able to buy the Leys Castle Estate from his brother Alexander, who could no longer afford the repair bills – the sum involved was £60,000 in the value of money at that time – a large sum.

Three weeks after his arrival in London, he wrote to Edmonstone, who remained in Calcutta for another two years. This is the somewhat abbreviated letter:

My dear Edmonstone,

I wrote to you at St. Helena, but as all the India ships had passed before our arrival, you will probably receive this account of my safe arrival in England before you hear of our having doubled the Cape. The voyage was altogether most prosperous.

The climate is shockingly disagreeable but healthy none the less. I had a little cold for a day or so and am now in astonishing health. Your brother and his family are in the country so I shall see nothing of them until the winter, nor shall I, of course, have an opportunity of seeing and reporting on your children. But the Lumsdens, who live within a few doors of me and by whom I am almost daily informed, say that Archy is well and that your other little ones are thriving.

My sister is with me in town and left your son (John Elmore), a half-pay Lieutenant in Invernessshire, living with my relations, which he seems to prefer to his own, naturally enough, poor fellow, having been brought up with them since his childhood.

I have met with a number of old friends and a very great number of acquaintances and they all look happy enough. I spent the other morning with Sir George Barlow, who seemed very happy to see me. Lord Wellesley I have not been able to have sight of and Lord Teignmouth was not at home when I called. Some of the Directors have been civil – I dined with them all by invitation of the Chairman. I know nothing of their sentiments of the subject of Lord Moira's conduct to myself.

God bless you, my dear Edmonstone. My sister desires me to give you her kind regards. Give my warmest regards to Mrs Edmonstone and believe me – ever most affectionately.

Yours John Baillie

Another letter dated 15 January 1817, again abbreviated:

My dear Edmonstone,

I have been more than six months in England and Scotland and have not heard from you once. This, I have to confess, is surprising, I have heard from my brother and son that is the one who was removed from Lucknow and the other without hope of employment. This you may believe is disturbing and has a tendency by no means unnatural to impress me with a mortifying conviction that I am forgotten by my friends in Bengal. Of my situation and prospects in England I can say nothing that is satisfactory. The Government and consequently the Directors seem resolved to support my Lord Moira. And, of course, I have nothing to look for but continued injustice and oppression, should I appeal the decision.

I have left a card at your brother's but I have not had the pleasure of seeing him. I called on your sister at Cheltenham and kissed your three little girls. The boys, that is, Archie and Fred are, at present, I believe with your brother and I have heard that they are healthy and promising. The dear lads, who were brought up by my sister, unquestionably do credit to her care of them and are, in every way, entitled to your Name and the countenance of your Family, though, unfortunately for them, deprived of the one and enjoying little of the other.

John has lived with me for nearly five months and is still with one branch of my family. I shall endeavour, if I can see your brother, to persuade him of the necessity of placing John on the full pay of the Army and, if possible, in an Indian Regiment – his appearance is just as respectable as that of any young officer in His Majesty's Service.

Poor Alick has been brought up in a line that I would not have approved – he is truly an amiable youth and would do credit to a more honourable profession that of a Manufacturer in Glasgow.

My fortune with all my encumbrances is scarcely sufficient for my comfort – yet many are comfortable with less. Perhaps I shall learn to be so hereafter – if not, and Lord Moira comes home, then I will probably return to Bengal, while India is subject to the Government of this man, I can never wish to be there.

God bless you. Pray try to do something for my son and brother. I should certainly have exerted myself under similar circumstances for yours and I, therefore, have a right to appeal to a friendship, as sincere, should be active.

With warmest regards to Mrs Edmonstone, I am, ever affectionately, yours John Baillie.

No replies have been seen to either of these two letters or for that matter any other letters which Edmonstone may or may not have written to Baillie regarding his sons and, indeed, one can perhaps detect an element of froideur, given his criticisms of Edmonstone's apparent neglect of his two surviving sons, namely John and Alexander by his Indian lady in Calcutta.

He was only 44 years old when he returned from India, so there was time for him to start another career and, like many such men, he found it in the House of Commons. First of all, he had to find a seat. At the General Election of 1818, he offered himself as a man 'unconnected with any person or party' for the venal borough of Hedon, which he had been cultivating for several months, but he then withdrew. He also tried his luck at Anstruther Easter Burghs, but made little headway against the Lord Advocate. He then tried again at Hedon and having secured the backing of the Tory Corporation and having also bought the freedom of the borough for 200 guineas, he then went on to win the seat at the General Election in 1820.

In 1823, when he was appointed to the Board of the Honourable East India Company, he naturally voted against the reform of that Company. For the General Election of 1830, he abandoned Hedon and managed to secure his unopposed return for Inverness Burghs, where his family had influence, at the expense of Robert Grant, the brother of Charles Grant, whom we have met before in connection with the Clapham Sect. When he was elected, this was what he said:

> I am a friend to rational freedom of every kind and to every country . . . but too partial to existing institutions . . . to subject them to the hazard of subversion for the chance of speculative improvement . . . I think well of the present Government, especially Wellington and Peel . . . while they follow the same course . . . they shall generally have my cordial support; but I am not one of those who can be led by even the strongest partiality for a minister to lend my support to any measure, which either my conscience or my judgement disapproves.

He successfully contested Inverness Burghs as a Conservative in the General Election of 1832, but four months later, he died at home, in London on 20 April 1833, probably from a heart attack at the early age of 61, and was interred seven days later in the St Marylebone Chapel Vault. By his Will, he provided handsomely for all his children, who had survived him. His English and Scottish estate was sworn under £20,000, for some reason in the province of Canterbury, while the entailed Scottish estates, which would have gone to John Wilson Baillie had he survived, went instead to his daughter Ann and her husband John Frederick Baillie of Dochfour.

Well before his death, he was appointed Doctor of Law at King's College, Aberdeen University and he had also been elected a Fellow of the Royal Society. He was also, along with Edmonstone, a Founder Member of the Royal Asiatic Society.

His was not such a brilliant career as that of Edmonstone, and it ended badly with his dismissal as Resident at Lucknow by Lord Moira. On reading all the papers, one has to admit that perhaps it might have been deserved – he had overreached himself – nevertheless there is little doubt that he was in his day and particularly in his Bundelkhand and Fort William College days, one of the most able officers in the service of the East India Company and one of their most distinguished Orientalists.

Appendix

Copies of letters sent to the Edmonstone Family by Margaret Baillie of Leys Castle, Inverness, regarding John and Alexander Elmore (nee Edmonstone), two of the Scottish-Indian children of Neil Edmonstone. In a number of cases, these letters are quite long and have been abbreviated.

Letter date 23rd May 1811

My dear Sir,

I have the pleasure to acknowledge receipt of your esteemed favour of the 3rd, concerning a Bill of Exchange, £22–10s. Agreeable to your wish, I have drawn the money and shall endeavour so for to direct the boys in the outlay that the greater proportion may be applied for useful purposes.

I always feel ashamed when you talk of obligation to any part of our family, knowing that you have conferred so great benefits and given such uncommon proofs of Friendship to John Baillie as none of us can ever repay. I shall be extremely vexed and mortified at your removal of the boys from here till their future pursuits in life render it necessary, particularly as I believe such a determination proceeds from your displeasure at my having sent the eldest boy to College without your approbation, which I certainly would never have ventured on had there been time to consult you on the subject, but I mentioned to my brother the reasons that induced me to take such as step and hoped that they might be sufficient to excuse it.

I have never considered the charge of the boys troublesome – on the contrary the hope of being in some measure useful to them afforded me infinite pleasure and I shall ever be most warmly interested in their welfare and happenings.

John has recently expressed a wish to go into the mercantile line should he remain with me. I propose if agreeable to you that after spending one more year at his education, he should be under the direction of a respectable Gentleman in trade to ascertain whether his liking for business may be permanent. Alick, although rather slow in learning, now gets on much better and is a boy of uncommon kind disposition and I shall indeed be both surprised and disappointed if he does not turn out remarkably well. The boys entreat me to present their respectful duty to you. They take the opportunity of enclosing an answer to their Mother's letter.

I remain always, My Dear Sir, with great respect, your Obliged Humble Servant. Margaret Baillie.

Letter to Neil Edmonstone dated 7th July 1812.

My Dear Sir,

Your agreeable favour of the 11th December afforded me very sincere pleasure as it answered the painful idea of your being dis-satisfied with the mode of education adopted for the boys, particularly sending John to College. I now conceive that the only objective arose from a fear that I might give the boys ideas inconsistent with your views for him, to avoid which I constantly endeavour to impress his mind with a connection that such education be given solely for the purpose of better enabling him to work his way through the world.

I do not apprehend that any material addition to the ordinary allowance can at present be requisite for John since all I propose is to place him with a gentleman who transacts business in the banking line, merely to qualify him for keeping accounts correctly and to occupy the time until all his studies are completed and he is of fit age for entering into business.

I believe Brother John intends sending his eldest boy George to London in a year or so time hence, to finish his medical studies and as John will then have done entirely with school, I thought it might be proper to remove him from here and place him more immediately under the direction of your brother Sir Charles Edmonstone. I trust you will see no necessity for me to correspond with anybody else except yourself or my brother John, as I should feel rather reluctant to enter upon the subject, as I am totally ignorant of the circumstances which placed the boys under my control.

I cannot discover that Alick has yet a decided preference for any profession, but he is of so amiable a disposition that I know that in all respects he will conform to your wishes. I must confess that he has hitherto been rather backward with his books, especially in classical studies for which he appears to have no great relish – however in a mercantile line that would not be very necessary and as Alick has begun of late to apply himself much better and certainly does not want for abilities, I have no doubt about his turning out well.

I enclose letters from both the boys to their mother – they entreat me to present their respects and duty to you.

Letter to Sir Charles Edmonstone dated 28th August 1813

Dear Sir,

Your brother Mr Edmonstone's letter of 6th February which I received last week led me to expect the honour of hearing from you and I now have the pleasure of acknowledging your favour dated the 2nd inst. In obedience to your commands I shall be most happy to give you as much information in my power respecting the Elmores.

John is nearly seventeen and Alick has entered his fifteenth year. They have been educated at the leading house here and have had every advantage generally bestowed on private gentlemen in this county. The eldest was three months at King's College, Aberdeen, where I presumed to send him along with my brother's son without any previous direction, but I have since had the happiness of receiving Mr Edmonstone's approbation. Alick, not having any great flair for classical learning, did not go to college, but left the grammar school within these few months and now bestows all his attention on French and Arithmetic.

They are now eleven years under my care and with truth I can say I have never known any boys of more docile and tractable dispositions, they are also very affectionate and most grateful for any great offers done them. John is decidedly inclined to the mercantile line, indeed his great wish is to go out east to Bengal, failing of which with your agreement John would have no objection to go into a counting house in London, he writes a good hand and has a sufficient knowledge of figures.

As you are now acquainted with their history, I think it right to observe that the shade in their complexion is little inconspicuous since John might pass for a very dark native of Britain and Alick would never be supposed by people unacquainted with his birth. Permit me to express the high sense I have of your condescension in attaching a weight to my opinion, regarding the future destination of the two boys. They are both extremely averse to the Army, although surely a most honourable profession. Being much attached to my young charges and sincerely interested in their future welfare and success?

Letter to Sir Charles Edmonstone dated 7th September 1813.
Dear Sir,
I should have earlier done myself the honour of answering your favour of the 1st inst. but judged it reasonable to allow John a little time to consider and adjust his mind to the disappointment he appears to feel at losing his long and cherished hope of getting out to India. Being most desirous to conforming with your wishes and views for him, he will not object to entering a forwarding house in Glasgow, but seems dreadfully averse to the Manufacturers which he says he can by no means bring his mind to. The fact is that, though without a legal claim to any rank in Society, he is sufficiently proud to have a great desire to be considered a gentleman, therefore recoils at any employment which he imagines might retard his being received as such, feeling as he does the misfortune of his birth. He eagerly grasps at what affords the quickest prospect of getting over it and with this idea formerly thought of the Army but, as this idea did not appear to proceed from any decided partiality for the Army, I rather dissuaded him because, although a genteel line, a Subaltern's pay scarcely provides a subsistence. Etc

Letter to Sir Charles Edmonstone dated ten days later 17th September 1813.
Sir,

I was yesterday favoured with yours of the 13th accompanied by Mr Edmonstone's letter and a perusal of it has fully convinced me that he does not wish the boys should go to India, therefore attempting to send either of them would be very wrong since he is certainly the best judge of the difficulties attending their comfortable establishment there.

As you condescended to leave it optional to me, I thought it right to let John know Mr Edmonstone's sentiments on the subject and read out to him that part of the letter you took the trouble to send, hearing which made him see immediately the propriety of giving up all idea of India – indeed I am persuaded the desire first arose from a wish to be near to and under the more immediate protection of a father he so much respects and loves and whose expressions of affection he says compensates for a disappointment arising from the unfortunate circumstances of his birth.

John also appears hugely grateful for your condescension and the warm interest you have taken in him and he desires me to inform you that he decidedly prefers the Army but at the same time will cheerfully go into the mercantile line at Glasgow, if you think it proper, since he wishes in all respects to conform to your pleasure and says his greatest wish and happiness shall ever be to deserve your approbation and that of his father.

I sincerely trust that he will conduct himself so as to effect satisfaction; at present he is certainly as free from either vicious habits or inclinations as any creature can be and is of an obliging and conciliatory disposition. The only fault I can find in him is a thoughtless indolence of mind which prevents his making the improvement in acquiring all the information I would wish. He is, however, very young and a little experience may remedy this defect; on the whole I have every hope of his turning out well; yet deemed it proper to make this remark as even my affection for John would not lead me to deceive you.

I return Mr Edmonstone's letter and I beg him to express my sense of goodness in his sending it.

I have the honour to be
Sir,
With great respect your obedient and humble servant
Margaret Baillie

Letter to Sir Charles Edmonstone dated 17th January 1814
Sir,

I have the honour to acknowledge your favour of the 6th which I should have taken an earlier opportunity of answering but we spent the Holy Days with some friends in the country from whence Elmore did not return until yesterday.

I immediately communicated to him your intentions and entreated him seriously to consider the advantages he might expect from entering the commercial line with your countenance and support but find him averse to anything except the Army on which he continues entirely bent and most impatient to see himself in a red coat. God grant that he may not repent when it is too late.

I sincerely regret his having chosen a profession so little likely to be profitable yet I am fully convinced to any other.

I have the pleasure to assure you that Alick is quite of a different opinion and says he is determined not to follow John's example but will soon sometime knows that he is most happy to try his fortune in trade either at Glasgow or wherever else his friends think proper.

I have lately written to Mr Edmonstone to mention Alick's wishes and have at the same time informed of your goodness and kind indulgence to Elmore who entreats me once again to express you his gratitude.

I remain always,

Sir,

With Great Respect

Your Humble and Obedient Servant

Margaret Baillie

Letter to Sir Charles Edmonstone dated 4th February 1814

Sir,

Owing to the difficulty of travelling, I did not receive your favour after post hours yesterday and have lost no time in replying to it.

Elmore is extremely grateful for your kind condescension to allowing him a choice, but as the destination of both Regiments is said to be the same and he has no acquaintances in either, it cannot make any difference in which the Commission is purchased. Perhaps going among strangers may rather be an advantage as I think that those who are ignorant of his history will scarcely know it from his appearance, which upon the whole is certainly prepossessing and his complexion not darker than I have seen in general of the natives of this country.

I have the honour to be Sir,

With great respect your obedient and humble servant

Margaret Baillie

Letter to Neil Edmonstone dated 29th May 1815.

Dear Sir,

Although I have not been favoured with any answer to my last two letters, I trust you will excuse my troubling you with a few lines to introduce my nephew George Baillie, who goes out as Surgeon on the Castlereagh Country Ship, as my brother's last letters gives us reason to hope for his speedily leaving India and has some fears his son may not overtake him, which would be a great loss and disappointment to the young man should this happen, I presume to entreat your advice as to what course it will be most prudent for George to take, since I know there is no friend on this earth on which John would rely so much.

My nephew can afford you every information regarding your boy John Elmore, who corresponds regularly with me and I have the truest satisfaction in hearing most favourable reports of his conduct and character from all quarters. Indeed, I am assured that there is no officer in his Regiment of the same rank more respected than John.

I am immediately writing to your worthy brother Sir Charles Edmonstone about some situation in the commercial world for Alick, who is still here, as promising a boy as could be wished, except that he has no turn for classical learning. I enclose a letter from him. John informed me that he had the pleasure of writing to you lately.

I have the honour to be, Dear Sir, with great esteem your obedient and humble servant,

Margaret Baillie

And a letter from Alexander Elmore to his father Neil Edmonstone dated 29th May 1815,

My dear Sir,

We have been greatly disappointed at not having had the happiness to hear from you for a very long period.

My brother writes to us frequently. He is still in Ireland and continues very fond of the Army. I have no wish for a military profession and am very desirous to try my fortune in the commercial line as Sir Charles Edmonstone seemed to approve of that plan formerly and that it would be also be agreeable to you.

I hope it may please him to provide a situation for me in the course of this summer for although reluctant to part from my closest friends, I do wish to attempt doing something for myself.

My dear companion, George Baillie, if spared, will reach Bengal and will deliver this and give you all particulars.

I am, my Dear Sir,

Your Affectionate and Dutiful Son

Alexander Elmore

I have found it impossible to find out what eventually happened to these two Elmore sons of Neil Edmonstone. Perhaps someone with more time might be able to trace them and ascertain whether they married and had children.

The Report By Captain John Baillie Of The State Of Affairs In Bundelcund Dated 16Th December 1805

The Province of Bundelcund during the Government of Rajah Chutter Sol, its last sole possession, was justly estimated to produce a yearly Land Revenue of One Crore of Rupees; its Capital and only strong Fortress of Calingar resembling in its situation and exceeding in its size and natural strength, the Fortress of Gwalior, being built upon a high rock of great extent, which forms one of the range of mountains extending from Rotas to the Confines of Ajmere.

2   The principal Residence of Rajah Chutter Sol and the Metropolis of the Country, which he governed, was the City of Purnea situated above the Ghats or beyond the range of mountains above described, of about fourteen Casses from Calingar. In the neighbourhood of this City are the valuable and celebrated diamond mines of Punna, which formed a source of considerable public Revenue, as well as for private profit, to mercantile adventurers during the Government of the Native Chiefs of Bundelcund and of its late Mahratta Conqueror.

3   From the City and Diamond Mines of Punna and the once populous flourishing City of Chutterpore below the Ghats, which was founded by Rajah Chutter Sol and formed occasionally the place of his Residence, almost the whole of that Species of Revenue, which is denominated in Lacs, may be said to have been exclusively derived, for no other Town or Commercial Market of importance is found to have existed in Bundelcund, till after the establishment of the Maratta influence and Government. The Lacs Duties, which were levied on the City of Chutterpore alone, are stated upon good authority to have amounted at one time to more than four Lacs of Rupees per annum and those of Punna, with its Diamond Mines, to have been nearly an equal sum.

4   Both these cities are now comparatively desolate and though included in the Portion of Territory, which it would be expedient for the British Government to select under the Deed of Option by the Peishwa, they are both at present held by refractory Bundelah Leaders.

5   During the Government of Rajah Chutter Sol, the Province of Bundelcund was invaded by Mohummud Khan Ramgurh, the Pathan Chief of Furrackabad and the Peishwa Bajee Rao was invited from the Deccan, for the purpose of repelling this invasion.

6   The expulsion of the Afghan from Bundelcund through the successful exertions of a Mahratta Army was followed by Rajah Chutter Sol's adoption and by a distribution of his territory among the two legitimate sons of the Rajah Herdee Lall? and Juggat Roy, and his son by adoption Bajee Rao.

7   By this arrangement, the Peishwa became the legitimate and rightful possessor of a large portion of territory in Bundelcund, which was the earliest territorial acquisition of the Mahratta Government in Hindustan.

8   This portion of territory, considerably extended by subsequent conquests, is now, with the exception of a few small districts, which are in the possession of the British Government, held tributary to His

Highness the Peishwa by Rao Shere Bhoo Subahdar of Jhansee and Rana Gobind Rao of Calpee who, as the subjects of the Mahratta Government of Poona, have placed themselves, during the present War, under the immediate protection of the British influence and power in the province of Bundelcund.

9 The two remaining shares of the possessions of Rajah Chutter Sol continue to be held in small portions by the numerous descendants of the legitimate sons of Chutter Sol or by the nominal adherents and rebellious Servants of the declining branches of that family, until a long series of domestic dissensions and Civil War in the Province had paved the way to its entire subjugation by a foreign power.

10 Sindia, in his last and successful attempt to establish the Mahratta power and influence in the northern Districts of Hindustan and the Imperial Court of Delhi, was attended by a strong reinforcement of troops from the Deccan under the command of Alee Bahadur, who was a grandson of the first Peishwa Bajee Rao, being the son of Shumshere Bahadur, who was the off-spring of an illicit transaction between the Peishwa and a Mussulman concubine.

11 The avowed object of the Peishwa in detaching this body of troops under the Command of Alee Bahadur to the assistance of Madhoojee Scindia was that of securing his own rights, as the Head of the Maratta Empire, even such parts of Hindustan as should be conquered by the Mahrattas and, in particular, of obtaining the exclusive possession of the Northern Districts of Doab, which were to be placed under the immediate management of Alee Bahadur as the relation and representative of the Peishwa.

12 On a former expedition of Madhooje Scindia to Hindustan and, immediately after the assassination of Apareeal? Khan, the Imperial Minister of Delhi, a number of the Mussulman Nobles and other powerful adherents of that Chief and of his Predecessor Najief Khan, had abandoned the Mussulman faction and influence at Delhi and had attached themselves to the Mahratta Leader.

13 Among those persons was the late Rajah Himmat Bahadur, a powerful Commander of a large body of horse and of a numerous party of Gosains or Nangahs, a peculiar class of armed beggars and devotees, who are generally known in the Northern Provinces of India and of whom Rajah Himmat Bahadur was the Spiritual Head as well as the Military Commander.

14 The character, which Rajah Himmat Bahadur had borne in the service of Dowla, Najief Khan, Apareeal? Khan and others, through which he had successively passed before his introduction into that of Scindia, was of a nature, whether justly or imperfectly appreciated, which together with the

subsequent conduct of that Chieftain, had induced Scindia towards the close of the year 1788 or beginning of 1789, to deprive him of the high rank and influence, which he possessed and to meditate the seizure of his property with a view of putting him to death.

15 Rajah Himmat Bahadur apprized of Scindia's design, while repairing to his tent for the purpose of paying an accustomed visit at the Durbar and with being unprovided with the means of defence, determined suddenly to seek refuge and personal safety under the principal banner of the Mahratta Empire, which had been entrusted on this expedition to Alee Bahadur, as a relation and representative of the Peishwa and was guarded by a select body of troops under the Nawab's immediate command.

16 Of this measure, the immediate effects were to frustrate the designs of Scindia against the person and property of Himmat Bahadur, to produce a breach between the former Chief and the Representative of the Peishwa and to defeat the views of the Peishwa and of Alee Bahadur, in the possession and management of a great portion of Hindustan over which Scindia now determined to establish his own independent authority.

17 Alee Bahadur being thus disappointed in his views of aggrandizement in Hindustan, unable to cope with Scindia in the field and unprovided with the means of supporting the Army, which he had led from the Deccan, was preparing to return to Poona, when Himmat Bahadur, who was a native of Bundelcund and possessed considerable influence in that province and had, at one time, subjected a large portion of it to the authority of the Nawab Vizier, suggested the entire conquest of Bundelcund, as a proper and very easy object of his Protector's ambition and power.

18 An Agreement was accordingly concluded between the Nawab and the Rajah, by which a large portion of the Province, when conquered, would be consigned to the independent management of Himmat Bahadur and its Revenue to be exclusively applied to the payment of a body of troops, which the Rajah engaged to furnish and maintain in the service of Alee Bahadur.

19 The distracted and turbulent state of the Province of Bundelcund, which had long been a scene of domestic dissension and civil war between the legitimate descendants of the Rajah Chutter Sol, afforded at this time a peculiar encouragement to the ambitious views of Alee Bahadur, seconded by the personal influence of Rajah Himmat Bahadur over many of the native chiefs and territories of Bundelcund.

20 Of the territory, which had descended to the two legitimate sons of Rajah Chutter Sol and had been divided in unequal portions between

them – the larger share or that which was possessed by Rajah Hindu had passed from the possession of the grandson Hindooput to that of two rebellious servants of his family named? and Khan Rajah Chabic, the former of whom had established an independent authority at Punna and the latter had obtained possession of the Fortress of Calinger with the districts surrounding that Fortress.

21 The possessions of Rajah Juggut Roy after a long and severe contest between his second son and his two grandsons Goman Sing and Khoman Sing, the children of the eldest son of Juggut Roy, had been first distributed among the three and afterwards entirely usurped by the two latter, whose posterity was now contending in their turn for the sole possession of the whole of the inheritance of Juggut Roy.

22 Rajah Beejy Bahadur of Churkharee, the son of Rajah Khoman Sing, having been disappointed in his ambitious view of subjecting the other branches of his family and the whole of their possessions, to his own immediate authority and being unable to cope with his competitor, Arjun Sing, the Dewan or Minister of Rajah Bulu, an Infant and the grand nephew Rajah Goman Sing, was induced by the advice of Himmat Bahadur to invite the Mahratta invasion, and on the condition of his being protected and secured in the possession of his Fort of Churkharee and of a territory of 4 Lacs of Rupees, to yield every assistance to the Invader.

23 By this arrangement, a considerable obstacle to the advance of Alee Bahadur's army was removed, a number of less powerful Zamindars under the influence of Beejy Bahadur though with him the descendants of Chutter Sol, were induced to follow his example in joining the Mahratta Chief and the only powerful opponent of his progress was Arjun Sing, by whose valour the possessions of that branch of the family, to which he adhered, had not only been maintained but had even been considerably augmented by a partial conquest of the hereditary possessions of Hindu Lah? from the Rebel Hoozany, whom Arjun Sing had slain.

24 The progressive conquest by Alee Bahadur of a large portion of Bundelcund was greatly facilitated in the second year of his invasion by the defeat and death of Arjun Sing, who was slain and his Master taken prisoner in a memorable battle, which was fought near the Fortress of Ajy Gurh, a place of considerable strength situated at nearly an equal distance from Calinger and Punna and commanding a pass through the mountains from the former to the latter place.

25 The possession of the Fort of Ajy Gurh and the establishment of Alee Bahadur's authority over the City and District of Punna almost immediately followed the defeat of Arjun Sing, and Alee Bahadur, after

having occupied a few succeeding years in endeavouring to settle
his new territorial acquisitions and in punishing and depriving of their
Forts the remaining turbulent Zamindars, prepared to undertake the
conclusion and the permanent establishment of his conquests, by
commencing the siege of Calinger, for which purpose he had previously
engaged the assistance of a few European officers with some regular
infantry and guns.

26 About this period of time, the Minister and the Government of
Poona being jealous of the independent authority of Alee Bahadur in
Bundelcund and desirous of appropriating the future revenues of the
valuable possessions which he had conquered and Alee Bahadur, on the
other hand, looking forward to the Government of Poona for occasional
supplies of money and for reinforcements of troops in time of need,
an arrangement was concluded between the parties which, though it
gratified the immediate wishes of both, was not followed by any solid or
permanent advantage to either.

27 By this arrangement, the sovereign and paramount right of the Peishwa
over all the conquests of Alee Bahadur in Bundelcund was declared
and acknowledged. A Grant of the Government of these territories was
given by the Peishwa and accepted by the Nawab in the form, which is
usually practised at the Poona Durbar, with regard to all other Governors
of distant Provinces and with a reinforcement of Maratta troops, some
confidential servants of the Peishwa were despatched to Bundelcund
for the purpose of superintending and controlling the Collections and
Disbursements of the Public Revenue.

28 But these measures tended neither to accelerate the complete
establishment of Alee Bahadur's authority in Bundelcund nor to produce
any accretion of Revenue to the Peishwa from the portions of it, over
which his authority had been established.

29 The crafty Policy of Himmat Bahadur, who was jealous of the growing
influence of the Peishwa's servants at Alee Bahadur's Court and who
foresaw in the entire Settlements and the tranquillity of the Country, the
downfall of his own power and the resumption of the Territory which he
held in Jaidad, was uniformly, though secretly, occupied in applying the
influence, which he possessed over the Native Chiefs of Bundelcund,
to excite disaffection and revolt against the Mahratta Government and
to produce commotions and rebellion in every district of the Province,
which was not constantly occupied by Alee Bahadur's troops.

30 The disturbances, which were thus excited by the secret influence of
Himmat Bahadur or by the restless and turbulent dispositions of the
Native Chiefs of Bundelcund, precluded the application of the whole of
the Mahratta Force to the accomplishment of the only object, to which it

could have been applied with any reasonable prospect of success, the capture of the Fortress of Calinger.

31 The operations of the siege of Calinger, which at an early period had been converted into a Blockade from the want of a battering train, were protracted, although never totally relinquished during a period of several years, owing to the numerous and frequent detachments that were necessarily made from an Army, which together was scarcely adequate to the purpose of ensuring success, and the death of Alee Bahadur towards the close of the year 1802, while his Army was cantoned before Calinger, left his project of the entire conquest of Bundelcund, in which a period of nearly fourteen years of constant warfare had been occupied, not a step further advanced than it had been in the third year of his invasion.

32 Shumshere Bahadur the eldest son and Representative of the Nawab Alee Bahadur was at the period of his father's death in the 18th year of his age and resided with his mother at Poona, where he had been brought up under the immediate care of his relation and sovereign the head of the Mahratta Empire.

33 The rebellion of Jaswant Rao Holkar and the disaffection or supineness of the other Mahratta Chieftains had occasioned about the same period of time, the expulsion of the Peishwa from his Capital and Government and Shumshere Bahadur had attended him on his flight to Bassein, but had returned shortly after with the consent of the Peishwa to Poona for the purpose of preparing to assert his birthright in the Province of Bundelcund.

34 Rajah Himmat Bahadur, whose influence and power in the Province had lately been increased by the accession of a body of infantry under the command of a European officer named Mieselback, professed at first his intention of supporting the right of Shumshere Bahadur and of maintaining the Government of his father's possessions in his name and behalf until his arrival in Bundelcund.

35 For this purpose, avowedly, he selected from the several Mahratta leaders, who remained in Alee Bahadur's camp, the nearest Mussulman relations of the late Nawab and a person who, from his long residence in Bundelcund under the exclusive authority of Alee Bahadur, might be considered as attached to this family alone and unconnected with any other Mahratta party.

36 This person named Ghuree Bahadur, the maternal cousin of the late Nawab, was accordingly declared the Regent during the absence of Shumshere Bahadur and to him were committed the management of the territory and the custody of the personal property, to a large amount, of the deceased Alee Bahadur; Rajah Himmat Bahadur, retaining as

before, the exclusive management of his own districts and an increased influence over the mind and councils of the Regent and of the native Chiefs of Bundelcund.

37 About this period of time, the declared hostility of the several subordinate Chiefs of the Mahratta Empire to the beneficial arrangements, which were concluded by the Treaty of Bassein, occasioned a formal declaration on the part of the British Government of their intention of maintaining the provisions of that Treaty and this Declaration was immediately followed by offensive operations on the part of Scindia and of the Rajah of Berar and by the no less hostile, secret and cautious measures of aggression on the part of Holkar.

38 As the plan of hostile operations, which was suggested by the latter Chieftain, the invasion of the British territories in the Doab and a predatory invasion into the Districts of Mirzapore and Benares, by the route of Bundelcund, would appear to have formed one of the measures to which the greatest importance had been attached and for the execution of this measure, the Nawab Shumshere Bahadur would appear to have been originally selected as a proper instrument by the united Council of all the Confederate Chiefs.

39 A Summud was accordingly prepared under the Seal of Ameel Rao, the brother of the present Peishwa, whom Holkar had raised to the Musnud, conferring on Shumshere Bahadur, the succession to his father's Government of Bundelcund, and letters were despatched to Rajah Himmat Bahadur and the several other Chieftains in that Province, apprising them of the departure of Shumshere Bahadur from Poona and calling on them to assist and be obedient to him in the execution of the measures, which had been planned by the Mahratta Chiefs and to ensure the success of which a considerable portion of the Mahratta army in Hindustan under the control of Ambajee Ingla was also destined to cooperate.

40 Rajah Himmat Bahadur, foreseeing in the success of this latter plan of the Mahratta Chiefs, an immediate diminution of his own authority in Bundelcund and having some grounds to apprehend the personal enmity of Shumshere Bahadur or, perhaps, duly appreciating the power of the British Government and its known observance of the principles and maxims of just policy and public faith, determined to abandon the Mahratta interests and to seek the permanent establishment of his influence with the aggrandizement of his possessions in Bundelcund, by assisting in the transfer of the Province from the Mahratta to the British Empire.

41 A negociation was accordingly commenced on the part of Rajah Himmat Bahadur with the Civil Officer at Allahabad, through the medium of

Colonel Mieselback, whom this Rajah had detached for that purpose and his proposals having been communicated to Government, the acceptance of these proposals and the occupation of the Province of Bundelcund by a Detachment of the British Forces were considered as just and necessary measures of precaution and defence against the hostile designs of the Mahratta Chieftains, of which the Government had previously been apprized (vide secret instructions to Mr Mercer 22nd July 1803).

42 By an Agreement concluded at Shapore on the 4th September 1803 between Mr Mercer on the part of the Honble East India Company and Colonel Mieselback and the Nawab? on the part of Rajah Himmat Bahadur, it was provided, among other stipulations, that a portion of territory in Bundelcund, yielding an annual revenue of 20 Lacs of Rupees, should be ceded in Jaidad to the Rajah for the maintenance of a body of troops under his command in the Company's service, and in consideration of the great advantages, which were expected from the junction of the power and the influence of Himmat Bahadur and from his zealous cooperation with the British Force in their occupation of Bundelcund and the establishment of the British authority in that Province, a permanent Jagir in the Company's commission was also promised to the Rajah, the extent of it to be proportionate to the Benefits, which might afterwards be derived from his adherence to the tenor of his engagements.

43 The immediate advantages, which flowed from this arrangement, were to the British Government the great facility and assistance, afforded to a detachment of their troops in crossing the Jumna into Bundelcund, which might otherwise have been vigorously opposed by the united forces of the Mahrattas and of Himmat Bahadur, and to the latter Chieftains, the attainment of a rich fertile territory of more than double the extent, which he had proposed under the former Government, without any considerable increase of his former Military Establishment.

44 The Districts, which were specified and assigned to Rajah Himmat Bahadur by Mr Ahmuty, who succeeded Mr Mercer in the conduct of affairs in Bundelcund confirming, with a few trifling exceptions, the whole of the territory contiguous to the west bank of the Jumna from Elahabad (Allahabad?) to Calpee and the possessions of those Districts by the British Government, whether they be under the immediate management of its Civil Officers or of a faithful native, must ever be of a great political and commercial importance, as protecting a large portion of our territories in the Doab and securing the free navigation of the Jumna for a space of at least an hundred miles.

45 The yearly revenue of those districts in the interior of Bundelcund, which were assigned to Himmat Bahadur under the management of his representative, was stated by this Chief to be only Rupees 15.33,184 but the general belief of the country has estimated it at 18 Lacs of Rupees and there is little doubt of their producing more than this latter amount under the immediate influence of the wise and just regulations of the British Government in India.

46 During the negotiations between the British Government and the Rajah Himmat Bahadur, the Nabob Shumshere Bahadur had arrived in the Province of Bundelcund after a tedious march from Poona by the route of Nagpur, on which he was attended by a limited number of followers and towards the end of which he had been joined by a few of the adherents of his father, who advanced from Bundelcund to meet him.

47 From the circumstances of Shumshere Bahadur's unauthorised journey by the route of Nagpur and his having evaded a junction with a predatory leader in the service of Holkar, who was accompanied with a numerous Army on the western frontier of Bundelcund, the inference of his never having cordially acceded to or having, at an earlier period, relinquished the hostile designs of the Mahratta Chiefs against the British Government, may very fairly be deduced and the justice of this inference was, shortly afterwards, confirmed by his endeavouring to conduct a friendly negotiation through the medium of the British Resident at Lucknow.

48 But, as the previous political arrangements of the British Government precluded the recognition of Shumshere Bahadur's rights of succession to the conquests of his father in Bundelcund, the alternative of implicit submission on a promise of personal protection and some further provision for his maintenance and his immediate evacuation of Bundelcund was all that could be then proposed to him and his delay in acceding to this proposal was followed by some operations against him on the part of the British Detachment, which prevented their taking possession of the fortress of Calinger and occasioned the reduction of some other fortresses and Districts by the Native Chiefs of Bundelcund, who took this opportunity of resuming their ancient territories and rights under the pretence of submission to the British Government or of hostility to the Mahratta forces, which our Army was employed in subduing.

49 About this period of time, a proposal on the part of His Highness the Peishwa was made to the British Resident at Poona, for the cession of a portion of territory in Bundelcund in lieu of the Districts in the Deccan which had been ceded by the Treaty of Bassein and in consideration of an increase of the Subsidiary Force, which had originally been stipulated to be provided by the British Government to the Peishwa.

50 The proposal having been accepted by the British Government, a Deed of Cession to the Honble Company for a territory in Bundelcund of 32 Lacs and 16,000 Rupees, in lieu of Subsidy of 4 Lacs of Rupees, was prepared and transmitted to the Presidency and corresponding details of Agreement between the two States were added in the form of a supplement to the Subsidiary Treaty of Bassein.

51 By this arrangement, the Peishwa whose authority over the conquests of Alee Bahadur in Bundelcund had been hitherto merely concessional and who had never derived any revenue from the territory, which Alee Bahadur possessed, was enabled to apply the revenue of that territory to the payment of the Subsidiary Force, which protected his hereditary dominions, while, on the other hand, the British Government acquired a legitimate and unquestionable right of Sovereignty over a valuable territory of great extent in Bundelcund, which must otherwise have been relinquished at the conclusion of the present war.

52 The occupation of the Province of Bundelcund by the British troops during the War was an indispensable means of the defences of the Company's territories in the Doab as well as of the towns and Districts of Meyapoore and also the City of Benares, and our possession and government of a large portion of Bundelcund, even in times of peace with the leading powers of India, must ever be considered as one of great civil and commercial as well as of political importance.

53 The turbulent and restless disposition of the natives of Bundelcund is well known to be such as, under any other than the British Government, would render the navigation of the Jumna and the tranquillity of our possessions in the Doab extremely precarious and doubtful and in danger of occasional molestation to the great prejudice of our Civil and Commercial concerns.

54 A new system of political conduct in Bundelcund was obviously prescribed by the terms of this arrangement with the Durbar of Poona, to the immediate accomplishment of the salutary objects, of which not only the agreement with Rajah Himmat Bahadur but also the subsequent diminution of the authority of Shumshere Bahadur and the tacitly authorised encroachments of the native Chiefs, were decidedly prejudicial and hostile. Tho' the Northern Frontier of Bundelcund, which had been held by this Chief as Tributary of the Peishwa, was immediately occupied by British Troops, but by a subsequent arrangement with Nana Govind Rao, after he had evinced submission and attachment to the views and interests of Government and had joined the Detachment in Bundelcund, all his Districts including Mahobar in that Province with the

exception of Calpee and of a few villages to the northward on the banks of the Jumna, were restored to him and the only question regarding this Chieftain, which remained to be decided, is that of his obtaining from the more remote territory, the revenue of the British Government

55 The Nawab Shumshere Bahadur, who had uniformly professed implicit submission to the will of His Highness the Peishwa and to whose principal adherents, as the Minister of his late father, the instrument of Cession by the Peishwa was addressed, feeling naturally the severity of the only alternative, which the British Government under existing circumstances could have offered to him, endeavoured to preserve his authority in Bundelcund by requiring the assistance and cooperation of the other tributaries and descendants of the Peishwa's Government on the northern frontier of the Province and of a few of the Native leaders with interests in Bundelcund.

56 Among the Dependants of the Government of Poona, Nana Govind Rao of Calpee, whose valuable District of Mahobar lying in the centre of Bundelcund, tho' distinct from Alee Bahadur's conquests and consequently excluded from the objects of the Deed of Cession to the Honourable Company, had nevertheless been seized by Rajah Himmat Bahadur as a part of his Jaidad, under the authority of the British agent, was one of the first to unite his force with that of Shumshere Bahadur, in opposition to the British.

57 In consequence of this improper conduct on the part of Nana Govind Rao, by which he had unquestionably, tho' inadvertently, placed himself in the situation of an enemy to the British Government, the Fort and District of Calpee, situated on the west bank of the Jumna, and some other Districts equivalent in land and money to the District of Calpee and which it must be highly expedient to retain in our possession, or his obtaining by our mediation at the Poona Durbar, a remission of the Tribute, which he formerly paid to the Peishwa, to whom our general right of selection from the whole of his territory in Bundelcund or even our right of conquest from his Tributary and declared Enemy at the time, might successfully as well justly be seized.

58 Another less important question, arising from the establishment of the British Authority over the District of Calpee, related to a Jagir of 52 villages, yielding a revenue of nearly a Lac of Rupees, which was granted by the Peishwa to the late Nawab? Moolk? Jhansi, is now, with the exception of three villages reserved by Nana Govind Rao, in the possession of Nuressood? Daula, a son of the deceased Nawab.

59 To this Jagir, a claim of rights has lately been preferred on the part of the Nawab Moullar? Jah, who stiles himself the eldest legitimate son and representative? Moolk and whose claim apparently supported by the

Peishwa, has been transmitted by the British Resident at Poona where Jah resides.

60 The several Documents by which the counter claims of these contending brothers and supporters were submitted to Government by the late Board of Commissioners for the affairs of Bundelcund, and they consist chiefly of contradictory declarations in the form of last Wills and Testaments by the Nawab? Moolk, who would appear to have frequently changed his sentiments and views respecting the succession to his Jagirs, but even attentive perusal of these documents did not suggest any valid ground to the Commissioners for the removal of Nuree? and Dowla, from the exercise of a right of possession, which he had held previously to and at the period of the British conquest of Calpee and in which his conduct had uniformly exercised the most steady attachment and fidelity to the British interests and views.

61 While the British Detachment was occupied in the siege and conquest of Calpee and the surrounding Districts, a conciliatory negotiation had been opened up with the Nawab Shumshere Bahadur and the other dependants of the Peishwa, as well as with some independent Zamindars on the North Western Frontier of Bundelcund and the result of this negotiation was the personal submission of Shumshere Bahadur and his surrender of the few forts and Districts, which remained to him, on the promise of a provision either in land or money to the extent of 4 Lacs of Rupees from Accession, to be set and fixed by the British Government, in concert with His Highness the Peishwa, from the remaining territory or revenue of Bundelcund, after the accomplishment of the objects of the Deed of Cession to the Company of a territory of 36 Lacs and 16,000 Rupees.

62 This arrangement received the immediate sanction and approbation of the Governor-General in Council, who was pleased not only to ratify the terms of the Agreement with Himmat Bahadur, but also to suggest to the Peishwa the justice and expediency the extending these provisions, which had been assigned to that Chieftain, by vesting him with the management of the Peishwa's remaining territory in Bundelcund.

63 With this latter suggestion in favour of Himmat Bahadur, the Peishwa has since complied but the accomplishment of the benevolent intention of both Governments and the exercise of the trust which has been conferred on Himmat Bahadur in Bundelcund, must depend on the entire subjection of the remaining Districts of that Province, which are now held by refractory Bundelah leaders.

64 With the Subhadar of Jhansee and the Rajahs of Dutteoo and Shumshere?, whose submission to the British Government and junction

with the Detachment on the North West Frontier of Bundelcund had immediately preceded or followed the surrender of Shumshere Bahadur, conciliatory arrangements were concluded at the same period of time and received the ratification of His Excellency the Commander-in-Chief.

65 The immediate object of these arrangements was to secure to the several Chieftains, the unmolested possession of their ancient territorial rights and by ensuring their zealous cooperation with the British forces on the frontier to present the strongest possible barrier against the hostile and predatory inroads, which were then meditated by Holkar and Ameer Khan.

66 The importance of this object during the present War with a reference to many of the Chieftains in the interior as well as on the frontiers of Bundelcund, has been already sufficiently demonstrated and its importance, with a view to the future tranquillity of the British possessions on the west bank of the Jumna, would appear to be equally obvious, while no danger, inconvenience or expense can be produced to the Honourable Company by maintaining the relations and adhering to the terms, which were established by the arrangements in question and Articles of Agreement with the Subhadar of Jhansee dated the 6th February 1804.

67 The accomplishment of the Civil Objects of the Deed of Cession to the Honourable Company of a portion of Bundelcund or, in other words, the realisation of an amount of revenue proportioned in any degree to the Subsidy in lieu of which this territory was ceded, had been hitherto suspended by the necessary effect of the previous arrangement with Rajah Himmat Bahadur, and by the encroachments of the Native Chiefs of Bundelcund, whose power and influence in the Province had never been effectively suppressed during the Government of Alee Bahadur and who took advantage of the consistent employment of the regular forces and of a large proportion of the troops of Himmat Bahadur on the frontier and in the more general operations of the War, to attempt the resumption of their ancient territorial rights.

68 To preclude the more general and success of this attempt and to put a stop to the extending encroachments of the rebellious Bundelah leaders, the application of an irregular force consisting of two Brigades or nine Battalions of Matchlock men with 17 Field pieces of ordinance, which had been received into the British Service from Rajah Ambajee Ingla, was the only coercive measure, which appeared to be practicable during the continuance of the foreign War and the adoption of this measure, giving effect to the implicit submission of Nawab Shumshere Bahadur and accompanied by every conciliatory effort with the Native Chiefs of Bundelcund, followed by the establishment of British authority over a territory of 12 Lacs of Rupees in the interior of the Province, acclusive of the Jaidad of Himmat Bahadur and the Fort and District of Calpee.

69 To the situation and conduct of the Native Chiefs of Bundelcund, whose subjugation to the Poonah State through the medium of Alee Bahadur's conquest, although disavowed by these Chieftains and imperfect in itself, was the legitimate foundation of the right now asserted by the Company, the only principle of conciliation and pacific measure which could apply, were those of considering them as the subjects of the British Government by transfer from the Peishwa and holding out to them the security and undisturbed possession of such parts of their ancient rights, as were held under Alee Bahadur's Government and consequently excluded from the objects of the Deed of Cession by the Peishwa, on the conditions of their allegiance and fidelity to the Honourable Company, their renouncing all views of future aggrandizement and their abandoning such parts of Alee Bahadur's conquests, as had been reserved by them, subsequently to his death.

70 To the influence of this principle though subversive of their former views in the reduction of Himmat Bahadur's power, which had tacitly, if not explicitly, been encouraged by the early consent of the British Officers in Bundelcund, a few of the most powerful Zamindars, after some struggle and opposition to the irregular force, which was employed in the interior, had evinced their entire subjugation, and arrangements for this were concluded with the Rajah of? Mylepore? and?, which have received the ratification or are now under the consideration of Government and under the obligation of Rajah Beejy? Bahadur's?, in despatches of the 18th August and 2nd September 1804.

71 Rajah Bukht Bulu of Banda, formerly mentioned in this report, and Rajah Jelo Sing, who is also the descendant of a branch of the family of Chutter Sol and possessed, at one time, considerable influence and power in the Province, were precluded from the benefit of the above principle, as applied to the other Chieftains, by the circumstances of their possessions having been recently reserved by the former Government and their having an actual provision at the period of the introduction of the British Authority in Bundelcund.

72 As it appeared to the British Agent and has since been established by unquestionable proof that both of these Chieftains had enjoyed at one time considerable grants of land under the Government of Alee Bahadur and as the permanent tranquillity of the Province of Bundelcund, under any foreign authority, must depend upon a liberal consideration of the Claims of its ancient possessors, whose influence and power to excite commotion are by no means suppressed, it has been judged to be expedient to grant suitable provisions to the two Rajahs in question and

the suggestions of the Board of Commissioners to that effect namely of a provision of Rupees 36,000 in land and money for Rajah Bukht Bulu and of Rupees 24,000 for Rajah Jelo Sing as proportioned to their ancient possessions, are now before the Government for consideration and decision.

73 The amount of these provisions and the extent of all the Jagirs, which are held by the Native Chiefs of Bundelcund must, of course, be considered as on behalf of the Peishwa rather than the Province, being in reality the grants of the former Government and excluded from the objects of the Deed of Cession of a territory of 36 Lacs and 16,000 Rupees.

74 By the measures, which have thus been adopted and as related in the foregoing sheets, every hereditary Chieftain, who possessed power or influence in Bundelcund, has been conciliated and placed in due subjection to the British Government of that Province and the British authority may be considered as established over a portion of Alee Bahadur's conquest, which yields a clear revenue at its present reduced estimate of 28 Lacs of Rupees, including Rajah Himmat Bahadur's Jaidad and exclusive of those casual acquisitions which were foreign to the Deed of Cession by the Peishwa and may be estimated to produce yearly revenue of 4 Lacs of Rupees.

75 What remains yet to be affected with a view to the complete accomplishment of the joint objects of the British Government and His Highness the Peishwa in the province of Bundelcund with the only and apparent means of the accomplishment, shall be related in the sequel of this Report.

76 From the best and most authentic information, which has hitherto been obtained, respecting the extent and value of the conquests of Alee Bahadur in Bundelcund, it would appear that the full amount of the gross revenue of the territory which he possessed, was never more than about 52 Lacs of Rupees including Jagirs and provisions to the Native Chiefs and Zamindars, which extended to nearly 8 Lacs of Rupees per annum and estimating the revenue of the Districts now under the British authority with those of Himmat Bahadur's Jaidad at 39 Lacs of Rupees, whereas after deducting Jagirs, they are here estimated at only 28 Lacs.

77 But setting this difference of estimated revenue, which cannot at present be investigated, totally aside, the territory which remains to be reserved by the British Government on their own account and on behalf of the Peishwa, involves only three or four districts yielding a gross revenue of five Lacs of Rupees including Jagirs and a territory of unknown extent and revenue above and below the Ghats from which, including the City and Diamond Mines of Punna, Alee Bahadur could never have realised a greater sum of 8 Lacs of Rupees per annum.

78　The whole of the territory, which remains to be reserved, forms a part of the inheritance of Rajah Hirdee Jah, the oldest son of Chutter Sol, whose posterity, as has been briefly stated, were entirely dispossessed and seized by their rebellious Servants being Beny Hooganj and Khouin Chobey.

79　An illegitimate male descendant and the widow of Rajah Hindooput are the only surviving representatives of this branch of the family and they are maintained in indigence and obscurity, but deprived of any sign of influence by the descendants of the rebellious Servants of their House.

80　Goudha Chobe retains possession of the Fort and District of Calinger, another refractory Bundelah possesses the Fort of Azygurh and District of Jeypoor Huldee, two of the sons of Beny possess Houyoore and a considerable portion of the territory beyond the Ghats and? an obscure Hindoo of the Deccan? Tribes formerly in the service of? Sing, the son of Hindoo Put, holds the Fort of?, the town of Chutterpore and the greatest part of? below the Gath.

81　The submission or suppression of all these persons is indispensable to the complete accomplishment of the joint objects of the British Government and of His Highness the Peishwa in the province of Bundelcund and the general history of the Country from the earliest period, as well as more particularly from the commencement of Alee Bahdur's invasion and the uniform observations of the British Agents, since the Country has been occupied by British troops, suggest the capture and possession of the Fortress of Calinger, as the only effective means of suppression of all the disaffected and rebellious leaders and of the permanent tranquillity of the British possessions in Bundelcund.

82　The character and conduct of the several persons above mentioned during the Government of Alee Bahadur, since the occupation of the Province by the British troops, have been such as might, consistently with justice and sound policy, preclude any negotiations with them, except upon the basis of implied submission to the British Government and reliance on its clemency.

83　So their possessions of the Forts and Districts, to which they hold no legitimate title, could be asserted at any period of their usurpation and the proofs of this hostility and disaffection to the British Government and to the Peishwa as well to their own heredity Chiefs, whose influence and authority and their maintenance and existence, depend on a more efficient Government of the Province, have justly subjected these persons to the dispossession of the fortresses and lands by their occupation, of which the good order and Government of the Province and the tranquillity and happiness of its inhabitants have ever been precluded and disturbed.

84 The natural strength and extent of the Fortress of Calinger was the only obstacle to its immediate capture by a British regular force, if the more general operations of the present war had permitted, the application of even a limited force to that purpose and there was every ground to believe that appearance of a regular force with a battering train before Calinger would have produced the submission of the Bahadur, whose internal means of defence are in no degree proportioned to the natural strength of the Fort or to those of any hereditary Zamindars and possession of a Fortress of far inferior strength to Calinger.

85 The Garrison of this Fortress, which to be efficient, must consist of at least 3000 men, has never been estimated at more than 500 men and the natural distrust, attending a treacherous and unjust acquisition, has precluded the admission of any greater number into the Fort, so that its present Garrison consists of little more than 400 men, unprovided with proper arms and ammunition and impeded in the due exertion of their natural means of defence, by the presence of their wives and children, who are retained as pledges of their fidelity and by the fears of the Keladar himself, whose family, with a large proportion of his wealth being lodged in Calinger, may be considered as inducements to his surrender at an early period of the siege.

86 The Capture and Surrender of the Fortress of Calinger would in all probability be followed by the evacuation of Ajy Gurh, which is very inferior in its strength and by the voluntary submission of the remaining disaffected leaders, to whom adequate pensions might be assigned without material expense to Government or burthen to His Highness the Peishwa, whose remaining share of Bundelcund might justly be chargeable with this expense, and thus it might be fairly presumed that, by the active operations of a limited regular force for a few months after the conclusion of the foreign War, the whole of the Province of Bundelcund would be placed in the quiet possession of the Honble Company or under the influence and control of the British Government, which would tend equally to the accomplishment of our Civil and Political views.

87 To the complete establishment, however, of the civil objects of Government in the Province of Bundelcund or to the realisation at a moderate expense of the Revenue of this valuable Possession, a measure of importance and of considerable delicacy in the execution would still be wanting, namely the reduction of the numerous irregular forces, which have hitherto been maintained in the Province and for whose services after the capture of Calinger, no further occasion would exist.

88 Regarding the reduction of the Brigades of Ambajee on the conclusion of the War, the terms of their admission into the British Services preclude any degree of hesitation or even political discussion. The Proclamation of the Governor-General in Council is sufficiently explicit on this Subject, but the resumption of Himmat Bahadur's Jaidad, although consistent with every principle of justice and proceeding on a declared and acknowledged right, (See Dispatches of the 6th and 20th June 1804 to G. Mercer Esq) is a measure of considerable delicacy and admitting in the practical detail of some political discussion.

89 That the original views and expectations of Himmat Bahadur, in his alliance with the British Government, embraced not only a perpetual Grant of his Jaidad in Bundelcund with his permanent and increasing influence in that Province, but also a considerable Jageer (namely the Tullacha of Belaspoor, Secumdera yielding a Revenue of a Lac of Rupees) in our more tranquil Possessions in the Doab, there can be no reason to doubt, although the terms of his Agreement with Mr Mercer do not, by any means, authorise such an expectation.

90 If Himmat Bahadur, therefore, had survived the conclusion of the War, his known character and his power and influence in Bundelcund might have posed considerable obstacles to a beneficial arrangement of the affairs of that Province for the Company, which might materially affect his own ambitions and views. But, by the death of Himmat Bahadur, the obstacles to such an arrangement are now entirely removed and the few following considerations are all that appear in justice to be requisite, with a view to the resumption of the valuable Districts, which were assigned to him immediately on the conclusion of the War.

91 The Services which have been provided by Himmat Bahadur and by the Troops under his command, though by no means proportioned in their value of so large a portion of the Public Revenue as is now assigned for their payment, yet when estimated with a due consideration of the influence and power, which he possessed and of his means of opposing the British views in Bundelcund, had he adhered to the Maratta Interests on the commencement of the War, must justly be considered in establishing the Title of his Representative and Family to an adequate and even a liberal maintenance.

92 The circumstance too of having possessed a considerable Jaidad under the former Government of Bundelcund and a degree of power and influence, which after contributing to, or rather of itself, conducing the success of Alee Bahadur's invasion, could never in justice or in policy have been reduced by that Chieftain and was in fact equal if not superior

to his own, is obviously entitled to consideration both by the British Government and of the Peishwa with a view to a liberal decision on Himmat Bahadur's claims.

93 In the Districts which were held by the Chieftain during Alee Bahadur's Government and which the general Sentiments of the inhabitants as well as the consciousness of his own power and influence had led him to consider as a property and the future inheritance of his Family, he had constructed several Forts at a very considerable expense and had supplied them with Military Stores and other means of defence, by which he might have successfully resisted the attempts of the former Government to subvert his authority in Bundelcund.

94 For the power, influence and territory, therefore, which Himmat Bahadur possessed in Bundelcund and which his Family might have inherited, if it had not been transferred to the Company for the eminent Services which he had rendered to Alee Bahadur, and ultimately to the Poona State in the subjugation of a large portion of the Province, which is now applied to the Peishwa to the payment of our Subsidiary Forces and for the less important though still considerable advantages, which the British Government derived from their Interests in the commencement of the present War, it could appear to be but just and reasonable that the Representative and Family of the late Rajah should possess in the character of Jageerdars from the Honble Company, the means of dignified and affluent retirement and that the Peishwa's Possessions should be burthened with a large portion, if not the whole, of the expense.

95 The possession of the Zamindars of Bolaspoor Secundera in the Zillah of Cawnpore had been uniformly looked forward to by Himmat Bahadur as the Reward of his Services to the British Government. The faithful companion of his fortune and his constant adherent during all the vicissitudes of his Military career, Rao Subsooh Rao was the Zamindar and Farmer of this Etaka, which he had relinquished with his Mukhee Malekana, in consequence of a difference with the late Collector of the District and to which it was the ancient wish of both these associates to return in the characters of Jagidar and Farmer.

96 Rao Subsooh Rao died a few months before his Master and his son Rao Gaman Sing succeeded to the command and influence, which his Father had possessed, over the Troops and Councils of the Rajah and which are now increased in his person over the infant Son and Representative of the Rajah and the acting Manager of his Affairs.

97 From this circumstance, the expediency of a Grant of the Etaka in question, as a provision for the family of Himmat Bahadur in preference to any other, if their claims be admitted to be just, would appear to

deserve consideration because, although the right and power of resuming the Jaidad without any previous adjustment of the terms of its resumption be unquestionable, the proper execution of a measure, which involves the obtaining the quiet possession of several Forts, the dispersing and dismembering, without commotion, a large body of armed Men linked together by powerful Sirdars, whom the Inhabitants of the Country have long been accustomed to consider as their Governors, each Sirdar is, in fact, the Possessor of a Jaidad and the sudden establishment of the British System of Government in a Country, which has been so differently ruled, must require great delicacy and caution on the part of the Person, who executes it and even some sacrifices or concessions by the Authority, which prescribes such a measure more particularly in critical times.

98 It was owing to this consideration alone that a suggestion of the expediency and indeed necessity of postponing the resumption of Himmat Bahadur's Jaidad was offered to Government on the occasion of his Death and which the predatory irruption of Ameer Khan, with the circumstances attending that irruption, seemed to threaten the suspension for a time of the British Authority in Bundelcund.

99 The same consideration, though its influence be greatly diminished, would lead to the postponement of this measure, till a regular Military Force can be employed in the interior of the Province and till the active operation of that force or negociation, aided by its presence, shall have produced the surrender of the Fort of Calinger and Ajygurh and the submission of the refractory Bundelas, when the obvious inutility and inefficiency of Himmat Bahadur's Troops and of every irregular force in the British Service would naturally suggest to their leaders that the period of their reduction had arrived and would facilitate the means of their reduction.

100 A number of the present Sirdars might wish to become Farmers or Managers, under the British Government, of the Districts which they now hold in Jaidad; Kuncham Geer, who has at present the chief commands and Rao Goman Sing the most powerful of his adherents, would retire to the Jaigeer and Zamindaree of Secundera, which they would manage under British control for the benefit of the Heir and Family of the Rajah and the Widow with the Infant Son would take up their residence in Benares, where a house has been prepared for their reception.

101 In addition to the Grant of the Jagir, some compensation for the value of their Military Stores and particularly for those in the Forts, which Himmat Bahadur had constructed, might naturally be expected by the Family and their request might be urged on the grounds of Arrears being due to the Garrison, which would impede their surrender of the Forts.

102 The justice and expediency complying with this Request to preclude any delay in the completion of so important an arrangement and to secure the immediate surrender of the Forts are sufficiently apparent and a few less important questions might arise in the progress of the Arrangement, which it is unnecessary here to discuss and would by no means be difficult to determine.

103 By the conclusion of this arrangement with the Representative of Himmat Bahadur following the Capture or Surrender of the Forts of Calinger and Ajy Ghur and the establishment of the British Authority at Purnea and Chutturpoor, the means of determining with precision the relative Territorial Rights of the Honble Company and of His Highness the Peishwa in Bundelcund and of appropriating to each the specific Districts and ascertained Revenue, which should belong to them, would no longer be difficult or doubtful.

104 The selection of the District, which it is expedient for the British Government to retain, must be prescribed by the situation exclusively and it is suggested to be the following on the supposition of the clear Revenue of the several Districts amounting in aggregate to no more than the sum of 36 Lacks and 16,000 Rupees, which cannot, of course, be ascertained till the Districts be in our possession.

1. The several Districts in the actual possession of Government including Calpee and a part of Bypoor on the bank of the Jumna of all of which the clear revenue, at a very low estimate, is Rupees 14,00,000.

2. The whole of Himmat Bahadur's Jaidad in the interior of that Province, estimated according to his Statement at 15,33,184. Brought forward 14,00,000 equals 29,33,184.

3. The Districts of Calinger, Jeypoor, Huldee and part of Cutola below the Gauts estimated, as formerly stated, at 5 Lacks of Rupees but chargeable with the Jageers and Provisions to be made to the Native Leaders, who may become submissive to the British Government without coercive measures, 5,00,000.

4. The City and Diamond Mines of Purnea with a portion of Territory adjacent which may produce a Revenue of Rupees 2,00,000 – a Grand Total of Rupees 36,33, 184.

105 Should the revenue of the Districts above described be found upon investigation to exceed the Estimate, which has been stated, the surplus might properly be applied to the extension of the Provisions for Shumshere Bahadur, whose condition as the sole Possessor of the

remaining Districts of his Father's acquisition in Bundelcund, will be found to be very short of his natural Claims and expectations.
SIGNED J. BAILLIE
SIGNED N.B. EDMONSTONE
SECRETARY to the GOVERNMENT

APPENDIX to the NARRATIVE of TRANSACTIONS in BUNDELCUND

1   To secure the internal tranquillity of the Province of Bundelcund, supposing it to be free from the danger of foreign invasion, during the early progress of returning the Jaidad, the presence of the whole of the Detachment which is now serving on the North West Frontier or of a Detachment of equal force in the interior of the Province, would appear to be indispensable.

2   The distribution of the Regular Force in such a manner as by placing a strong Detachment in the Neighbourhood in each of the most populous Districts of the Jaidad, to preclude the danger of insurrection or afford the immediate means of quelling it, would also be expedient.

3   The previous reduction of the Forts of Calinger and Ajy Gurh would, in a great degree, supercede the necessity for both these measures, because it would suppress the spirit of insurrection and depredation throughout the Province – it would put an end to the hopes of all those who are disaffected to the British Government; and it would confirm the fidelity and allegiance of a great number of the Inhabitants of Bundelcund who, though cordially attracted to our Government by personal and selfish considerations, are yet diffident of our intention of retaining the possession of the Province, and might be induced to join in an attempt to excite commotion from the fear of offending the more early established authorities.

4   The Body of Irregular Troops maintained in the Jaidad, may be estimated to amount in the whole to the number of at least nine thousand men, of those about 2500 are efficient Cavalry, commanded by Sirdars or Resaladars in the proportion of one to fifty horsemen, but among these Sirdars, there are perhaps twenty, who possess considerable power and influence in the Province, as holding portions of the Country by assignment in Jaidad for the payment of their Troops. Fifteen hundred Sepoys under the Command of Colonel Mieselback and three subordinate Officers are dressed, armed and disciplined in the European manner and are provided with English Muskets and a few serviceable field Pieces of Ordnance are attached to this Corps for the payment of which, a valuable District contiguous to the Jumna assigned in Jaidad to Colonel Mieselback.

5   Of the remaining irregular Infantry, nearly 3000 form a Body of Gosains or Nangahs armed with Rockets, Matchlocks and Bludgeons, who were brought over by Kunchum Geer from the refractory Bundelah leaders in August 1804 and the remainder consists of about 2000 Matchlock Men and others, who are employed to garrison the Forts and as artificers in the Park and Arsenals.

6   As an important measure preparatory to and indicative of the intended general resumption of the Jaidad that of placing the Districts Serounka? and Luckampore, which are now held by Colonel Mieselback, under the immediate authority of the Collector of Bundelcund, but as the Corps Commanded by Colonel Mieselback has been hitherto extremely useful in the Province and its retention in our Service for the interior duties of Bundelcund after the reduction of Ambajee's Brigades might be attended with beneficial effects, it is suggested that the Corps be retained in the Company's Service for the first year after the resumption of the Jaidad, and that its allowance be paid from the Treasury.

7   Colonel Mieselback would readily acquiesce in this arrangement, the Revenue of his Districts would do more than compensate the additional disbursements from the Treasury, and the faithful attachment of Colonel Mieselback's Corps to the British Service, with his personal influence over many of the Sirdars in the late Rajah Himmat Bahaddur's Army might, under proper control, become an useful instrument of the tranquil and successful progress of the subsequent arrangement with Himmat Bahadur's family and dependants.

8   Another important preparatory measure towards the resumption of the Jaidad is the dismissions from the British Service and the removal from the Province of Bundelcund of the body of Gosains or Nangahs. The character and conduct of this lawless and predatory Banditti, who formed a necessary but troublesome appendage to the Troops of Rajah Himmat Bahadur in the service of the former Government and whose admission into the British Service was highly expedient, if not indispensable, at the critical period at which they were introduced (see Public Despatch under date the 13th August 1804) are such as would render their continuance (as a body of armed men) in any part of the Honorable Company's Dominions extremely prejudicial to the Civil and Commercial resources of the Districts which they occupy, and even formidable to the tranquillity and happiness of the Inhabitants of those Districts.

9   From the terms and circumstances under which the Nangahs were admitted into the British Service, the great disinclination of the Native Chiefs in general to expand what they consider their private treasure in the payment of their troops, the inadequacy, perhaps, of Kunchum Geer's means to the regular payment of the Nangars, who constituted a supervenient burthen in the Jaidad and the limited pecuniary aid, which has been granted to him for this purpose (see public letter to G.Mercer Esq dated 9th December 1804 Para 9), it is more than probable that a large sum of Arrears of Pay must now be due to the Nangahs and that this Amount would be claimed from the British Government in the event of their immediate dismission from the Service.

10 The strict justice and great political experience of complying with this request in order to secure the peaceable retirement of the Nangahs from the Province of Bundelcund and their engagement of not entering into the Service of any Bundelah leader nor attempting to disturb the tranquillity of the British possessions in that Province are suggested as Subjects, which are highly worthy of consideration, with a view to the resumption of the Jaidand.

11 By the adoption of the two preparatory measures which have thus been suggested, it is highly probable that the representative and managers of the Affairs of the late Rajah Himmat Bahadur would be induced of their own accord to propose their retirement from the British Service and to seek the fulfilment of their original expectation of a Jageer in the Doab, as the means of an honourable retreat. A few of the most respectable Commanders of his Army, being Zamindars of our possessions in the Doab, would probably express an inclination to remain in the British Service and the employment of a select body of five hundred of the best horsemen to be attached to Colonel Mieselback's Corps, might form a subject worthy of consideration.

12 Among the Claimants on the British liberality at the period of the resumption of the Jaidand, the Nawab Myhoodeen Khan, who was the principal Mediator in an arrangement between the British Government and Rajah Himmat Bahadur and whose influence over the minds and councils of the late Rajah and his successor have uniformly been excited to promote the views of Government, might be employed as a useful instrument of facilitating the proposed measure and a moderate provision in his Native Country of Delhi, where he professes some claim as a Jageedar under the Government or in Bundelcund, by his employment in the British Service, might be held out to him as the reward for his fidelity and zeal in aiding the proposed arrangements.

13 The sons of Rajah Omerau Geer, the brother of Rajah Himmat Bahadur, have also considerable claims together with the Rajah's Widow and Child for a provision from the British Government. These persons had long held important Military Commands and possessed exclusive Jageers, in the Service of the late Rajah, who had adopted them as his own children and declared the eldest of them to be his successor before the birth of Narinder Geer.

14 A suitable provision for each of these persons might be promised to be made payable from the produce of the young Rajah's Jageer, the revenue of which should be distributed or applied to the maintenance of the family under the control of the British Government and the just claims and expectations of all the persons, whose rights and interests would be materially affected by the assumption of the Jaidand, might be fulfilled in such a manner as would greatly facilitate the execution of the measure in question and preclude the imputation of injustice or illiberality, which might otherwise prevale to the prejudice of the British interests in Bundelcund, notwithstanding the unquestionable right on which the resumption of the Jaidad would be founded.

15 The foregoing remarks, in addition to the suggestions which have been offered in the concluding paragraphs of the Narrative of Transactions in Bundelcund, are all that would appear to require immediate consideration with a view to the resumption of the Jaidand.

16 In the progress and result of so important a measure, it is probable that many other subjects of discussion might arise, which it is impossible at present to foresee or judge of with any degree of certainty or precision, but there might safely be and committed to the discussion of the persons, who might be entrusted with the execution of the measure, if acquainted with the disposition of the Natives, though possessing little previous knowledge of the particular history and present of Bundelcund.

SIGNED J. BAILLIE and
N.B.EDMONSTONE
Secretary to the Government
26th September.
TO CAPTAIN BAILLIE
Etc etc etc

Sir,

1 The readiness which you have manifested to undertake the duty superintending and carrying into effect the arrangements connected with the proposed resumption of the Jaidad Lands, assigned to the late Himmat Bahadur in the Province of Bundelcund, has afforded great satisfaction to the Honorable Governor General and I am now directed to communicate to you the Instructions of the Governor General for the regulation of your conduct in the execution of that duty, and to explain to you the nature and extent of the power and authority, with which the Governor General deems it necessary to vest you for the purpose of

carrying into effect the Civil and Political arrangements contemplated with the Province of Bundelcund.

2   The Governor General has now judged it proper to record upon the proceedings of Government, the able report, which, at the desire of the Governor General, you prepared upon the affairs of Bundelcund together with its Appendix, containing your sentiments with regard to the measures to be adopted for the tranquil resumption of the Jaidand and to the arrangements with which it is connected.

3   The Governor General deeming it to be proper that you should be apprized of the grounds upon which the British Government founds its rights to resume the Jaidand, with a view to enable you eventually to meet the pretensions, which may be urged on the part of the Family of Himmat Bahadur to the perpetuity of the Grant under the terms of the arrangement concluded with that Chieftain, I am directed to state to you the sentiments of the Governor General upon the merits of this question.

4   The obligation imposed upon the British Government to secure to Himmat Bahadur, the possession of a Jaidand to the extent of 20 Lacks of Rupees for the maintenance of troops, must be considered in the first place with reference to the views and intentions of the British Government respecting Bundelcund at the time when the engagement with Himmat Bahadur was concluded. The Province of Bundelcund was, at that time, considered generally to belong to the Peishwa. The detected intrigues of the Mahratta Confederates indicated the adoption on their part of a systematic plan for the application of the local Military power and resources of that Province to the Invasion of the Doab upon the grounds, therefore, of the definitive alliance then established with the Peishwa, as well as upon principles of self-defence, the British Government was justified in endeavouring to establish in the Province of Bundelcund an arrangement calculated not only to defeat the projects of the Confederates, but also to afford to the British Government the Military and Political advantages of the local situation of that Province, leaving for future adjustment the admitted rights of the Peishwa, and it was considered, that our occupation of the Peishwa those rights of which he had become deprived by the usurpation of his servants. This was the object and foundation with regard to Bundelcund and the aid of Himmat Bahadur was solicited to facilitate the accomplishment of the proposed arrangements under a promise of assigning to him a Jaidand of 20 Lacks of rupees and on the condition of his faithful services, a Jageer in the Doab. It was not then in the contemplation of the British Government to establish its authority, laws and regulations in the Province of Bundelcund, in other words to annex that Province to the

Honorable Copany's Dominions, and the grant of the Jaidand to Himmat Bahadur had reference to his future condition relatively to the Peishwa.

5   By the transfer, however, to the Company of a portion of the Peishwa's possessions in Bundelcund, estimated to yield a Revenue of 36,16,000 Rupees in exchange for an equivalent, the circumstances of the case were entirely altered. The allegiance and dependence of Himmat Bahadur were transferred with the Territory. It cannot be supposed that the British Government would have accepted as an equivalent for 36,16,000 Rupees a possession, which involved the perpetual alienation of near two thirds of that amount. But Jaidands granted for the support of Troops to be employed in the service of a State, are in their nature, not reasonable when the service of the Troops is no longer required. How far it might have been deemed advisable and just on the grounds of merit and the essential services of Himmat Bahadur to resume the Jaidand during his life is a distinct question. But admitting even the right of Himmat Bahadur to hold such Jaidand under the engagement concluded with him, that right was not declared by the engagement and cannot be construed to extend to his heirs and successors.

6   Upon these grounds, therefore, the Governor General entertains no doubt whatsoever of the right to resume the Jaidand Lands, granting at the same time a compensation to the Family and the amount of the Jageer proposed to be assigned to Himmat Bahadur must be considered to exceed the admitted though not the personal profits of the Jaidand.

7   I am now directed to state to you the sentiments of the Governor General with regard to the measures to be pursued for the actual resumption of the Jaidand referring to your Report on that subject.

8   The Governor General concurs in opinion with you relative to the facility, which would be afforded to the tranquil resumption of the Jaidand by the presence of a considerable body of British troops in the interior of Bundelcund and you are apprized of the actual transmission of orders to Lieutenant Colonel Martindell, commanding the British Detachment in that Province, directing him to withdraw the Troops under his command from their advanced position on the North Western Frontier to the interior of the Province. The Governor General is also aware of the great importance of obtaining possession of the Forts of Calinger and Azygurh with a view not only to the tranquil resumption of the Jaidand, but also to the effectual establishment of our Authority within the Ceded Territories of the Province and to other objects, which will be explained in a subsequent part of this Dispatch, connected with the Peishwa's share of Bundelcund, for the right of the Peishwa to the occupation of Calinger and Azygurh previously to the Cession of Territory in Bundelcund

considered as a right founded in the Conquests of Alli Bahadur, no doubt can be entertained and the British Government is at liberty to consider that right to be transferred under the option of a selection prescribed by the terms of the Peishwa's grant. The Governor General, therefore, deems it advisable to render the occupation of those Forts the earliest objects of attention, and as the possession of Calinger would probably produce the immediate surrender of Ajygurh, it is sufficient at the present moment to consider the means of acquiring possession of the former.

9 It appears by your report that the Fort of Calinger is at present in the possession of the descendant of two rebellious servants of the Purnea branch of the Family of Chutter Sol, and that the only surviving members of that Family are a Female and an illegitimate son of a lineal descendant of that Family. But although the Governor General is satisfied of the right of the British Government to the possession of Calinger, it is not at present his intention to authorise the prosecution of the siege of that Fortress. The Governor General entertains a confident expectation of obtaining possession of it by means of amicable negotiation and this expectation is augmented by the intelligence lately received from the Magistrate in Bundelcund of the assassination of the Killadar by his brother and the dissensions prevailing in the Family. The conduct of that negotiation will form a principal part of the duties of your Mission.

10 Such a negotiation will, however, be materially facilitated by the appearance of a resolution to obtain possession of the Fortress by force of arms and with that view, the Governor General has determined to authorise the adoption of every measure, short of the actual prosecution of hostility, by directing Lieutenant Colonel Martindell to make the preparations required for a siege and to occupy with the main body of the Force, the position which would be most convenient if the siege were actually intended. The Governor General has also directed two Howitzers with the necessary proportion of Military Stores to be conveyed to the Detachment from the Fort at Allahabad; a copy of the Governor General's instructions to Lieutenant Colonel Martindell upon the subject is enclosed for your information.

11 You will observe that the Governor General has not deemed it necessary to apprize Lieutenant Colonel Martindell of his resolution to abstain from the prosecution of the siege – the powers vested in you with regard to the employment of the Detachment under the command of Lieut-Colonel Martindell are expressly defined by those instructions, and will enable you to arrest the progress of the preparation for the siege at such time as may appear advisable as well as to direct the Services of the Detachment to other objects connected with the resumption of the Jaidand.

12 Your presence with the Detachment and its assigned position will enable you to employ every means of obtaining possession of Calinger by negotiation and at the same time to carry on the details of the measures connected with the tranquil resumption of the Jaidand with the best prospect of success, you will be cautious, however, not to authorise the progress of measures indicative of an intention to prosecute he siege of Calinger to such an extent as may render the declared or manifest relinquishment of that operation discreditable to the reputation of British arms.

13 With regard to the terms to be offered to the Killidar of the Fort of Calinger as the price of the surrender, the Governor General is of the opinion that the grant of a Jageer in the vicinity not exceeding 30,000 Rupees per annum, and the value of the ordnance and Military Stores in the Fort would be an equitable compensation and you are accordingly authorised to propose these terms – a similar adjustment with the possessor of Azygurh will also be approved by the Governor General.

14 The Governor General leaves to your discretion to judge of the time at which it may be expedient to declare to Koor Kunchum Geer, the Manager of the Jaidand, the intention of resuming it – enclosed you will receive Letters from the Governor General addressed to the Manager and Rajah Narinder Geer, notifying your mission for the general purpose of concluding certain arrangements directed to the improvement of the Administration and the affairs of the Province and to the adjustment of all points in which the interest of the Family of Himmat Bahadur are concerned and referring them for further particulars to your communication. These letters are in reply to addresses from Narinder Geer and Kunchum Geer which have been brought to this place by their Vakils. Copies of them are also enclosed for your information. Unless any of the measures immediately connected with the resumption of the Jaidand, such as the disbandment of any of the Troops supported from the resources of the Jaidand or the adjustment of the claims of any of the Chiefs attached to the Family can be adopted without disclosing the intended resumption, it seems advisable that the communication of that design and the execution of those measures should, as far as may be practicable, coincide in point of time with a view to preclude the plunder and exaction, which any considerable interval of time between the publication of the proposed resumption and the introduction of the British authority into the Territory composing the Jaidand, might afford the opportunity and the temptation to practise.

15 In the appendix to your report you have stated as measures preparatory to the resumption of the Jaidand; firstly, that of placing under the immediate authority of the Collector of Bundelcund, the Districts of

Terannha and Luckunpoor now held in Jaidand by Colonel Mieselback, and secondly the dismission and the removal from the Province of Bundelcund of the body of Gosains or Nangahs now supported from the resources of the Jaidand.

16 You have stated the first of these measures to be easy of accomplishment, it is not necessary, therefore, to regulate the moment of its adoption with reference to the observations contained in the 14th Paragraph. The Governor General concurs in your suggestion of maintaining Colonel Mieselback's Corps in the service of the Company for a certain period of time, or at least to render its reduction a measure ulterior to the dismission of the troops of Himmat Bahadur. This Corps may perhaps be usefully employed in effecting the resumption of the Jaidand.

17 With regard to the second measure above stated, every facility will be afforded in the accomplishment of it by the presence of Lieutenant Colonel Martindell's Detachment, and by enabling the Collector of Bundelcund to supply funds for the payment of the arrears due to the Nangahs. In addition to the cash, which may be accumulated in the Collector's Treasury, a further supply of 2,75,000 which has arrived at Allahabad on its way to Cawnpore, under charge of Captain Carpenter, has been ordered to Banda, and the Collector has been instructed to hold at your disposal, the whole of the Treasure in his hands. A copy of the orders issued to the Collector upon this subject is enclosed for your information. I am directed, however, to intimate to you the necessity of applying such part of that Treasure in the discharge of the heavy arrears, due to the Detachment under the Command of Lieutenant-Colonel Martindell, as the indispensable wants of the Detachment may require.

18 In conformity to the suggestion in the 14th Paragraph of the Appendix to your Report, you are at liberty to retain for the present in the British Service, a few of the most respectable Commanders of the late Himmat Bahadur's Troops, being Zamindars of our possessions in the Doab. The Governor General also approves of the employment of a body of Horsemen to the extent which you have suggested, provided it should appear to you to be a measure intimately connected with the tranquil resumption of the Jaidand. Both these measures, however, must be considered as a temporary matter. They appear to the Governor General to be expedient merely with a view to preclude the injurious consequences of disbanding the whole of the Troops of the late Himmat Bahadur at the same time. The Governor General trusts that the whole of those troops, together with the Corps of Colonel Mieselback, may gradually be disbanded and you will be pleased to keep this object constantly in view.

19 The Governor General also approves the suggestion contained in the 12th Paragraph of the Appendix to your report relative to a provision in favour of the Nawab Wudycooden? Khann, you will hereafter be pleased to submit to the consideration of the Honorable the Governor General, the precise mode and extent of provision, which you may think it advisable to assign to him.

20 The Governor General considers the arrangement proposed by the 14th Paragraph of the Appendix to your report for the maintenance of the sons of Rajah Omrao Geer and the several branches of the Family to be entirely advisable, if it can be satisfactorily accomplished. The Governor General considers it to be a duty imposed upon the British Government, under all the circumstances of the late Himmat Bahadur's conduct and the resumption of the Jaidand, to secure a suitable provision for all the branches of the Family.

21 The Governor General relies upon your discretion to make all the authorised compensation with every degree of economy consistent with the principles of equity.

22 The Governor General is prepared to fulfil the obligation of assigning to the Family the Jageer of Secrunda in the District of Cawnpore and you are authorised to afford Kaur Kumchum Geer every necessary assurance upon that subject, but it may be advisable to suggest to his consideration, that the full benefit of this intention may be hazarded by any overt or clandestine attempt on his part or on the part of any branch of the Family, to impede the tranquil resumption of the Jaidad, and that every practicable extension of favour and indulgence may be expected as the reward of a contrary course of conduct?.

23 The Governor General entirely concurs in the opinion suggested in the 101 Paragraph of your general report that the family of Himmat Bahadur will be entitled to receive the value of the Ordnance and Military Stores in the several Forts within the Jaidand, and the adjustment of that value will, of course, form a part of your duties.

24 The Governor General understands that the Grant of a Khelant to Rajah Narinder Geer is greatly desired by Kumchum Geer and is of the opinion that it would be proper to confer Khelants both on the Rajah and the Manager at proper Seasons and you are authorised to confer Khelants upon those Chieftains in the name of the Governor General under the decease of Himmat Bahadur, and you will observe that an intimation to this effect is contained in the Governor General's Letters to those persons, you are also authorised on the same occasion to confer suitable Khelants on the Sons of Rajah Omrao Geer and on any other of the principal Sirdars or most powerful adherents of the late Rajah

Himmat Bahadur on whom the Conferring this mark of the Governor General's favour may be deemed by you to be expedient.

25 The Governor General is aware that various other subsidiary questions, connected with the resumption of the Jaidand, are likely to occur during the progress of your proceedings – under these Instructions such questions you will, of course, submit to the Governor General.

26 I now proceed to state to you, by direction of the Governor General, the nature and extent of the further powers vested in you for the completion of these arrangements contemplated within the Province of Bundelcund.

27 The Governor General deems it proper to vest in your hands exclusively the temporary Civil jurisdiction over the resumed lands of the Jaidand, together with such other lands as may be placed under the authority of the British Government by the result of the proceedings which you are authorised and directed to undertake by the instructions contained in this Despatch.

28 You will accordingly consider yourself to be vested with the functions of Collector Magistrate in the assumed lands, the Governor General deems it proper that you should take the oaths of Magistrate before the Governor General previously to your departure for Allahabad.

29 In your capacity as Collector, you will proceed to form the Settlement of the assumed Lands, according to the best information you can obtain with regard to the assets of the Country, limiting the term of the settlement to one year, and granting Pottahs and Sunnuds agreeably to established forms. You will be careful to correspond regularly with the Board of Revenue on the subject of the settlement, reporting your proceedings from time to time, for the information of the Board, and paying due regard to any suggestions and instructions you may receive from that Board relative to the settlement. The Board of Revenue will be instructed to transmit to you the forms in which you are required to keep your Revenue accounts. You will be pleased to transmit to the Board of Revenue and to me for the information of the Governor General at the earliest practicable period of time, an estimate of the produce of the assumed lands and of the charges upon them.

29 As the exercise of the functions of the Judge and Magistrate of Buncelcund relatively to persons residing within the Jaidand Lands, under the Instructions with which he has been furnished, might materially interfere with and impede the conclusions of the several arrangements, which are committed to your charge, the Governor General has been pleased to direct, that, for the present, the Judge and the Magistrate of Bundelcund will consider the functions of his authority to be limited to those Districts, which are in the actual possession of the British Government and that he will refrain from issuing any judicial process or exercising any of the functions of his office connected with the rights

and persons of the Chieftains residing within the limits of the Territory in the occupation of the British Government or of their adherents without your previous concurrence, you are, however, directed to concur with the Judge and Magistrate in the adoption of every measure, tending to the Establishment and improvement of the general Police of the Province and to support the efficiency of his authority within the limits of his jurisdiction, by the influence of your own within the Districts placed under your charge. The Governor General trusts that this defined distinction of authorities will preclude their collision and tend to the efficiency and support of both.

30　The Judge and Magistrate of Bundelcund has further been directed to deliver over to you on your arrival at Banda, the whole of the political and other records of your late Office of Agent for the Commander in Chief in Bundelcund, together with Copies of the Proceedings of the late Board of Commissioners for the Affairs of that Province and of all the Political Dispatches transmitted, and received by Mr W.H. Brookes and by the Judge and Magistrate since your departure from Banda. A Copy of the Instructions issued to the Judge and Magistrate upon this occasion is enclosed for your information.

31　The 8th Paragraph of this Dispatch refers to the accomplishment of objects connected with the subjection of the Peishwa's Share of Bundelcund and I now proceed to communicate to you the Governor General's Instructions with reference to these objects.

32　You have been verbally apprized of the circumstances under which the Peishwa's Brother Amrut Row is at present residing within the Company's Territories and of the Governor General's extreme anxiety to relieve the British Territories from the inconvenience of his presence and the Public Finances from the burthen of his Stipend, with the least practicable delay; you are informed that every effort, which has been employed to induce the Peishwa to provide for his Brother by the Assignment of a suitable Jageer, has failed of success and that the Governor General considers himself authorised by every principle of public justice and equity to establish Amrut Row in the possession of a Jageer within the Territory belonging to the Peishwa even without his concurrence and consents, after the most mature deliberation the Governor General is satisfied that the least embarrassing arrangement with respect to Amrut Row will be to assign to him a suitable provision within the Peishwa's Share of Bundelcund.

33　The Governor General bears in mind the proposition made under the Authority of Government to the Peishwa to assign the whole of his reserved Territory in Bundelcund to the management of Shumshere Bahadur and the Peishwa's concurrence in that proposition. The

Governor General however is not aware of the existence of any positive engagement with Shumshere Bahadur pledging the British Government to establish him in the management of that Territory; but under any circumstances the Peishwa must be considered to be at liberty to revoke the Arrangement, and the provision proposed for Amrut Row may justly be carried into effect, under the supposed exercise of that right.

34 But rather than abandon this Arrangement which affords the only prospect of relief from the extreme inconvenience of Amrut Row's continuance within the Company's Dominions and from the heavy burthen of his Stipend of 8 Lacks of Rupees per annum, which, by the terms of the engagement concluded by Sir Arthur Wellesley with Amrut Row as chargeable from it's commencement to the Peishwa, the Governor General will be disposed to grant a compensation to Shumshere Bahadur, if it should ultimately appear to be necessary on grounds of justice and expediency, at present, however, the Governor General is disposed to think that the advantages of retaining the management of that portion of the Peishwa's Share of Bundelcund, which will remain after the Assignment of the proposed Jageer to Amrut Row, will constitute a sufficient provision for Shumshere Bahadur. It is, of course, to be understood that the Stipend of 4 Lacks of Rupees at present assigned to Shumshere Bahdur will cease when he shall be placed in possession of the prescribed portion of the Peishwa's reserved Territory.

35 The general Arrangement therefore, which the Governor General is anxious to accomplish is to assign in Jageer to Amrut Row, a Territory out of the Peishwa's reserved Share of Bundelcund, yielding a Revenue of 8 Lacks of Rupees per annum and to deliver over the remainder of the Peishwa's Share to the management of Shumshire Behauder.

36 For this purpose, it is obviously necessary that the whole of the Peishwa's reserved Territory should, in the first instance, be subjected to the British Authority. From every information which the Governor General possesses, the accomplishment of this object appears to depend exclusively upon the previous possession of Calinger and Ajygur, and the Governor General is led to entertain the fullest confidence that the possession of these Forts will, without any hostile effort, place the whole of the Peishwa's reserved Share of Bundelcund at the disposal of the British Government. At this moment, it is impracticable to prescribe the proceedings to be adopted for this purpose after the Fort of Calinger shall have been surrendered to the British Government. It is sufficient at present to apprize you of the Governor-General's intentions and to signify to you generally the Authority of the Governor General to enter into Negociations with the occupants of that Territory for their submissions of the Authority of the British Government asserted on the part of the Peishwa. The progress of events will suggest the proper time for requiring Amrut Row to proceed into Bundelcund for the purpose of assuming charge of the Jageer to be assigned to him. You will, however, consider the early accomplishment of this Arrangement to be an object of the greatest importance.

37 I am further directed to signify to you that the Settlement of the Claims of the Bundelah Chieftains of the Rana of Culpee and of the Nawab's Nasser oo Dowlah and Moolah Jah will also form a part of the general duties of your Mission, most of these Questions are already under a reference to the Supreme Government and you will hereafter receive Instructions with regard to the final adjustment of them founded on the Documents in the possession of Government. It will also be your duty to endeavour to affect a Settlement with Khour Lonce Jah and the Macander Rajah Ram in the event of their submission.

38 You have been informed under the immediate Authority of the Honble the Vice President in Council of the extent of your allowances and authorised Charges during your Mission to Bundelcund with the exception of the necessary establishment of Public Servants.

39 The Governor General is informed of your desire to have the assistance of Mirza Mohummed Jaffer's abilities in the conduct of the important Duties now committed to your Charge. The Governor General is fully apprized of the Merits and Services of Mir Jaffer in the discharge of the Duties of Superintendant of the Revenue, and, in the essentials, and which he afforded you in your Negociations and Arrangements, during your former employment in Bundelcund as described in your Official Letters to my address of the 29th December 1803.

40 The Governor General is aware of the exigency and importance of the Services of a Native Officer as peculiarly qualified to be the immediate instrument of accomplishing the detail and importance of this important and delicate Negociations and Arrangements connected with the objects of your Mission and the Governor General is induced by the high Opinion, which he entertains of the abilities and integrity of Mirza Jaffer, founded in his successful exertions in the accomplishment of the arduous duty of disbanding the Vizier's superfluous Troops under the direction of the Resident at Lucknow in the year 1801/2, to authorise the re-appointment of Mirza Jaffer to the situations which he formerly held under your Authority in Bundelcund, with the same Allowance of 1,000 Rupees per Mensem to commence from the 1st of the present Month.

41 The Governor General is further pleased to authorise you to entertain the following Establishment of Native Servants viz;

An English Writer   Rupees 60per Mensem
A Moonshee with
2 Mohurrirs   Do   150
A Nazir   30
3 Chabdars at 8 each   24
3 Santaburdars at 7 each   21
4 Spearmen at 6 each   24
1 Jemmadar and 20 Chaprassis 120
1 D and 20 Sawars at the established Rate of Pay.

42 You will not, of course, entertain the accustomed Establishment of a Collector, until your Duties as Collector shall have commenced by the actual resumption of the Jaidand.

43 I am directed to inform you that the Governor General has been pleased to appoint Mr Wauchope to be your Assistant, with a Salary of 400 Rupees per Mensem and the usual deputation Allowances.

44 Lieutenant Colonel Martindell is authorised to appoint an Escort of the Strength usually assigned to Officers in Political Situations to attend you during your employment in Bundelcund.

45 You will consider your Official designation to be that of Agent to the Governor General in Bundelcund.

I have the honor to be etc (Signed)

N.B. Edmonstone

Secretary to the Government.

To Captain J. Baillie.

Glossary

Bahadur	a hero or champion
budgerow	a boat with no keel used for river travel
cass or cess	in Bengal a distance of around 3 miles; in Bundelkhand a distance of around 2 miles
Diwani	the right to receive the revenue of Bengal, Orissa and Bihar conferred on the East India Company by the Moghul Emperor in 1765
Doab	the region between the Rivers Ganges and Jumna in upper India
Durbar	a court or levee
Firman/farman	an instruction
Gosain	an armed Saiva ascetic
Haft hazari	a commander of the Deccan Light Horse
Hircarrah	a messenger
Jaidad	a revenue assignment of property specifically earmarked for the payment of troops
Jagir	an estate
Jagirdar	the owner of a jagir
Khelat	a fort
Killadar/keladar	a garrison or fort commander
Kshatriya	the Military caste
lakh	one hundred thousand rupees
Mofussil	out stations in the Indian provinces
Munshi	a native teacher of languages
Nangah	a naked warrior ascetic
Nawab	a chief governor of a Moghul province
Palkee	similar to a palanquin but instead of a box, a hammock
Peischcush	a rental tribute
Peshwa	the chief minister of the Mahratta powers
Rani	a Hindu Queen
Ressaldar	a cavalry commander
Sanyasi	a man who renounces worldly life

Sirdar	a Military commander
Summud	a deed of grant
Vakil	an authorized representative/ambassador
Zamindar	a landowner
Zillah	a British administrative district in India

Further Reading

Archer, Mildred. *India Revealed: The Art and Adventures of James and William Baillie Fraser, 1801–35*. Cassel. London, 1989.

Bengal Obituary. Thacker and Co. Calcutta, 1851.

Bennell, Anthony. *The Making of Arthur Wellesley*. Orient Longman. Bombay, 1997.

Bhatt, Ravi. *The Nawabs of Lucknow.* Rupa and Co. Delhi, 2006.

Callahan, Raymond. *The East India Company and Army Reform, 1783–1798*. Harvard University Press. Cambridge, MA, 2008.

Cardew, Sir Alexander. *The White Mutiny – a Forgotten Episode of the History of the Indian Army by Sir Alexander Cardew K.C.S.I.* London: Constable, 1929.

Chancey, Marla Karen. *In the Company's Secret Service: Neil Benjamin Edmonstone and the First Indian Imperialists, 1780–1820*. Dissertation. Florida State University Libraries, 2003.

Chatterji, Dr Nandalal. 'Lord Hastings, Colonel Baillie and the Oudh Loans'. *Journal of the Uttar Pradesh Historical Society*, vol. 1 (1953): 52–62.

Cooper, Randolph. *The Anglo-Maratha Campaigns and the Contest for India.* Cambridge University Press. Cambridge, 2003.

Dalrymple, William. *White Mughals: Love and Betrayal in Eighteenth-Century India.* HarperCollins. London, 2003.

Edwards-Stuart, Ivor. *The Calcutta of Begum Johnson.* BACSA. London, 1990.

Fisher, Michael. *A Clash of Cultures: Awadh, the British and the Mughals.* Sangam Books. London, 1988.

Fisher, Michael. *Indirect Rule in India: Residents and the Residency System, 1764–1858.* Oxford University Press. Delhi, 1991.

Hickey, William. *Memoirs of William Hickey.* Edited by Alfred Spencer. Hurst and Blackett. London, 1925.

Llewellyn-Jones, Dr Rosie. *A Fatal Friendship: The Nawabs, the British and the City of Lucknow.* Oxford University Press. Delhi, 1985.

Llewellyn-Jones, Dr Rosie. *Lucknow Then and Now.* Marg. Mumbai, 2003.

Losty, J. P. *Calcutta, City of Palaces: A Survey of the City in the Days of the East India Company, 1690–1958.* British Library. London, 1990.

McGrigor, Mary. The Persian Translator. *The Life and Times of Neil Benjamin Edmonstone.*

Moon, Sir Penderel. *The British Conquest and Dominion of India.* Duckworth. London, 1989.

Pearse, Hugh. *Lake's Campaigns in India: The Second Anglo-Maratha War, 1803–1807.* Leonaur. Driffield, 2007.

Pemble, John. *The Raj, the Indian Mutiny and the Kingdom of Oudh 1801–1859.* Farleigh Dickinson University Press. Rutherford, NJ, 1977.

Pinch, William. *Warrior Ascetics and Indian Empires.* Cambridge University Press. Cambridge, 2006.

Pitre, Brigadier K. G. *The Second Anglo-Maratha War, 1802–1805: A Study in Military History.* Dastane Ramchandra. Poona, 1990.

Santha, Kidambi Srinivasa. *Begums of Awadh.* Bharati Prakashan. Varanasi, 1980.

Spiers, Malcolm. *The Wasikadars of Awadh.* Rupa and Co. Delhi, 2008.

Index